The Savvy Guide to Making More Money

Susan Hayes is managing director of Hayes Culleton, an international financial training company. Susan has brought the company to markets across the world and was nominated for the Enterprise Europe Network Rising Star Awards in 2011. In addition, she contributes regularly to the media – including the *Sunday Independent*, the *Sunday Times* (Malta), RTÉ, TV3, 4 FM, Newstalk and Today FM – on matters relating to economics, financial markets and entrepreneurship. In 2008 she wrote a digitized module, 'Introducing Wall Street to the Classroom', to make the stock market approachable and accessible for second-level students. She is also co-author of the Leaving Certificate textbook *Positive Economics*. Her first book for the general public, *The Savvy Woman's Guide to Financial Freedom*, was published in 2013. Susan is from Cork and has a BSc in Financial Mathematics and Economics from NUI Galway.

Praise for *The Savvy Woman's Guide to Financial Freedom*

'Last night I was able to see areas where I can cut my costs, and how I can do that. **And for the first time after several months of going into overdraft, this month, because of sticking to the budget, I had £311 left in my account.** Now I can use that towards clearing off my credit card debt. In the past I could only pay a minimum amount on the card; now I know that if I stick with the budget I can clear that debt. I got the enthusiasm to start doing this from reading your book'
Thandiwe Mtetwa, enterprise lecturer

'Your book was not only a first step in financial guidance, it actually allowed me to think for myself in making steps 2, 3 and beyond. This is, I suppose, the difference between your book and the other books out there that "promise" to change everything. The "others" miss the point that, at the end of the day, it is imperative that the individual is not only told what to do, but **they get to be in control and get creative with their own ideas and wants**' Catriona Plunkett, aviation sector

'To say Susan provides **a hefty intravenous shot of positivity** through everything she does is an understatement. However, as we all know, positivity is a vastly abused and misunderstood word these days – so it's important to contextualize Susan's version of it. It's an attitude of **reality tempered by change and possibility** – of newness and active engagement in making a difference in one's own economy'
Olwen Dawe at Irishbizwoman.blogpost.com

'**This girl practises what she preaches**, and she is on a mission to help women (and men) to gain financial independence, whatever that might mean to them. "**It means different things to different people**," she said, adding that for one person it might mean the freedom to take Wednesdays off, or to earn another £5,000 a year, while for another it might mean making half a million pounds' Amanda at Candis.co.uk

'Taking Control: So I sat in a coffee shop and did all my figures, I worked out what I had earned and what I needed to earn to pay it all off and to be financially free, **even doing the exercise felt liberating**. I took the first positive step to financial freedom and it felt good. I took my own advice and I got organized, I took Susan's advice and got savvy'
Ciara Conlon, the Productivity Coach

'The tone of *The Savvy Woman's Guide to Financial Freedom* is **very friendly, warm and conversational**, as if all the advice is coming from a (very expert!) girlfriend over a latte' Sheena Lambert at Writing.ie

'She encourages positive thinking, and pushes you to work hard. Whether dipped into or read from cover to cover, this book has most of the answers. Follow Hayes's advice, and **you are well on the way to achieving financial independence**' Sophie at Modern Young Finance

The Savvy Guide to Making More Money

SUSAN HAYES

PENGUIN

IRELAND

PENGUIN IRELAND

Published by the Penguin Group
Penguin Ireland, 25 St Stephen's Green, Dublin 2, Ireland (a division of Penguin Books Ltd)
Penguin Books Ltd, 80 Strand, London WC2R ORL, England
Penguin Group (USA) Inc., 375 Hudson Street, New York, New York 10014, USA
Penguin Group (Canada), 90 Eglinton Avenue East, Suite 700, Toronto, Ontario, Canada M4P 2Y3
(a division of Pearson Penguin Canada Inc.)
Penguin Group (Australia), 707 Collins Street, Melbourne, Victoria 3008, Australia
(a division of Pearson Australia Group Pty Ltd)
Penguin Books India Pvt Ltd, 11 Community Centre, Panchsheel Park, New Delhi – 110 017, India
Penguin Group (NZ), 67 Apollo Drive, Rosedale, Auckland 0632, New Zealand
(a division of Pearson New Zealand Ltd)
Penguin Books (South Africa) (Pty) Ltd, Block D, Rosebank Office Park,
181 Jan Smuts Avenue, Parktown North, Gauteng 2193, South Africa

Penguin Books Ltd, Registered Offices: 80 Strand, London WC2R ORL, England

www.penguin.com

First published 2014
001

Set in 12/14.75pt Dante MT Std
Typeset by Jouve (UK), Milton Keynes
Printed in Great Britain by Clays Ltd, St Ives plc

A CIP catalogue record for this book is available from the British Library

ISBN: 978–1–844–88328–8

www.greenpenguin.co.uk

MIX
Paper from
responsible sources
FSC
www.fsc.org   FSC™ C018179

Penguin Books is committed to a sustainable
future for our business, our readers and our planet.
This book is made from Forest Stewardship
Council™ certified paper.

To Ardle

Contents

Contents

Introduction

Famous entrepreneurs are not born under a lucky star that gives them the ability to make money: it's a skill that can be learned, developed and called upon as often as necessary.

As I write these very words, the world is gripped in the latter end of a recession that is forcing many people into a very lean time. Money-saving experts are regularly featured in the media. However, when your income, as well as your savings, seems to be dwindling by the day, there comes a time when it's just exhausting to be forever worrying about the money going out. You can't live on bread and water alone.

Through these pages, which were carefully written with you in mind, I want to help you to alleviate the panic that comes from thinking about money. Let me shine a light on how to focus on the things you can do, which will help when all you feel like doing is burying your head in the sand. This book will go a very long way towards improving your financial well-being, and, as you will see time and time again throughout the coming chapters, I speak from a wealth of experience.

When I'm interviewed on various media, people often ask, 'Finance is a wide area that can cover a plethora of topics – what do you specialize in?' I answer that I focus on personal finance, investment, entrepreneurship and economics. More often than not, my answer is followed by, 'How do you make more money? What's the secret to riches?'

There isn't a hidden secret to making money; it's a skill that can be learned and developed. And once you've acquired that skill, you can rest assured that, whenever you need to increase your earnings, you'll have a proven system that will enable you to do just that, one that works every time, and one that you can scale up or down depending on the amount of time and energy you have available. I want to banish the many prejudices and misconceptions that keep people in difficult places, full of worry and anguish. I want to show that money is simply a tool, a means to an end, and not that monster always hounding you, leaving you confused, angry and exhausted from never having enough.

In this book you will find many stories that are about me: not because I have an inflated sense of self, but because I practise what I preach. I won't recommend that you do something unless I've tested it myself and found a way to make it work. I've been there and done that, so that hopefully you'll be able to benefit from my experience and learn from my blunders – and perhaps even get a laugh out of them.

You need to widen your view of what is possible. If just reading this introduction brings up your resistance, if you feel a gulf of scepticism opening, perhaps you're my ideal reader: someone who most needs to change their mind-set and someone who stands to benefit the most from it. You might see a drastic difference in your life, once you become more flexible. We all have people in our lives that rely on us, and many things – some welcome and some not so welcome – that restrict what we can do with both our time and our money. However, it is important to remember that there is much within our control. Leave 'reality' – that mighty dream-crusher – aside for a moment, and think of what your life could be. All the completely 'out-there', unrealistic dreams I have dreamed – of setting up my own company, of expanding internationally, of writing my own books – have come to pass. I'm going to work hard to achieve many more totally absurd, unrealistic dreams in the years to come.

Before you embark on your money-making journey, there are a couple of things that I need to tell you. First of all, I have written this book so that it can become your point of reference. Wherever you are on your income-generating path – just finishing your education; out of the workforce and wanting to generate a new income; currently employed and looking to earn a little more; working in a sales role within an organization; or seeking to optimize an existing business – you will find something tangible with which to move forward. The fundamental steps that lead to €5,000 or €5 million are the same, but the amount of action, belief, effort and attitude that you need to put into those steps varies enormously, depending on the result that you wish to obtain.

Ideally, you should go through the book once, step by step, trying out the strategies that I suggest. By the end, you should be well on your way to reaching your goals. You can then go back to the beginning and tackle each step from a more informed place, reaping more and more benefits, refining processes and turbo-charging your progress with each successive read. This is exactly what I'm doing at the point I've currently reached in my career: ready to move on to the next stage in my business, I'm returning to my original principles and starting again, only from a higher vantage point than the one I held when I first started out.

Yes, making money is a repetitive process. It involves repeating the same processes until they work. There's no magic pill, no instant transformation, no miracle: people who are successful at making money are just like the rest of us. Do you think you're no good at making more money? Do you think only someone like Steve Jobs can work this magic? Let's say you're looking for a specific object (your keys might be a frequent culprit) in a room. Let's say the light is off and you can't find those keys, because you can't see them. Would you get angry at yourself for 'never having been good at finding things in a pitch-black room'? Would you give up and say you're not cut out for this? No. You'd just switch on the light. It's precisely this shift in mind-set that I want to encourage you to adopt: if you're not making as much money as you'd like to, perhaps it's because you've not realized that the way you're going about it is having a limited effect. So you blame yourself, when in fact you just need to change tack and find that light switch . . . and if the batteries get low, you can recharge by reading this book.

So you try something: if it works, you do it again and create a wonderful success loop; if it doesn't, I suggest that you go back to the drawing board and try something else. You can then cruise at this altitude or you can start all over again and aim higher, becoming bigger and better. On some occasions, life may drop you from a plateau's height and you'll need to pick yourself up and get going again. I have included a huge number of money-making principles in this book, and they have stood me and others in good stead over the years. Being enterprising is mostly a matter of changing your mind-set to 'Can do, will try, will try again'.

Making more money is certainly not *only* about becoming an entrepreneur or setting up a business. Being enterprising as an employee is not only possible but exhilarating and rewarding. Nor are there age limits or constraints. In this book I share my experience of developing a varied portfolio of income streams during my full-time study in college; of being an employee with much of my role dedicated to sales; of taking the incremental journey of setting up my own business. Curiosity and creativity are basic human needs that can be fulfilled whether you're in business for yourself or an employee, and whether you have high- or low-risk tolerance. Thinking what you might offer your employer, researching the problems you could solve for them, increasing the value you bring to your job, knowing who influences their decisions – all these approaches are exactly the same if you're developing a product or service for your own business. Your offering must always be truly helpful and you must always know who or what influences your target market's buying decision. Making more money is about solving a problem for somebody, or giving them pleasure, fun, entertainment. And this is as universal as the rhythm of the seasons.

Because making money is a skill, it's absolutely necessary that you take action and practise, practise, practise. You *will* get better with each successive round. All of the steps that I describe in the book are essential – but it's also vital to move beyond learning them to the point where you apply them. You can do market research until the cows come home, but if you don't work out an action plan based on that market research and then implement it, your bank balance will never improve, because, to go back to my metaphor, you didn't turn on the light to find your keys. Many of the steps

I describe can become very comfortable zones in which you can stagnate if you don't use what you've learned to progress to the next stage. 'Oh, I'll just do a little bit more market research, just a tiny bit, and then I can actually put my offering out there.' The moment you actually make money is the one when somebody agrees to buy what you're offering – and this is the only thing that matters. Not your number of Twitter followers, nor the list of vacancies that you printed off, nor the feedback from your focus group.

That's why I urge you to adopt what people in business circles call Key Performance Indicators, or KPIs. (I use some business language in the book, because, no matter what your situation, I will be sharing with you the proven tips and techniques that successful businesses – small, medium and large – use to make more money.) In the coming chapters I show you how to put this framework in place in your own life, and how to measure your success within it. It's very important to track your actual progress, so that you can gather information and then, on the basis of that information, go back to improve what needs to be improved, or gather strength from seeing positive trends even when the going gets tough and you're not making any visible (to the human eye) progress. KPIs are quantifiable outcomes that you regularly log into a document of some sort (I like spread-sheets). If you've ever gone on a diet – say, by joining WeightWatchers – and tracked what you were eating, how you were exercising and the amount of weight lost, you've already used KPIs. KPIs remove the emotions and mood swings that could jeopardize your success, and show you, black on white, when you're on track and when you need to correct course. The numbers never lie. I will be talking about KPIs right throughout the book, and you'll really come to love getting everything down on paper and checking in with yourself regularly.

So what are you waiting for? Is there anything holding you back? Do you think you lack time, or experience, or you don't know the right people? Excuses have a 100% rate of success. 'I don't have any time', 'I'm not a natural salesperson', 'I'm not an entrepreneur', 'I'm no good with money', 'There's a recession', 'Unemployment is up'. Some of these barriers are real; some of them are only barriers of perception; but, either way, you can work through all of them.

Don't wait until . . . until the recession is over . . . until the children leave for college . . . until you enrol on that course. The perfect moment will never come. This little voice telling you to wait a little bit, to make sure there are no risks, to spend a long time looking before you leap – it's your comfort zone speaking. It will keep you in the place you're currently in, if you listen to it. Things will never begin easily, and there will be a learning curve at the start. It's not as if, once the stars align, you can suddenly have your rags-to-riches story and then cruise into the sunset. You'll have to take one step at a time. But you'll learn and discover much in the process that will enable you to move towards your financial utopia. I absolutely encourage you to share the things that you learn from this book with as many people as you possibly can. My dream for this book is that it reaches a multitude of people who truly want to better their lives financially and in other ways.

It's my duty not to conceal from you the fact that you'll meet frustration and disappointment along the way. Not everything you try will work the first time around. But those setbacks are stepping stones to your success. Don't just give up at the first hurdle. I have seen this many times in my own career: even when it seemed all hope was lost, things did work out in the end. You just need to actually begin, and to find help along the way. Your results might be a bit wobbly at first, but you have to start somewhere, just as you did when you first learned to talk, walk, read, do maths, ride a bike, swim.

Another problem is that the mystique surrounding business often causes people who are very enterprising to think that they're not doing anything particularly remarkable. My aunt used to collect flower-heads, store the seeds and grow her own flowers to sell the year after to complement the family budget. In her overwhelmingly busy life of taking care of her family, she had found the time to be ingenious and resourceful to add some cash here and there. And, still, when I tell her that I admire her business savvy, she says, 'Me?

But I'm not a business person, not like you.' To which I have to say, 'How about all the many different ways you've found over the years to improve the household's bottom line?' 'Ah, but sure I was only bringing in a couple of pound here and there. It's not like I had a logo. Ha, ha!' As if that mattered one blind bit, as if that alone was a red badge of entrepreneurship.

Reading my aunt's story, you might be thinking, 'Well, I've done similar things in the past. There was the time when I . . . And that other time when I . . .' Exactly. That's what I mean. You're already thinking enterprisingly. You already have it in you to make more money. This book is here to make the process faster, smoother, easier. If you've made money before and thought it was down to luck, I'll show you that it wasn't: that it's a skill applied to a process, and that it's repeatable.

So let's get started.

STEP ONE

Understanding what new income
would really mean to you

1. *Finding your motivation and self-belief: why are you doing this?*

One balmy evening in Malta, I was having dinner with a really good friend who was preparing for a job interview the next week. As we were enjoying local delicacies and listening to the waves in Spinola Bay, she shared with me how this interview was the step-up in her career that she had been waiting for – a golden opportunity. I was pretending to be the interviewer, and giving feedback on her answers, and encouraging her to believe in herself and to up the ante. However, my usually calm friend reacted angrily to my comments and eventually spat out, 'What would you know anyway – when did you ever go for an interview?'

Of course it was just a bad case of the nerves and our friendship didn't suffer, but her reaction got me thinking. Admittedly, I have never gone through the rigours of an HR psychometric test or a five-person panel interview in which I have to elaborate on my CV with a view to securing a full-time, wage-paying job in the traditional sense. However, every single time I have pitched to a client, applied for funding, met a prospect for coffee, I have been 'interviewed for a job'.

We tend to think being self-employed and being employed are two completely different things: as if people who run a business, or who are financially self-sufficient, have a totally different set of skills, in comparison with a person who works in an office or on a building site or in a classroom or a hospital. The things they do might technically be very different, but at some point both groups have somehow successfully persuaded someone to buy from them.

Business people write brochures and post sales copy on a website, while employees-to-be write a CV. Business people ask for 'testimonials', while employees-to-be ask for references. Business people anticipate objections that relate to price when they hear a sales pitch, while employees-to-be develop their own answers to sticky questions like 'What is your greatest weakness?'

The employee has just one customer (this is actually called a 'monopsony' in economics), and they are looking for a much larger sum of money than the business person, who is pitching for a smaller amount but from a larger number of people. The business person has to have a diversified portfolio of incomes. So if you have ever worked a day in your life and got paid for it, you've demonstrated the ability to make money. We just need to refine and optimize the process until it is scaled to the level that you want to reach.

That night in Malta, my friend said to me, 'I could never do what you do.'

What exactly did she think was so difficult?

'Trying to sell to people all the time and get money from them and always keeping an eye on the competition.'

'Isn't that the same as your applying for this job, getting paid and working your way up, so that you can get a promotion in the future?' I said.

So if you think that you could never do what I do, I have to tell you: you're already doing it every day. The only difference is that I have had to ask for the sale multiple times, and not just once every ten years or so. As a result I have more practice, and I have had to develop and refine a system that will increase my chance of making the sale. This is what I would like to share in this book. But, first, let's address some legitimate doubts you might have.

You think you should wait out the recession, or at least wait for better economic times, before trying something new

'So, Susan, why did you set up your business in a recession?' If I have heard this question once, I have heard it a hundred times. I didn't set up a business during a recession; I just set up a business . . . and it so

4

happened that, in terms of macroeconomic statistics, a recession was going on. I had some skills and abilities, a bucket-load of enthusiasm, ready-to-pour action and a dream. That's it. The opportunity was there – irrespective of the economic situation.

Now I have a Company Registration Number, a VAT number, an accountant, company stationery and a business card sporting 'Managing Director' as my title. However, you don't need all of these trimmings to make more money. From the time I was in secondary school to the day that the company was incorporated, I generated several streams of income – some clear-cut, some opportunistic, some foraged. They all had one thing in common: I simply sold something at a higher price than what it cost me (often my time and labour). You don't need to have a business to make this book work for you; all you need to have is the money-making muscle that enables us to survive and thrive financially.

Some people might say that a recession is the best time to set up a business, and others might totally disagree. I don't think the larger economic picture should really be the 'deal-breaker': both boom and bust periods create specific playing fields, and both have drawbacks and advantages. During hard economic times, people might have less money to part with, and they might be looking to save rather than to spend. But suppliers might be more likely to offer discounts and special deals – which means that you might be able to run a business with less money than would be required in better times.

During times of economic prosperity, consumers and businesses can be severely time-pressured, with the result that they are looking for value over price; so suppliers have to demonstrate that they can provide that value, while also competing on price; and consumers can be at the mercy of 'cost-push' inflation (i.e., when businesses put up their prices because the cost of their own inputs has risen). There are some businesses that might disappear in the depth of a depression or at the height of a boom, but the owners can absolutely take the skills they developed in a previous business and start again, whether that be in a new venture or in employment. The ability to apply one's skill to the process of making more money is the same, despite the ebb and flow of the products and services that comprise the offering.

You'll never find the time

I'm always intrigued by how often people say 'I don't have any time', despite the fact that we all have the same twenty-four hours to work with. Yet some accomplish far more than others in that time. Perhaps you think, 'Oh, hang on, I know the ones you're talking about – I'm not RoboCop, I couldn't turn into a workaholic.' But if something is really important to you, you will prioritize it and make the time – you know you've done it in the past.

In deciding whether to take on my final professional exam last year, I had to consider if I would have the time to devote to it. I was already working morning to night during the week and a couple of hours on Saturday and Sunday. I was really scratching my head as to where I might be able to find 'study time'. I started off by isolating an evening here and there in which to study, and incrementally built it up, so that, by the time I had three months to go to the exam, I was able to switch off the laptop on Friday evening and leave it completely unattended until Monday morning; I also managed to clear two nights a week when I would just dive into the books.

I did cut out a couple of things, but what made the difference was my efficiency. Nature abhors a vacuum, so often a task expands to fill it. In my case, I had to cut out anything that was not absolutely essential and compress what had to be done into whatever time I had available, while still giving it the attention it deserved. I took nine months of little bits and pieces of time and turned them into a good stab at a very difficult exam. That was a particularly intensive stretch of tight time-management, but I have plenty of ongoing methods of making the best of the hours in my day. For instance, I watch my one guilty-pleasure soap on the TV player while I'm making dinner at night, and I often choose to use public transport so that I can read the paper on my journey.

How about you? Let's say that you do have a busy life – and, for 99% of us, 'I don't have the time' isn't just an excuse, but feels like truth. You may have an elderly parent, a child with special needs, an insanely busy job or a new baby who hasn't got an 'off' button; hence you're not in a position to pick and choose your free time. I completely understand and acknowledge that. Still, I'm asking you to focus not on the time you don't have but on the time that you do. For example, let's say that you have ring-fenced four precious hours per week to relax in front of the TV. Imagine that, for three months, you used three hours a week to grow your revenue instead of watching the box. Three hours a week, three months – what could you achieve? Rather, what couldn't you achieve?

If you really want to find time in your day, I suggest that you take ten minutes to write down how you think you'll spend every day next week. Next, write down how you *actually* spend your time in half-hourly slots, starting from this minute. You must include time spent on social media, a phone call with a friend, gazing into space, just being tired, reading a magazine in the bathroom (yes, everything). It's a very simple thing to do, but it will tell you exactly where your time has gone, as opposed to where you think it's going.

Write down all the things that you would like to do and slot them into your diary. If you physically can't do so, you now know why you never get on top of things or feel that you don't have any time to do anything. I didn't realize that I was setting myself up to fail each week on achieving a to-do list when I hired my personal assistant. In the first two weeks, I had to document all of my tasks, appointments, commitments, etc., for her to put in the diary. She has a fantastic sense of humour and after yet another casual 'Will you put in three hours for *x* and two hours for *y*?' from me, she said, 'I suggest that on your next trip to London we schedule you for a visit to Hogwarts School of Witchcraft and Wizardry, where I'm sure you'll be able to purchase a magic wand or at least a time-travel spell.' I had to truly document every single thing that I had to do before I realized why things weren't getting done: it was simply impossible. Therefore, I had a choice between doing fewer things or doing things more efficiently.

So start making a schedule, try out a time-budgeting strategy, identify where time is leaking out of your life to no purpose and then figure out ways to work your time to produce better results. After all, time is money . . . literally.

You need to figure out your priorities

Getting on top of things is a matter of doing things, yes, but also of eliminating anything that isn't a priority. So what are your priorities? If you could make more money by working overtime, would that be a priority?

There are many people who would be delighted if their employer approached them to offer an extra five hours' work per week at time and a half. By following the steps in this book, you can create that new 'employer' – a customer who will be delighted to pay you that extra money for the products or services that you will provide. Imagine you're working in an office and your boss is in the next room, and for €2,000 she needs somebody to do something that you would really love to do. You can get up off your chair, walk into the room, mention that you have the skills to do the job, and say you'll do it for exactly the amount of money that she had in mind – or you can go home that evening and do nothing. Although this is a hypothetical scenario, you are probably making this sort of choice every day – that is, every day that you don't search out the opportunity that could be waiting for you in the next room.

You're waiting for the perfect idea

But, you say, you don't know what you could possibly sell: 'If only I could come up with an idea.' For some reason, people think that they have to come up with an 'idea' before they can make more money. Well, my own idea is to charge people a pound for every time that I hear that and then I can be a millionaire. You don't need an idea that will be revolutionary, but simply something to sell, which is anything that people value and would be willing to pay for. Do you think your plumber or the owner of the dry-cleaner's waited until they had the perfect original idea before they started to make money?

For International Women's Day last year, I sponsored a lunch for the Roscommon Women's Network, a charity in the Irish midlands. Over a coffee before I stood up to speak, I was chatting to one of the staff and asked her what people could give to the organization if they didn't have cash to spare. She said they could offer their time: cover reception, produce a newsletter, talk to any contacts who could help to promote the charity or just listen to people who wanted to talk. I brought up those points from the stage, and afterwards a woman meekly approached me and thanked me. I really didn't know what I had done for her, but she said, 'I never realized that as a retired old woman, I had anything to offer to anybody any more. Now I know that I can help out this great cause simply by giving them my ears and attention.'

Don't wait for the light bulb to go off: engage with what's going on in your head and that will be enough. When you then combine intention with action, you'll be amazed at what you can achieve.

Trying something new seems overwhelming

I might be having a go at all the barriers that are holding you back, but deep down I know where you're coming from. The idea that you could increase your revenue seems overwhelming, because – and I'm assuming this is the reason why you picked up this book – you're not quite sure where to start and you can feel the panic mounting. *All those things that need to be done. And they need to be done now!*

At a dinner party in London one evening I saw a heated exchange between two brothers. Arthur was highly motivated, successful and always looking for ways to climb the career ladder. Nick was a hard worker, wanted wage stability and considered work to be a means to fund other areas of his life – and it was with Nick that the conversation had started, because he wanted to make more money in order to fund more leisure.

Arthur started off by telling Nick that he should set up a small business, and then in a couple of months employ somebody else, and then buy a van, and then take on another two people, and then expand UK-wide, and then, and then, and then . . . He took out a sheet of paper, drew a stick man at the bottom corner of the page with a staircase leading to the opposite top corner – where I thought a listing on the London Stock Exchange would materialize. Nick took the pen off him and said, 'Let me draw you another picture.' He drew a square box on the other side of the page and said, 'This is the size of my flat – how can I set up a business in this? I would need a secretary to take bookings, a filing cabinet, a computer, a second phone line, a canteen . . .' I thought he was going to say that he needed to rent a tower on Canary Wharf, such was the amount of space that would be required. The brothers were talking two completely different languages.

There were as yet no bookings to take – so why did Nick focus on the secretary?

Nick was overwhelmed by the idea of generating a self-employment income, never mind setting up a business (and he wasn't helped by Arthur's 'taking over the world' ambitions on this occasion). Both had a desire to make money, but they had diametrically opposed views of how much, how soon and how to get there. If you feel that making money is a mind-boggling concept and you wouldn't know where to start, I'll share with you the step-by-step framework that you can follow. You'll know at every stage what the next step is; and if you lose your way a bit, you'll always be able to find your way back to the previous one.

Sometimes we're just crushed by the sheer enormity of the task.

We feel completely paralysed, like a deer in the headlights: instead of doing what we can, instead of doing what would work, we freeze and our mind draws a blank. But we have to realize that there is a method that we can follow, that can get us going. There is a small step we can take right now.

Once, when I was at college, I sat down with a life coach and told her that, although it was my dream, I really couldn't imagine ever having an international business. I could never imagine saying to somebody 'Well, I'm in New York next week on business, but maybe we could meet after that' with a straight face. She matter-of-factly replied, 'Do you know anyone who does that?' I rolled my eyes and said, 'Of course, I read about lots of people who do' – and then she gave me a look that said 'What's the problem, then? If it's possible for other people, why not you?'

Roll forward a couple of years, to the time when I actually had started my own business. I was consumed by a burning ambition to take it international and yet also by that same sticky feeling of doubt, wondering whether I ever really could. However, I decided that, no matter how small the opportunity, I was going to go for it and leave the feelings of fear, doubt and uncertainty at the door. I pictured this as putting them away in a mental box, which worked surprisingly well.

Two days later I got an e-mail from the Dublin Chamber of Commerce: a trade delegation from Malta was coming to Ireland in a couple of weeks and were open to setting up meetings. My first reaction was 'What could I possibly say if I were to meet somebody on this mission?' Then I reminded myself to take the emotion out of it and to simply, mechanically reply to the e-mail, asking to set up some appointments. After all, all I had to do was to type a couple of words and press 'Send'.

I followed through and met with two companies on the day they visited Ireland, but I went in thinking, 'If I'm honest with myself, this is really a bit of a waste of time, as I have no intention of actually going over to Malta or doing anything with these people. I'm just keeping a promise to myself that I wouldn't turn down any opportunity that came my way.' I went home afterwards, sent them a LinkedIn invitation and was ready to leave it at that.

Over dinner that Friday night, I was talking about the week to my fiancé, who is also my business partner, and I heard the words 'Will I go out to Malta?' come out of my mouth. Again, mechanically, I looked up flights and saw a return ticket for €30. I went through the motions of booking it, and when I clicked 'Confirm' I was thinking, 'I don't really believe that I'm going to go, but it's only €30 to feel like I'm living my international dream.' I decided to play along with my own game. I got a quote for a hotel, and it was very reasonable, as January was totally off-peak in Malta.

I then sent an e-mail to the two people whom I had met in Dublin and asked if they would be interested in meeting me while I was on my 'visit', but I genuinely thought I would afterwards say that something had come up and that I wouldn't be going after all. However, when it was apparent that Ryanair, the travel agent and the two contacts all actually believed that I was going to Malta, I started to say to myself, 'Maybe I will go, meet these two people, contact the Irish Embassy, write a blog post about my experience and spend the rest of the time working on the laptop, pretending that I'm actually busy in Malta.'

I decided to go one step further. I contacted the International Department in the Dublin Chamber and told them that, following the trade mission that they had hosted, I was planning to visit Malta myself. Did they know of anybody that I could meet while I was there? That's when the magic happened. They contacted Finance-Malta on my behalf, and that organization offered to introduce me to any of its members who might be interested in the financial training that we offered. Within a couple of days, I had an itinerary of fifteen meetings, a driver supplied by Malta Enterprise and a plan. There was no backing out now. But maybe, just maybe, I could actually do this?

Today, 60% of our revenue comes from abroad, with 5% from Malta, I travel abroad on business at least once a month, and I'm a patron member of the Irish International Business Network. It all started because I took one mechanical step after another. The belief that I could actually do it wasn't a prerequisite – that came afterwards.

If you feel that you really can't make more money, not because of any concrete reason but because of a feeling inside, let's start off with some small-ticket items. You don't have to believe that you can: just follow a couple of mechanical procedures, and if you really don't like having a better bank balance, you can resume life as it was.

It's important to think things through before you get going

Now I would like to turn to those impatient readers who are champing at the bit. I can hear you thinking, 'Come on. I've already blasted all those excuses, I know I have the time, I have an idea, I have everything. I'm ready to go. When does this book actually start?' I salute your enthusiasm and can-do attitude. Congratulations. Even though it feels strange to tell you to hold on, as I totally share your impatience, I nonetheless have to tell you that self-awareness, preparation and reflection are absolutely essential to your success.

Before you jump right in there, have a serious think about whether your plan will generate a profit (aka margin), how long will it be before you can reap the reward of your efforts in the form of money (aka sales cycle), and whether this route offers one-off or regular income (aka a replenishing market).

Let's say you're thinking about approaching your boss for a raise of €2,500 per annum or a bonus of €2,500. 'It doesn't matter,' you think, 'it's the same thing.' Or is it?

The two are very different:

A raise of €2,500 amounts to almost €50 per week over the year. There is a much smaller apparent impact on the employer when you ask for a small amount (which will subsequently occur often) than when you ask for a large, one-off number.

If you earn an extra €2,500 per year, how does that affect the tax that you pay? In fact, if you were to ask for €40 extra per week, would that keep you in a lower tax band? Would it mean that the lower raise would work out to the same amount as the higher raise after tax? If you take the entire amount on a one-off basis, how would this affect your actual after-tax earnings?

If you get a bonus of €2,500 this year, how can you ensure that you do the same again next year? If you get a raise of €50 per week, it's a new contract that will exist until further notice. You don't have to ask for it again.

Yes, it is easy to disguise procrastination as 'detailed planning' – something that you'll wish to avoid. Yet, it does pay (quite literally) to look into the future and to evaluate your options before embarking upon your journey.

You have the power to change your future

There is one last barrier that I need to address, and it is a big one. Ponder this. Isn't it incredible that there is such an enormous weight-loss industry, given that we all know how to lose weight – eat less and exercise more? Yet we pay inordinate sums of money in the hope that we can find the secret to weight loss.

I decided to lose some weight myself a couple of years ago, and I learned a lot about nutrition and the psychology of eating. I adopted strategies to measure and manage my eating. I developed ways of incorporating exercise into my day. However, none of that would have made a blind bit of difference if I hadn't acted on all of that knowledge. There wasn't a single coach or instructor in the world who could help me get a fitter, leaner, healthier body if I wasn't willing to swap carbs for protein and get my heart pumping.

As I was writing this book, many people would laughingly say to me, 'Do you have a treasure map in there that will bring me to the money tree?' There is nothing that I can present to you on a velvet pillow that will miraculously change your money-making ability.

However, there is massive monetizing power within your own hands – and I'm here to help you harness it.

Many of you reading these words haven't tapped into your revenue-generating power as of yet, for any number of reasons. Perhaps you didn't know how, or you needed a framework, or you were waiting for a push in the right direction, or you were at a different stage in your life, or you believed that it would all happen in the future. These are all perfectly legitimate, acceptable reasons. However, please remember that the responsibility now lies with you. I have poured time, effort, my life's experience and all that I can offer you at this stage into these pages. I'm handing the baton to you. You'll have to take it up and finish the race yourself.

2. *Before you go in search of success, you have to know what it looks like*

One day I gave a talk in a school and asked a group of sixteen-year-olds how they would know if they got rich. I got lots of answers along the lines of 'having a big house', 'owning nice things', 'not going to work', 'winning the Lotto'. I had to knock the wind out of their sails by saying, 'What if I have a big house, but I have a €1 million mortgage on it? Am I rich?', 'I have some lovely earrings that I consider to be nice things – does this make me rich?', 'There are lots of parents who stay at home to mind their kids, but have about €100 of spending money at the end of the month. Are they rich?' and 'There are lots of Lotto winners who are bankrupt only a couple of years after the big windfall.' By the end, the entire room was in a thoughtful trance about what 'being rich' really meant. Don't dismiss those answers as child's talk – when I've asked the same question of adults, I've got some similarly vague, ambiguous answers.

The thing is that, like these kids, we often don't think about what reaching our goals really means, whether we actually want them and, most of all, how we'll know when we've actually achieved them. Understanding your goals is vital to reaching them. There is a definite strategy to obtaining your goals, and it's this: you have to define exactly what success means for you, and then go after it. Don't keep subjecting yourself to failure by choosing goalposts you can't see.

I think it's important to make your goals measurable for a couple of reasons. First, if you achieve them, you can actually recognize them. If your goal is to 'be rich', what is 'rich'? You might work yourself ragged and never think you are rich enough, even though you have millions in the bank – after all, others have billions, so you could always be richer. Second, if a goal is clearly identifiable and measurable, you can see whether every decision that you make brings you closer to or further away from your desired result. Finally, you're far more likely to stick the course when the course is something specific. Things become possible as soon as you think about what you actually want in concrete terms.

Of course giving shape to your goal isn't the single factor in determining success, but it is absolutely essential. As previously mentioned, how can you score if the goalposts are invisible? Why would you spend time and money travelling to a destination that doesn't appeal to you? How can you ever get that wonderful feeling of achievement if you simply never notice that you have arrived? There is a lot of merit in simply thinking about what you want, why you want it and how you'll know when you can give yourself that metaphorical pat on the back for having achieved it.

The flipside of success – failure – is also something you should think about seriously. Given that fear of it often holds us back from ever trying, maybe you should ponder what failure is. What's the worst that could happen? I'm not suggesting you say this in a glib way just to dismiss your fears. Ask yourself seriously: what is actually the very worst that could happen? And how would you handle it? *What's the worst that could happen?* is one of the most helpful questions you can ask yourself.

Let's imagine that I went to Malta and came back, having met only rejection at every meeting. My ego would have taken one hell of a whack, but I would have learned a lot along the way. It would have cost the price of the flight and the hotel, but a holiday out there would have been costlier, as I would have had a lot more time in which to spend money. So, really, I had nothing to lose. If I hadn't gone, I may well have been musing about dipping my toe into international waters to this very day, and I would have lost out on tens of thousands of euros, dollars and pounds of revenue. Now that would have been a disaster. Not to mention that I wouldn't have been able to share the experience through this book.

So take ten minutes to think about what failure would mean to you. What if things went as badly wrong as possible? What would that mean to you and your family? Write it all down, put it away and revisit it throughout the course of this book, if you feel you need to, and see if it really stands up. My own definition of failure is not trying. Let's figure out what yours is and whether it's enough to hold you back from the very real chance of a better lifestyle.

Remember also that *What's the worst that could happen?* is essential in calculating how much risk you can afford to take on any one venture. If push came to shove, how exposed would you be? Plan accordingly.

Consider a timeframe for your plans – and give yourself a deadline

Visible goalposts also make it easier to commit. Consider some of the things that you've done in your life: things that you knew were going to be short term and that you subsequently gave your all. If you had known, at the beginning, that the activity would go on forever, would you have started in the first place?

Studying for my professional exam required nine months of submerging my head in the books at every opportunity, including evenings, weekends and bank holidays. It required an immense amount of discipline and meant that lots of visits, nights out and lie-ins never happened. However, I knew that it had a starting point and an end point, and that afterwards, no matter what the result was, I had done something productive with that discrete amount of time. I choose the word 'discrete' deliberately. In maths, there are two different types of curves: discrete and continuous. The first is a curve that has a starting point and an end point. It's clear, defined and easy to work with. The second is a curve, which can extend into infinity; it is much more complex to work with and impossible to quantify.

If somebody had offered me the choice between studying forever, with life as I knew it stopping in the name of quantitative analysis and fixed-income theory – and not studying at all, I would have chosen the latter. So I would suggest that you give yourself a discrete, finite amount of time in which to achieve a specific amount of income. If, by the end of that timeframe, it hasn't worked but you've still given it your all, I promise you that you will, nonetheless, be left with something productive, positive and tangible: at the very least some more money and improved money-making skills.

When I was nineteen, I went to Edinburgh for thirteen weeks. I set off on an adventure with one night booked in a hostel, a one-way ticket and one bag. I didn't have a job, didn't know anybody and had absolutely no idea what I would do when I got off the plane. It truly was the summer that I grew up. Over that time, I met friends for life, found two jobs and learned about budgeting the very fast way. As I look back, the amount of learning about life that I packed into those thirteen weeks was amazing and will forever stand out in my memory. I'm sure you do the same: recall your life in highlights – your school years, relationships, a time that you spent in a specific company or a period of living abroad. There are some occasions, weekends, days or nights, that stand out above all others: a wedding, a funeral, a birth, a graduation, a family reunion, a party. What if I were to ask you what you did during June 2003? Can you remember? Maybe if there was a hook or a key event that could bring you right back? Let's make the next three months of your life into just such a memorable highlight – those three months on which you look back and say 'I remember it well because I learned a skill that has brought me money, security and an ability to be more self-sufficient' or 'That was the time I learned how to negotiate' or 'I taught my children how to think entrepreneurially so that they could always find ways to generate money, no matter what situation or part of the world they lived in.'

Or simply 'That was the time I had so much fun pretending for a few weeks that I was a high-powered exec running a multinational – until I woke up one day and realized I had created a sustainable stream of income while playing make-believe.'

(The homonym 'discreet' is also relevant here. You might be

worried that people will talk about you if you're earning more money. You might also be worried that, if people know about your endeavour and you fail – whatever that means – they'll mock you. Let's start off by keeping your ideas, dreams, aspirations, worries, concerns and all other emotions strictly between the pages of this book. That's really how I envision it: as a trustworthy, loyal companion, one that will be there for you when things get tough.)

One step at a time

How can you handle the hard stuff, and still make headway?

The answer is simple: like anything that's worth achieving, it's one step at a time, and one thing after another. Once, addressing a group of disillusioned business people suffering from the recession in a highly competitive industry, I shared the stage with a sports psychologist. He likened the current economic environment to a marathon, suggesting that we imagine ourselves elbowing our way forward to stand at the starting line. He said, 'I would have Muhammad Ali in my ears saying, "I'm gonna show you how great I am." I would lean forward, with my fists clenched, gaze focused and ideally with some sort of cape flowing behind me' (to which the room erupted with laughter). 'However, as I get eleven miles in, my lungs feel like they're going to implode, my legs start to feel like jelly and the last thing I would want is somebody telling me that I can be the greatest. All I want to do is to stay alive, never mind get to the end. At this stage, it's all that I can do to run to the next tree, then the next tree, then the next and then I want to collapse under the tree after that. I break it down to literally one foot in front of the other, again and again, until I notice somebody out of the corner of my eye who has thrown in the towel. He drags himself off the road with that look of defeat that I will not bear. I will go on, I will keep trying, and if I am going to give up, it won't be until the next lap. By the time I've talked myself through all of this, I've regained my breath and the finish line is just two miles away. Now I have a renewed sense of vigour, and, as I see the finish line and my kids shouting proudly "That's my Daddy", I think that, although my muscles are probably eating themselves by now, I'm going to relish telling my wife that it was tough, but, hey, I could handle it . . .'

There are times when you will feel like you can do anything, and there are times when just being able to hold yourself together is a phenomenal achievement. There are times when a motivating quote will be inspirational, drive you forward, make you reflect and give you a lovely warm glow. There are other times when you think whoever came up with that quote hasn't a clue what you're going through. It's likely that both will happen to you along this journey, and on those down days just use any energy that you have to take one small action after another. One foot in front of the other. On the great days, remember your cape and be the Super(wo)man that you can be.

Take your dreams seriously

What you shouldn't do on a down day, though, is rubbish your dream and listen to the little voice that says 'And just who do you think you are, Mister/Miss Big Bucks?' That's why I'm asking you, right here at the start, to play like the big players. Do multinationals have quarterly reports? You'll have quarterly reports. Do multinationals have board meetings? You'll start to have board meetings, just as I did after just a few months in business. Best of all, you'll have Key Performance Indicators. If you're sniggering already, ask yourself: could it be that using KPIs is what got those big companies to where they are now? Could it be that KPIs can give you a way to make those goalposts visible? Reachable? You bet.

I love to read in the *Financial Times* about companies turning over billions and dream of what I would do in their situation. I soak up stories of multinationals and the twists and turns of their journeys, because I want to grow our company to a very high level. I have, admittedly, come out with some clangers over the years, when

Ardle (my fiancé) rolled his eyes at some of my outlandish ideas. I remember bounding up the stairs to him one night (that was before we had an office) and asking what he thought of having a 'casual Friday' policy in the company? He said, 'Are you seriously asking me what I would think if you wore a pair of jeans sitting in the room downstairs on a Friday, as opposed to a pair of black trousers?' I remember asking him if he thought we should grow via organic growth or acquisition. I should contextualize by clarifying that we had set up the company the previous day. However, I didn't see why I should wait to think about those things. After all, as the business was a discreet project, I was admitting those things only to him (and now I've let you in on my little secret too . . .).

Before you think that I live in a fairy-tale land that bears no resemblance to reality, let it be known that sometimes my 'corporate speak' has brought us fantastic results. One Friday in the office I was feeling really down; it seemed I was getting nowhere and I couldn't see how to change that. I felt stuck. We were just about three months into starting the company. I rang Ardle and said, 'Is there any chance we could just meet later this evening, identify what we're really trying to do and then start working on some strategies to move forward?' I christened this dinner our 'board meeting', and we've been having those meetings ever since, each and every Friday night that I'm in the country. Now what if I had said to myself that day, 'We don't turn over millions, so I can't meet my boyfriend that night to figure out what to do next . . . That would be a board meeting, and I'm not allowed to hold one yet.' Think of all the conversations, developments, reflections and actual productivity that wouldn't have happened because I'd held myself back by thinking, 'That's only what big companies do.' Calling it a board meeting might sound dramatic, but what do I care how it sounds, if the meeting achieves the same objectives as a board meeting? Why wait if something works now? I want to make something happen today, and use tomorrow to build on it. So why not make that first step happen now?

If you feel silly using terms like KPIs, would you still feel silly if you had the salary of those who work in highly successful companies and who receive six-figure bonuses? They don't have a problem with it – talking about KPIs is just normal to them – and they don't feel that they are mouthing big words. To them, they are just describing what they do (monitoring the progress of their business) in a convenient way.

Personally, I'm always modelling the level that I want to be at and then trying to break it down into a step-by-step journey to get there. Successful businesses use KPIs to make sure they are on target, so there's every reason why I should use them too. Success leaves a trail of evidence. Observe that evidence, then imitate and emulate, and you'll be successful as well. It's just a matter of finding someone to imitate and emulate. (We call them 'role models'.)

The importance of role models

I was thirteen, sitting at my school's awards ceremony: the deserving members of the class that had just passed were being honoured for their achievements. There were six people in particular wearing down the carpet to the podium. As I watched them go up and down, up and down, collecting their awards, I silently yearned to be like them. Throughout the next six years, there were lots of nights when sitting down to *Coronation Street* was more appealing than writing an essay; lots of Sunday afternoons when it would have been lovely just to sit in the sun instead of study; and lots of nights when my bed was inviting me to a restful slumber before my homework was done. However, I kept those six people in mind, and whenever I needed an extra boost, I would say to myself, 'Would they give up now? I bet if they were sitting here at 11 p.m. and wanted to go to sleep instead of work out this organic chemistry, they wouldn't give in. If they had the option of doing another exam question before finishing this weekend, they would.'

I was nineteen, standing at my school's awards ceremony. As I was presented with the Student of the Year award, I recalled those six names and thanked them for getting me through the harder times. Powering through, with the imagined help of those role models, absolutely made the difference. I also wholeheartedly encouraged the school to continue to put the time, effort and money into holding an annual awards ceremony, because that may well have been what enabled me to put the icing on the cake of my young academic life. You don't need to get awards and accolades to have evidence that you tried your absolute best. There were times when I pushed myself as hard as I could and only a couple of people knew about it. There were times when I gave it my all and, to onlookers, I failed, because I didn't make the proverbial grade. Others achieved more and got better results, but that didn't take away from what I had done. All that matters is that you try and that you put some effort into your ambitions.

I continue to have role models for a number of reasons. If I'm ever doubtful of my own ability to do something, I simply look to others to see how they have carved their path. They have the same twenty-four hours in the day that I have, so why shouldn't I be able to produce my own version of their success? I think it's also important to be able to empathize with them. If you feel that they started from a similar place to yours, it's much easier to believe that you can do the same as or possibly even better than they have done. I found it easy to identify with my role models in school, because they too were once in their first year like I was. I find it rather difficult to identify with companies that begin their story with 'We borrowed ten million in a high-stakes deal from the bank and then . . .' because our business didn't start like that. I remember one interview in which an actress was asked, 'So what's the first thing that you do when you go home after filming?' and she answered, 'I load the dishwasher and the washing machine.' The interviewer blurted out, 'So you're just like the rest of us, then', at which the actress laughed and said, 'Why, what were you expecting?'

It's best if your role model is engaged in something that you find relatively impossible to accomplish today. I think there is a difference between those who motivate you to do what you think you can already do, and those who can help you towards what you feel to be impossible. The latter are true role models. You may know already that you could earn an extra €200 per year if you really wanted to, but you may not believe that you could make an extra €20,000. There are people who can give you the boost that you need to bring in that extra €200. However, the right role model can bring the impossible within your grasp: their example can inspire your imagination and make you realize that you can do it too.

But it's easy to dismiss our dreams when we see other people achieving things and we feel that there is too great a gulf between us and them. One night I watched a video about two people who had set up an amazing education company with millions in turnover and hundreds of employees. I felt simultaneously inspired and bereft as I tried to imagine how we could follow in the footsteps of this organization when it was so far ahead of us. However, the video went on to say that the company had started off as just two people with knowledge that they wanted to share and a wish to use technology as their method. They grew by the inch, the yard, the mile and then at a rate of knots as they innovated, adapted and developed. The founder also said, 'There are so many things that we want to do, that will take us years to achieve, but I'm so looking forward to it.' I sat there thinking, 'She could be somewhere else looking at a video, just like me, and thinking what I'm thinking, only about another, bigger company.' If you're using the success of others to shoot yourself down: Stop. Right. Now. Don't turn their achievements into yet another excuse to do nothing. Stop comparing. Instead, let yourself be inspired, and start to do what you can do now.

I always make sure that when I admire someone, I tell them. There was a look of pure pride on one father's face that night at the school awards when I told the audience his son was among my six role models. I have often approached business people and told them that I follow their story, think they have done amazing work or have had a specific influence on my life. I'm sure you would agree that it makes you bloom when you hear that you have made a positive impact on another person's journey. After *The Savvy Woman's Guide* to *Financial Freedom* was published in 2013, I got some heart-warming e-mails from people who said they had found ways to improve their financial lives dramatically, thanks to the techniques that I had described. Other readers said that their outlook had been completely dark about the future for years, but the book had given them some strategies to follow and the confidence to follow through. I treasure each and every one of those messages.

Finally, if you feel that you can add value to your role model's life or business in some way, don't hold back. Life isn't a linear path. Don't think that just because somebody earns more than you, or is more successful in some way, you can't possibly help them. Who knows – they might be looking for a contact in the very company for which you're working. They might be forming a focus group and you'd fit the profile perfectly. They might be feeling down that day and your message could get them back on to their feet. Even if there isn't something that you can do for them right now, it never hurts to create a platform for good karma. Never, ever underestimate the power of telling someone, 'Thank you for doing what you do, it's inspiring.'

3. *Working smart . . . and measuring success*

When you're working towards a big goal, it's very easy to think that what you have to do is put in lots of time and effort. Of course, time and effort are both necessary – lots of time and plenty of effort, depending on the size of your goal – but just as important is the application of critical thinking to what you're doing. No point spending all your time and energy in ways that are not actually getting you to your goal. You do need to work hard, yes, but it's more important to work smart. This idea of working smart has been turned into an acronym – SMART – a handy reminder of an approach to goal-setting that I have found hugely helpful, and you will too.

SMART goals follow a simple, yet comprehensive pattern that ensures you have the best possible chance of achieving what you set out to do. The acronym stands for

- Specific – a goal that is clear, narrowly defined and that will allow you to focus
- Measurable – a goal that can easily be ticked as 'done' when achieved
- Attainable – a goal that is actually possible (even if it's ambitious)
- Realistic – a goal that can be achieved within the constraints of your life and environment
- Timely – a goal that has timed milestones

I recently used this framework to help my audience make the most of CorkMEET, an international conference with over 600 attendees, including people from all over Ireland, and delegations from Bristol and Northern Ireland as well as Slovenia. They were about to embark upon a three-day mega-networking blitz, and I was the first speaker. As somebody who has attended hundreds of these events over the years, I know all too well how you can drive home afterwards full of good intentions. Then exhaustion kicks in, and the urgent overtakes the importance of following up. I decided to speak to them about how SMART goals could frame their experience and help them to get the most out of it while their energy levels and expectations were still high. I suggested they map out their objectives in the following ways:

First, what was the one overriding aim of the three days? Make it **SPECIFIC**. Of course, everybody would say they wanted 'more business', let's take that as a given, but how do you actually go about that? This is the same trap as 'I want to be rich'. 'I want to be rich' doesn't tell you what you should do, right now. What does 'more business' mean to you, in detail?

'For example,' I said, 'there are several international and foreign-owned businesses in the room. Do you want to use this opportunity to start building your soft export approach? Do you want to meet new people with a view to identifying prospects, following up and subsequently turning them into customers? Do you want to take a look at the attendee list, and work out a strategy for meeting certain people within a specific industry, existing clients or pivotal decision-makers? Are you here simply to get some time off from your business, some headspace in which to get new ideas and consider your strategic direction? Did you sign up for this event to sharpen your sales pitch, or to build your networking skills? The point is that all of the above will lead to "more business", but if you focus on just one of them, you can be far more effective.

'The next thing to do is to **MEASURE** how exactly you're going to execute this plan. For example, if you're currently turning one in every three leads into a customer, and you want to find ten new customers, you either need to meet thirty new leads or you need to improve your conversion rate. If you want to expand into the Slovenian market, you need to create as many meetings as possible with the businesses on that delegation. You also need to look at the wider opportunities that may not be apparent. Could you write an article about your experience, put it out on to a number of social media platforms and invite your new contacts to share it? Could you approach the organizers about speaking at a future event? Finally, how many meetings can you realistically fit into the time that you have?

'This brings us neatly into the arena of **ATTAINABLE** and **REALISTIC**. When you first arrive at an exhibition or a conference, you're fresh, looking forward to all that could happen and the people you're going to meet. After two days of high-energy networking, your mind is in overdrive trying to spot opportunities and dealing with the late nights along the way. On the third day, you may be absolutely exhausted and simply want to curl up with a coffee and your e-mail. It's important to think about what your actual capacity is, and match it up with your measurable, specific goal. Over the next two days you're going to have at least six meetings scheduled, and there is the possibility that one person may not show up. There are two coffee breaks, lunch, dinner and an impromptu opportunity while queuing on the way in. This makes ten realistic possibilities for meeting a lead and making a contact.

'The last part of this process is actually to schedule in the time to follow up, not just assume that it will happen.'

This last bit was the **TIMELY** element of SMART. It was incredibly important that the people in the room made time in their diaries to reap the return on the time they had invested. They needed to schedule a half-day during the following week in which to send e-mails, LinkedIn invitations, make the introductions that they had promised, etc. If they were going to ask people to meet them for coffee, they should have time slots clearly marked out to facilitate this. In the new international business relationships that would develop, they would need to create time to have phone conversations and conference calls. Finally, out of respect to themselves and their time, I suggested that they earmark an hour, exactly one month later, in which to review their progress. Only then could they decide what the final impact of that conference had been.

This may sound like a lot of work, but take it from somebody who has learned the hard way through wasted time and money: this is the most effective way to put your effort into any endeavour, and to generate the best results from it. It eliminates procrastination, propels you forward and stacks the odds of success in your favour. You might think, 'Well, with that much work sunk into it, no wonder this formula works. It had better.' And this is exactly the message I want you to take away from this book: I can give you the framework that will speed up the process, but only you can put in the hours. And guess what? When you put in the hours in a SMART way, results are 100% sure to follow.

Networking to build your confidence and knowledge

On a side note, I would encourage you to attend some form of enterprise event in your local area, even if you don't have a business. First, it's very encouraging to see other people finding ways to make more money every day. It was inspiring to go to business networking events when I was in college, even though it scared the wits out of me, just to see how people lived the life towards which I was aspiring. When I hadn't a clue about how to expand internationally, I started going to international networking events in my own local area, so that I could build my network, my knowledge and my confidence.

Second, there is a lot of learning that can take place as you talk to people who are taking on challenges and achieving successes. I speak at lots and lots of entrepreneurial events across Ireland and the UK, and I can assure you that there aren't bouncers at the door who will tell you to go home if you haven't got your business plan in your pocket. As you introduce yourself, you can always say something along the lines of 'I'm interested in setting up a new business/ networking on behalf of my company and currently looking at all of my options', which is a broad opener that will enable you to fit right in. I would also suggest to people who are in employment to go to an industry event of some kind at least once a year for the very same reason. It's good to brush up your knowledge with different views, talk to other people in other companies and gauge how things are changing in your sector, from the perspective of employability as well as other things – you never know how that information and those contacts could benefit you in the future.

Finally, please remember that everything worthwhile takes time. The universal law of 'cause and effect' dictates that if you pour effort into something, there will be some effect, even if at first it's not what you expected. If you devote part of your day to doing something four times a week for three months (let's call this a discrete dream), there will be a result of some sort from this. We'll look at how to make that time as effective as possible in the next chapter, but, for now, please remember this universal principle: when you invest time and energy in something, results will always follow. This book is here to make sure that your efforts are channelled effectively, and not wasted.

If you're still not convinced that you can make more money by applying the principles in this book, well, then – prove me wrong. Regularly set aside a certain amount of time over a period of reasonable length, apply some focus and effective effort in earnest – and see if you don't achieve something positive; see if you don't learn something that will directly improve your career and home life. Have you ever heard the quip 'It took me twenty years to be an overnight success'? This is the only way to be a success: repeated action, after repeated action, after repeated action, until the 'boom' of a tipping point is produced. People will call it 'overnight' because they can't see the time and effort that went into it. To them, it seems that your success came out of nowhere, when you know all the hard work that it entailed.

The numbers don't lie

On a recent trip to the US, I watched a programme in which a Gordon Ramsay-style restaurant guru was sent to a restaurant to rescue the business. Running the establishment were a husband and wife, working themselves to the bone, and two daughters who never saw them in a good or energetic mood. The restaurant was losing money, and the owners' connection to their 'third child' was a highly emotional one. They took a bull-in-a-china-shop approach to increasing revenue and decreasing costs: they didn't think, they just went and did whatever they thought would prevent the doors from closing.

For example, the wife decided to paint the ceiling a different colour to improve the decor. The husband was buying and cooking in bulk, and serving defrosted food swimming in oil, in an attempt to save money. They were also pushing their catering by offering large discounts (which was proving to be an expensive, time-wasting, loss-making activity). The expert asked the couple what their biggest fear was and they said, 'We don't want to fail our daughters and ourselves.' To which he gingerly replied, 'But you're already doing that.' They both dissolved into tears.

Over the course of the show, the focus changed from revenue to profit, and the team examined how to increase the quality of the food so that they could charge more for it, how to change the items included in the catering offering, how to increase the spend of the customer, and how to build retention. Each one of these improvements led to greater profit and, predictably, by the end of the show, the business was flying and they all lived happily ever after.

When you know what you're actually looking for (i.e., profit, not just revenue), you can measure it effectively (revenue minus cost), and you can develop and execute strategies (as they did in the business on the TV programme); it becomes much easier to apportion your time, effort, money and resources in the way that is best for you and for your bottom line. If you don't have any focus, all of your efforts can result in a diluted, limited effect.

Once you have a clear vision of where you're headed, and you have a series of steps to follow, you need to make sure that things are kept on track, while you're working on a day-to-day basis. KPIs will give you that bird's-eye view of how well your revenue-generating efforts are going. KPIs will allow you to stay on course towards your goal, or to correct course if need be.

The key is to examine the most telling aspect of your activities, in order to find out if you're actually making progress or just trying to convince yourself that you are. One day I was speaking to B&B owner Padraig Sweeney, a great friend of Ardle and mine, and I asked, 'How is business these days?' He told me that revenue was at its best level in five years. I congratulated him and asked about his levels of occupancy. He dismissed my question, and rightly so: 'If I were to bring my price down to €10 per night, I could have 100% occupancy, but that would only serve to make us look good, and our accounts would suffer for my ego. It's really irrelevant.' So make sure that you measure carefully those elements that will lead to success: if you focus on the wrong indicators, they may tell you a twisted story and conceal a ticking time-bomb. This is why carefully choosing and monitoring your KPIs is not just make-believe for grown-ups; it can make or break your success.

My challenge to you – GROW MORE!

Now that our journey together is about to begin, I'm going to ask you to take this grid and fill it out as you go through the book. But, before you do so, stop and think. This is the ideal moment to identify your sweet spot when it comes to making more money. Remember that 'making the most money possible' is not always the best option: you could work twenty-four hours every day, and that might bring in a lot of money, but at what cost? You may just want to make an extra €100 per month and not have to do a whole lot in order to get it. You may want to set up a business to generate some more money, but also because the idea has been in your head for a while and you want to give it a try. You may want to earn an extra €1,000 per month and would be willing to work for it, because if you could manage to grow it, you would be able to start planning to leave your full-time job. You may want to increase the amount of money that you make without increasing the amount of time that you spend at work. You may want to contain your business into fixed hours and keep it from oozing into other areas of your life. You may want to take on a sales role in your job. You may want to make more money, without the need for confrontational conversations or having to act as a sales-person; you would just like people to ask you to do things and to get paid for them.

It's very important to understand your goals, realities and motivations. What do you really want? What do you really not want? What comfort-zone boundaries do you want to push? Now is a good time to fill out the top four slots in the grid.

Goals	Motivations
Realities	Overcome
Opportunities	Route
What are you going to do?	Evaluate

First, what is your money-making goal? Remember to follow the SMART acronym: rather than 'I want to make loads of money', replace it with something like 'I want to make an extra €1,000 per month within three months.'

Next, it may be obvious, but write down your motivations: why you would like this to happen? For example, do you want a better lifestyle, send your kids to college, take a month off work to go to Australia, extend the house, wean yourself off the credit card? Attaching values to a goal was described to me once as having the same effect as that of a hot knife through butter – you just cut through anything that's in front of you.

Now proceed to the realities section and write down all of the stumbling blocks that you might be up against. You might be thinking: I don't have the time; I don't want to fail; I don't think I can do it; I have a lot of responsibilities already; I'm too tired; I just don't think it will work; all I'll do is spend it when I get it anyway; people will expect me to buy them drinks on a night out or take them on holiday if they see me with too much money. Get it all out on paper.

Finally (for now), take each one of those realities and think of a single strategy for overcoming it. Come up with at least one. In some cases, you'll find that I've addressed the barrier in the book. In others, just giving the barrier some thought might enable you to come up with a solution ('If I were to set up a standing order, I could save some money after I make it instead of blowing it all'). Maybe you can adapt your plan to your realities ('I can't leave my children during the day, so I can see if there are ways to make money online while I'm at home').

Let's check in with this grid regularly throughout the book and fill out the remaining slots as we move through.

STEP TWO

*Identifying what you could
do in order to make more money*

4. 'I don't know what to sell'

As I went through college, I picked up jobs here and there. I didn't think I was acting entrepreneurially at all, really; I just brought in those extra couple of euros wherever I found them. Throughout my four-year degree I had a part-time job in a corner shop with regular shifts throughout the week. I answered an ad in the shop window; I was flexible with my evenings, weekends and holidays, which suited both me and the owners.

A student's social life generally takes place during the week, so I used to babysit at weekends. My cousin told her friends about my availability, and I happily exchanged my house for theirs on a Saturday night.

I gave grinds in subjects in which I had done well in my second-level exams. When a friend of my uncle was worried about how anxious his son was before his exams, my uncle asked me if I would help, which I gladly did.

Having been introduced to a stock market training company (now called GillenMarkets) through the Business Society in college, I worked as one of their investment club coordinators and generated a commission on training days and products. (Little did I realize that this company would become my full-time employer after graduation.)

I went to Edinburgh during my first summer in college and exchanged three hours' cleaning daily for my accommodation in the hostel where I stayed for the first three weeks.

In Edinburgh, I approached some recruitment companies about work and was subsequently placed with the MS Society Scotland as a receptionist, a job I held for the entire summer.

In between lectures, I used to fill out market research surveys and was paid with vouchers. I simply googled 'money for opinions' and some small revenue streams were waiting for me online.

During my second summer in college, my aunt got me a job working in the nursery department of a hardware store. I learned some of the best lessons in sales techniques ever while working there.

The student travel agency USIT was recruiting campus representatives. I did this for two years in exchange for travel vouchers, which I redeemed for a flight to Australia.

During the third summer, I started running mentoring sessions for people attending the GillenMarkets stock market training courses. I would follow up with a call after the seminar to ask them if they needed any additional help. Out of every ten people, I used to have at least one person who took up my offer to answer their individual questions, show them how to buy and sell online, look up dividends, etc. I have since spent years studying investment, but the knowledge that I absorbed that summer has never been matched in any book that I've come across. I continued this service well beyond my college years.

I approached the Students' Union and put an ad on their site to sell my textbooks when I didn't need them any more.

I also applied to distribute and collect the Census forms, but I didn't get accepted, as my interviewers felt that I didn't have the time. (They were probably right.)

I feel that I lived my college years to the full and beyond, thanks to all that I experienced as I worked. I didn't cost my parents an arm and a leg while in full-time education, but rather enjoyed finding ways to turn my time, energy and abilities into money. In addition, though I didn't realize it at the time, I was refining the skill of being able to be financially self-sufficient – one that I would use for life.

However, I burned myself out completely several times along the way. I said yes to everything and didn't think too much about it. In some cases, I was doing things that were totally unprofitable, and in other cases, despite the fact that I was making a certain amount of money, I could have used my time in better ways in the long term. In addition, I never really had a financial plan, as I thought I was far too young for that. I never sat down and worked out how much I actually needed to make to cover the year's expenses. I also found that the more I made, the more I spent. I could have managed my time better and made my money work more efficiently, if only I had had the framework that I'm describing in this book (and in the previous one). I don't regret how I spent a single day in college, but now that I've learned the lessons of hindsight, perhaps you can benefit from them.

The point of telling you all this is that at every turn I was able to figure out a way of making money without needing to come up with a big original idea. This chapter is the total antidote to the 'But I don't know what to sell. I don't have an idea . . .' conundrum. As I said earlier, it is a misconception that a revolutionary idea is essential before you can make money. So we're now going to explore what a money-making idea actually is, how to use my framework for generating ideas, and how to ensure a money-making idea 'has legs'. Finally, you'll learn about the three KPIs that will help you keep track of your progress along the path of turning an idea into money.

Our world is full of money-making opportunities

There is an abundance of ways to make money all around you: all you need to do is think. You could simply begin by taking a look at structures that are already in place:

- Become an agent for another company's products or services (Example: Amazon, Kleeneze, ClickBank, etc.).
- Buy a business (www.businessesforsale.ie).
- Take a franchise.
- Go to a recruitment agency to get a job.
- Look for seasonal jobs.
- Keep an eye out at your workplace for additional opportunities.

~ Commercialize research. I have met with several academic professionals who have the most amazing ideas for a new piece of technology, a biomedical process or a food supplement. However, they don't have any desire to bring them to market. They don't ever want to have to think about a sales pitch, raising money, creating invoices and the logistics of international expansion. That's where entrepreneurs can come in.

In addition, it's important to look within and see what you enjoy doing. Spend a few minutes writing down every single thing that you like to do. For now, please don't let any thought be an obstacle – we'll deal with 'How could I possibly make money out of that?' later. For example, I might like to:

~ Talk to other people.
~ Shop.
~ Relax.
~ Watch TV.
~ Eat in nice restaurants.
~ Spend time with my kids.
~ Travel.
~ Go on nights out.
~ Eat chocolate.
~ Run.
~ Go to the theatre.
~ Play football.
~ Write.
~ Paint.
~ Go to beauty salons.
~ Go to the gym.
~ Cook.

Let's take that last example – *I like to cook, but how can I turn that into something that people would pay me for?* Let's brainstorm some more.

I can think of over thirty ways to make money out of a love of cooking:

1. Write a cookery book and self-publish it: it could be recipes, or tips to improve your cooking skills, or ways to organize your kitchen.
2. Deliver a weekly or monthly meal plan to paying subscribers, consisting of a list of meals for the week, the recipes for each meal, a shopping list and an app that maps their progress.
3. Write a cookery blog or start a series of podcasts and then sell the advertising attached to the space.
4. Write a blog with recipes for unusual ingredients and sell those ingredients.
5. Write a blog in which you review kitchen utensils, knick-knacks, etc., and sell the best of them for a supplier on commission.
6. Develop your own innovative products to sell to the retail or industry markets (for example, while cooking you had an idea for a contraption that would halve prep time).
7. Sell your homemade cakes, chutneys, jams, etc., to give as presents.
8. Design a foodie experience for parties.
9. Give a 'foodie tour' in your local area.
10. Open a café/restaurant.
11. Supply a café/restaurant.
12. Work as a chef in a café/restaurant.
13. Open a cookery school.
14. Open a catering business.
15. Offer a specialized home dinner-party service.
16. Make dishes and cakes to sell at an artisan market.
17. Open a food-consultancy practice.
18. Open a restaurant-consultancy practice.
19. Become a food buyer for a restaurant chain and travel the world sourcing ingredients.

20. Organize a regular cake sale in your workplace.
21. Be a foodie mystery shopper.
22. Write a paid cookery column for a newspaper or magazine.
23. Produce a food magazine (on- or offline).
24. Become a celebrity chef/critic and get paid to deliver after-dinner talks (I can hear you saying 'but . . .' – remember what I said earlier about just putting everything down, no matter how outlandish it might seem!).
25. Produce a show where you travel to undiscovered places and showcase their cuisine.
26. Develop an 'add-water' product to sell in shops.
27. Create a supper club where you charge people to come to your home for a dinner party.
28. Start a specialized cake-making business.
29. Cater specially for children's parties (and joint-venture with other businesses selling into this market, e.g., bouncy castles).
30. Offer a niche business catering for weddings in marquees at home.
31. Sell ready-made picnic boxes in summer.
32. Sell Christmas hampers as corporate gifts.
33. Create a cooking-related world record while simultaneously raising sponsorship and a media profile.

Now it's only a matter of examining each idea within the right framework. Which one is feasible for you at this point? Which one can actually bring in money? Which one will you implement?

Remember that there are just two reasons why people spend money . . .

In *The Savvy Woman's Guide to Financial Freedom*, I encouraged readers to divide their spending into three categories: fixed (e.g., mortgage or rent, standing orders, etc.), variable (e.g., utilities, education costs, etc.) and discretionary (entertainment, gifts, etc.).

I could have streamlined it further and pointed out there are really only two reasons why people spend money:

∼ To solve a problem (mostly fixed and variable expenditure).
∼ To give pleasure (mostly discretionary).

If you look at every single purchase that you make, the intention behind the transaction will most likely fall into those two categories. You buy groceries so that you won't go hungry; you pay the mortgage or rent so that you will have a roof over your head; you go to the doctor to make you better; you pay for transport to get to work – all of these things are issues that need to be solved. On the other hand, you go out for dinner for the ambience of a restaurant; you go out on the golf course for enjoyment, fresh air and banter; you go on holidays to see new places, relax and have new experiences; you get a facial for some pampering – all of these things bring pleasure.

If we flip that around, we can separate the broad activity of making money into two categories: you provide a solution to a problem or you give pleasure. You don't need to come up with something revolutionary or that hasn't been thought of before or that will 'disrupt the market'. All you need to do is satisfy one of two basic human desires: the avoidance of pain or the enjoyment of pleasure.

This is the cornerstone of making money: make absolutely sure you're solving a real problem, or that you're giving pleasure. Having said that, let's see how we can refine your offering further.

A framework for brainstorming

Let's take a skill that you have and come up with as many money-making ideas as possible. Please, please, please, don't hold yourself back by thinking that it's outlandish, would never work or isn't practical. This exercise is just you and the paper – the only target is to get as many ideas on paper as possible. There aren't any rules. So here are ten questions to prompt the brainstorming process:

1. What are the most obvious ways you could use the skill?
2. Could you offer a specialized service to an industry?
3. Could you offer a specialized service to an environment?
4. Could you offer a specialized service to a demographic?
5. Could you train others?
6. Could you write a blog about it, attract readers and sell advertising? (Please note that blogs are a wonderful way to gain exposure, raise your profile and market your services. But you have to think about how it can generate money; you have to have a 'business model'. Just 'writing a blog' isn't a money-making idea.)
7. Could you create a novelty angle and raise sponsorship with media attention?
8. Could you start a joint-venture with another company and offer your skill as part of their enterprise?
9. Could you buy something and, with your particular skill, make it more valuable?
10. Could you create an output or result with this skill for those who don't have the time to do it?

Now let's take two theoretical examples: you might be an Excel pro; or you might love porcelain dolls. How can you turn those skills or tastes into money?

Skill: Excel

What are the most obvious ways you could use the skill?	I could create proprietary specialized spread-sheets and sell them to businesses with a view to focusing the business on the important aspects of the company (aka KPIs) or create useful spread-sheets where I work and get paid overtime.

Could you offer a specialized service to an industry?	Every industry has a financial element behind the business, so I could develop special spread-sheets for the legal, childcare, education sectors, etc.
Could you offer a specialized service to an environment?	I could provide specialized spread-sheets for a local shop, a household, a community centre, an office. I could also take on the task of building spread-sheets for my workplace, training all staff on how to use Excel as well as developing and monitoring KPIs in the business.
Could you offer a specialized service to a demographic?	I could create specialized spread-sheets for a student, a tourist, a backpacker, a retiree, a parent, a couple preparing for their wedding.
Could you train others?	I could sell Excel training webinars (see p. 51).
Could you write a blog about it, attract readers and sell advertising?	I could write about complex Excel formulas, create budgets and documents for download, produce step-by-step videos on YouTube. I could gather e-mail addresses, ascertain who my market is and then sell advertising.
Could you create a novelty angle and raise sponsorship with media attention?	I could create a mass conference call and set a world record for the number of people working on a collaborative spread-sheet at the same time.

(Continued)

Could you start a joint-venture with another company and offer your skill as part of their enterprise?	I could approach companies that offer Microsoft Office training and become part of their team.
Could you buy something and, with your particular skill, make it more valuable?	I could create spread-sheets cost-free, build macros and formulas, lock them down and sell them on a website.
Could you create an output or result with this skill for those who don't have the time to do it?	I could create a KPI spread-sheet, offer to input the information in a company's accounts, process it on the spread-sheet and present them with a report. (Note: this is a subset of management consultancy.)

Skill: Porcelain dolls

What are the most obvious ways you could use the skill?	I could create and sell porcelain dolls. I could appraise vintage porcelain dolls. I could buy, restore and sell vintage porcelain dolls.
Could you offer a specialized service to an industry?	I could make specialized porcelain dolls as wedding favours.
Could you offer a specialized service to an environment?	I could make specialized porcelain dolls for children's birthday parties.
Could you offer a specialized service to a demographic?	I could make porcelain dolls for mothers as a gift to their daughters on their graduation.

Could you train others?	I could hold a porcelain-doll-making class in my city.
Could you write a blog about it, attract readers and sell advertising?	I could travel all over the world meeting people who collect porcelain dolls, gather thousands of hits weekly from people who love porcelain dolls and then sell advertising to porcelain-doll providers.
Could you create a novelty angle and raise sponsorship with media attention?	I could create a porcelain doll of a global household name (after taking legal advice on how to do it without infringing any property rights), invite them to a Google Hangout where they would take questions from their fans, officially launch the doll and then auction it live online.
Could you start a joint-venture with another company and offer your skill as part of their enterprise?	I could team up with a porcelain-doll seller and act as their sourcing agent.
Could you buy something and, with your particular skill, make it more valuable?	I could buy battered, worn, second-hand porcelain dolls and carefully restore them, adding bespoke twists for the clients.

5. *Putting your ideas to the test*

I often sit down with a blank sheet of paper, tell my objections to keep quiet and just write and write ideas until I can't squeeze any more on to the page. I buzz with enthusiasm, and then I ring my fiancé and tell him about how I'm going to do this, that and the other until I'm almost out of breath as I'm saying it. He usually brings me down to earth by levelly asking me, 'So how exactly is that going to work, or, as you're always saying, where is the profit within the revenue?'

I want to give you a gold star if you've come up with new angles on making money, and I hope that you've surprised yourself with how many ways there actually are. Now it's time to move to the next stage: put those ideas through a funnel in order to find the best ones.

Six questions that will help to clarify your idea

Here are six questions to ask yourself. They can be used either to examine a money-making idea ('Is that idea more of a service, or does it need to be developed into a product?') or to further your brainstorm ('If that idea wasn't just a one-off, but could generate a recurring payment, how could you position it differently?').

(1) *Does it solve a problem or give pleasure?*

Make sure that you're not 'creating' a problem to fit around what you intend to sell. Does your product really, truly solve a problem to which people are actively looking for a solution? How would they themselves describe their issue?

(2) Are you creating a product or a service?

A service is often instantly available to go to market. For example, if I had been thinking about this earlier in my career, I might have articulated it like this: 'There are people who want to learn the practicalities of investing in the stock market. How can I add value? I can offer to mentor them and show them how to buy and sell shares, and I can start to offer this service right away.' With many other service-based business ideas, the same straightforward path exists from idea to selling, apart from other logistical issues: I might need to find premises and to get insurance before I offer Pilates classes, or I might need to get some compulsory qualifications or insurance before I can start selling a particular service.

A product will typically need a greater amount of time between concept and sale, unless you take a pre-defined route. My previous book, *The Savvy Woman's Guide to Financial Freedom*, is a product: once it's produced, I don't need to expend a lot of effort to sell one additional item. But it took eighteen months of intensive work on the part of the entire publishing team, in comparison with my almost instant stock market mentoring service. Alternatively, you could begin to sell somebody else's product on commission or through a franchising opportunity, which would speed up the process but would also see them keeping most of the revenue.

The other side of the coin is that a product is often much more scalable than a service. With my mentoring service, the limited amount of time that I have available means that the amount I can sell is also limited, since I'm selling my time. There are three ways around this. First, I could charge more, which would result in a greater amount of money. However, the value I provide would have to justify the increase in price; and I still wouldn't have any more time to sell. The second option would be to 'be in several places at the same time', which is absolutely possible. If I were to deliver my tuition on the internet to a much bigger audience via a webinar, I could charge each person, and the only limiting factor would be the capacity of the technology. This form of education isn't considered individualized mentoring, but rather large-scale training, so it would constitute a different offering with a distinctly different price point. The final option would be to productize the offering by turning it into standalone training, without any live, time-dependent link to me at all: I could record training videos or write a training manual to sell. This would be completely scalable: that there are only twenty-four hours in my day becomes irrelevant. But I'd be producing a product, rather than providing a service.

(3) *Are you creating something new or fitting in with an existing structure?*

If you want to start making money right away, but you don't have any ideas, you can always become an affiliate of a company, selling their product and generating a commission. Alternatively, you can build your own product or service from scratch. The first method is often easier, can allow you to start making money right away, has brand recognition, and may have support structures in place. All you have to do is make the sales and let the parent company deal with anything that goes wrong. However, you would probably receive only a fraction of the income that you could get if you were to create your own offering. For example, I could register as an 'affiliate' with Amazon. If I post an Amazon link on my website, and if people subsequently buy books as a result, Amazon will recognize that I'm responsible for those sales and pay me a commission, which would be a proportion of the profit. It would take no more than a couple of minutes to set this up, and any problems relating to the sale would be handled by Amazon itself.

Alternatively, you could write your own book (which I did). It will be much longer before you'll make any money. However, you can keep all of the profit from each book (after the publisher gets their share), as opposed to the proportion of the profit that you receive as an Amazon affiliate.

(4) Will your idea generate a one-off fee or regular payments?

Consumers generally prefer if there is a one-off payment for a product; a recurring payment makes them feel that they're tied to the vendor. But, at the same time, they prefer to hear a smaller number when they hear a price. I could suggest that you pay €500 a year for a widget or €50 per month. At first sight, you might be drawn to the lower number, even though you end up paying more, as 12 × €50 = €600. Consumers immediately consider the effect a currency amount will have on their lifestyle. If you spend €500 today and that represents all of your disposable income for a month, you'd have to live 'fun free' until your next wage packet: is the value you receive worth that? From that point of view, €50 is much more acceptable. You can have both the product and your social life – you don't have to choose.

On the other hand, businesses generally prefer to have customers sign up to a regular payment plan for a number of reasons. It spaces out cash-flow: instead of getting all the money in one lump sum, the business knows there will be a regular flow of income for the foreseeable future, or at least for the duration of the contract. Also, they don't have to go back out to resell to customers: customers continue to pay at regular intervals unless they actively stop the payment at their bank or credit card provider. This automated system results in higher sales than if they had to encourage the customer to come back into their shop or outlet every single time they buy. The only downside is that the business has to wait much longer in order to get the whole amount. In our example, they would need to wait ten months in order to receive the same amount as they would upfront. Also, if you're going to take regular payments, you need to have the infrastructure to do so: credit card facilities, encrypted storage of data and an administrative system to back it up. In choosing whether to charge a one-off fee or a regular payment, you need to work out your cash-flow cycle, the impact of the cost on the consumer and the technology logistics and regulation impact of your choice. If you're in employment, the equivalent to a regular payment might be the building of a higher salary into a contract or an increase in the number of hours that you're contracted to do.

(5) *Do you want to generate a high or a low margin?*

Why would anybody prefer to sell a product with a little profit, rather than a lot? For a company to charge a large amount of money for something, there has to be added value. Let's take the example of one-on-one mentoring versus a self-directed training product that I mentioned earlier. Consider the price I could charge if I were to give you my undivided attention for ninety minutes and answer all of your questions about investing in the stock market. Now consider a step-by-step guide that allows you to access high-quality learning, but that isn't tailored to you, and that's delivered without the potential for immediate feedback; your personal circumstances and learning style aren't the main focus. Since the mentoring service is bespoke, convenient and immediate, you might be willing to pay a much higher price for it. In general, we're willing to part with more of our cash if we're given exclusive treatment (as above); if there are more benefits (a hotel has a golf course and a swimming pool); if the service is more convenient (dry-cleaning is delivered); or if the product saves us time (the train instead of the bus). Hence, if you want to sell something with a higher margin, you need to be able to demonstrate how it has greater value than its cheaper competitors.

(6) *Do you want a high or a low volume of business?*

Again, at first glance, it might seem that it's always better to sell lots of something than a little. However, look before you leap. Let's say that, for some reason, I had a huge influx of calls for mentoring, and my diary was filled up every day for three months. This looks great. Now let's roll forward and look at the consequences. The phone rings the next day and somebody wants to make an appointment; I tell them that my next available slot is in four months' time. They decide that they want to go elsewhere and I lose that customer and every other customer who subsequently has the same experience. Also, let's say that I get completely burned out and that within two months the quality of my offering falls dramatically. I'm going to lose customers because they're not getting my optimal attention, which is what they're paying for. Finally, I'm so busy with all of these customers that I don't have time to write invoices, follow up on new opportunities and keep the business running. In fact, this 'high-volume' approach could sound the death knell of the initiative.

In this scenario, I would be much better off thinking deeply and seeking advice on how to drastically increase the value of the offering and treble the price – which would allow me to work less for the same amount of money. I'll get fewer customers, but I'll be able to give them a fantastic service, apportion time in such a way as to ensure that I have a good pipeline of future customers, and stay on top of the business without compromising revenue and profit. However, if I'm selling a book, I can work with the highest possible volume that the printers can handle, which is a lot. If there are 1,000 books sold in one day, it's not going to adversely affect the reader of any one of those books in any way – they're not going to get a lesser book. It's important to ask yourself exactly how much you can handle. If you're going to take on lots of overtime at work, will the quality of your work decline? That might put your job itself in jeopardy, or you might miss out on that promotion. If you're going to start providing mystery shopping for a company, how much time or energy can you really give to this opportunity? If you're selling a service, how many customers could you ably service? If you're going to sell a product, are there any limits at all?

'You could be on a beach earning a million'

I have often heard people promise that you could be 'making a fortune while you're in the Caribbean' when selling commission-based products. However, there is a very big caveat: a lot of hard work goes into making that happen.

I started working with a stock market training company called GillenMarkets at the tender age of nineteen, while I was still in college. I worked solely on a commission basis until I finished my degree, so I completely understand how it feels to be reliant on people signing up for a company's product as an income stream. Undoubtedly, it can be a lucrative source of revenue, but don't believe for a second that people will come knocking at your door to buy and then in no time at all you'll be swinging over a sandy beach sipping a cocktail (as this form of opportunity can sometimes be portrayed).

Earning money via commission is just like any other business: you need to find your market, articulate what's good about the product, deal with people's objections, follow up and collect payment. People will turn you down, you'll get disheartened, and you'll need perseverance and tenacity. However, again, just like any other venture, it can absolutely be worth your while, if you believe the product delivers value and if you're willing to put in a lot of effort. I had complete faith in the training courses on which I was generating a commission, and I treated it as seriously as a part-time job. I was rewarded commensurately, and I also learned a lot about business in general, time-management, marketing and sales. As a bonus, it enabled me to prove myself to the company, which offered me a full-time job upon my graduation.

Commission-based revenue can be a great way to get your feet wet. You don't need to come up with your own product because the structures are already in place and you can start right away.

However, I have sat through a couple of presentations in which the audience is shown images of smiling, picture-perfect couples above a caption saying 'They made €5,000 last month', followed by the stereotypical person in a bikini and sunglasses jumping in the air, captioned 'She made €3,000 this month . . . while on holiday'. Next, they pull out a simple, clean chart claiming that 'Ten customers = €100 of passive income per month' and then extrapolate it to 'One hundred customers = €1,500 per month'. Then comes the sweetener. 'If you can bring in somebody else to work with you, every penny they earn, you do too.' Your mind starts racing with ideas about who your first ten customers are going to be and how you can call up your cousin to join you in this get-rich-quick scheme. Before you know it, you're imagining yourself swinging in that hammock.

Absolutely, you can have all of this and work your way into the picture-perfect poster, but please let me give you a couple of questions to ask yourself, should you be presented with this opportunity:

1. Would you buy the product? If you were to sell the product to a close friend, could you stand behind it? Please remember that when people buy something, they buy into the person who sells it to them – you let them down at your peril.
2. Ask the presenter about the people who started and who are now no longer agents for the product. Why did they stop working with them? In many cases, the answer is that they had other commitments, they lost interest, or they didn't fit into the culture of the organization. Those are clues indicating the extent of the workload involved.
3. Ask about the support offered by the company. Watch out for a huge red flag with a flashing neon sign if there is a skimpy answer to this one. There is a lot of reassurance for you as well as for the customer if everyone knows that there's a 24-hour help desk with a free phone number and competent staff. Of course, every company isn't going to be able to afford that, but if they say, 'Ah, sure, you can call me any time', beware. If one person is truly that available, it means they'll be flooded with calls and won't be able to get back to you, so they're not really available at all.
4. Ask about the upfront costs – they might ask for a fee to get you started. In many cases, organizations impose a small fee to test motivation and to weed out time-wasters. In other cases, companies sell a dream and charge people a significant amount of money to get in the door, often with

timers and urgency tactics ('Get it now before it's gone. The price goes up tomorrow'), so that they can raise a lot of money on the night. Before you do this, check out the next point.

5. Ask about conversion – does the company have data on how many people buy, out of the number of people who initially show an interest? For example, if one person out of every two 'leads' buys, I would need twenty leads to get ten customers. Alternatively, if the conversion rate is low, I would need to improve it by talking to more targeted leads (i.e., people who are likely to actually be interested in buying). Such data will give you a much better sense of how much you actually need to do to arrive at your target amount. If you need to talk to fifty people before you can secure your first ten clients and your €100 of passive income, you may find that some of the shine has been taken off that initial offer.

6. It's often relatively easy to think of the first ten customers, but . . .

~ Your family and friends might love you, respect you and enjoy being around you, but they may not need this product and may be slow to part with their cash. Don't glibly think, 'My aunt will buy it, my mam will buy it, my cousin will buy it and my best friend could definitely do with this.' Treat them as you would any other customer.

~ Where are the next month's sales going to come from? And the next? And the next? You don't need to have names, numbers and addresses, but you do need to have an idea about where to start looking. Have you any marketing strategies in mind? How does the company support you in this?

~ If your mind is running away from you and you're already spending the €500 that you're going to make in a month, do a quick analysis on a piece of paper. How many clients would you need to generate €500? How many leads would you need to find in order to do that? Do you think this is possible? Are you willing to put in the work? OK . . . then go for it.

Being realistic about who is going to buy from you

I once had coffee with an aspiring entrepreneur who was eagerly, enthusiastically setting up his own business. He told me that there were 2,000 businesses in his city and that he was hoping to work with 2% of them, with a view to earning €40k within the year.

We often hear people talk about their market in large, macro figures, only to then go on to claim that they want no more than a tiny percentage of it within a certain timeframe. For example: 'There are 1.34 billion people in China, so I have to sell to only 1% of these people to become rich.' Now this fits into the SMART framework almost perfectly – apart from one big, big problem. It forgets about the *R* part. Realistic.

Let me put this another way. Up until now, businesses and consumers have been managing perfectly fine without your product or service. Your offering will either solve a problem or bring pleasure to them, but they may not necessarily be convinced that your solution is better than their current one, or that they want to spend money on the luxury you're selling. As a result, although an estimate like 2% sounds very small and reasonable, it doesn't sound so easily obtainable when stated as 'I want to get forty clients spending €1,000 with me by the end of the year. My conversion ratio is one in five, and therefore I need to organize meetings with 200 targeted leads and service forty clients.'

My aspiring entrepreneur should have considered whether his figure was realistic. He should have asked himself whether he'd be able to find a new client almost every week while simultaneously servicing a growing customer base. I pointed this out to him, and by the end of the conversation, looking a little deflated, he told me that he needed to go back to the drawing board and review his expectations.

When you're writing a business plan, dealing with officials, or looking for outside investment, including the broad macro figures that you can get from market research reports is a good idea, because it shows that you've taken the time to really look into the venture that you're about to begin. However, in practice, I believe that it's better to apply a micro approach. Here are two examples:

IDEA I: I'M GOING TO TAKE A DOOR-TO-DOOR FRANCHISE

Market: there are 300 houses in my area. I can cover thirty houses each evening by devoting three hours per night to delivering brochures to thirty houses; and I can do this three nights per week. Hence, I can visit my entire target market in one month, and that's taking into account something cropping up on at least two evenings that would prevent me from working on this project. In addition, I can invite the ten people in my office as well as ten households within my wider circle of family and friends to buy some products. As a result, I can reasonably expect fifty customers to provide me with a commission of €10 per month each on a regular basis, which would allow me to earn an extra €500 per month.

IDEA 2: I'M GOING TO START A MULTILEVEL MARKETING INITIATIVE, HOSTING PARTIES AND SELLING WARES TO A FEMALE AUDIENCE

Market: I know fifty women and could contact them via e-mail, text or letter. Ten may offer to host a party in their home or workplace with ten people, which would generate €200 for me per event. I can envision doing this within the next six months, generating €2,000 in six months. I would then follow up with the participants of the party, asking if they themselves would like to host an occasion for their friends. I can reasonably expect at least one person at each party to be interested, which means another ten opportunities of

€200 for each one. Hence, I could aim to make the same amount again in the following six months.

It's essential to consider who really might buy from you, how you might expand that number, how conversion could be measured and then increased, and how you might build up retention of your customers (i.e., how you retain a customer as a client so that they continue to buy from you). This is the first step in making sure that your idea 'has legs'.

6. Asking the right questions about your big idea – and what to do when you get the answers

Look how far you've come already! You've brainstormed lots of ways of making money and given them structure. Perhaps you've ruled some out and been convinced of others. Now we're going to come full circle and turn that page of ideas into an orderly, well-thought-out list. We're going to figure out your precise direction forward, so that your time and energy will be optimized, using those KPIs that I spoke about earlier.

There have been times when I've made the mistake of doing something that brought in money, but didn't make a profit. At other times, I didn't look into the future to see when the money would actually arrive in my bank account and whether I could sustain the wait. I'm not going to let that happen to you! The next four questions will enable you to take your best ideas and choose the right one for you.

1. How likely are you to get paid and how long is it going to take?

The first part of this question may have you wondering why on earth somebody would bother to work at generating money if they didn't think they would get paid. Yet many enterprises start off without this certainty. One of the key things that you need to do is to stack the odds in your favour.

For example, you might want to ask your boss for a raise but think there's very little chance of that actually happening. So imagine the next best thing that you could suggest – your Plan B (e.g., suggest ways that you could get paid for doing extra work) and then a backup plan for that, your Plan C (e.g., give them details of a training course that you would like to do to add value to your role in the workplace). If you get the first outcome, that's ideal, but, if not, you need to have a plan in place to increase the odds of a favourable result.

If you see a fantastic commission opportunity, you need to ask yourself if the company is reputable and has a demonstrable track record in paying out on time. If you have an innovative idea that you think is a guaranteed seller, do some market research and test it out on an honest group of people before throwing yourself into it. If you're on a night out and you casually mention to somebody that you could do some work for them, turn this informal proposal into something real if they reply, 'That would be fantastic, we should talk about that.' Next, you need to consider lead-in time. This is the gap between the point that marks the beginning of the sales process and the point when money starts to appear in your bank account. If you take on a large-scale project that aims to commercialize research currently at concept stage in a university, it could take months to build a prototype, more months (or even years) to take it to market and then even longer again before you actually see any money. While the rewards from this may be generous, can you sustain yourself and third-party costs until you get to that point?

Alternatively, you could start to give piano lessons or French-language grinds right away and get paid at the end of the session. However, this sales process actually begins when you start to advertise, and ends when the money appears in your bank account. The lead-in time is very short, but the potential to make money is a lot smaller.

For people who are already in business, it's important to take account of the sales cycle per customer and per product. For example, you may sell the same number of identical products to two different clients. However, one pays promptly and the other drags it out well beyond their credit terms. In the interim period, you might have to buy stock on a credit card, which incurs interest, or you may not be able to do something because you don't have the funds (which you're owed) to hand. As a result, the second customer is not really identical to the first customer, and it's important to be aware of this. Perhaps you could reward the former to show appreciation of their timeliness; and, in the case of the second client, you could apply a small interest charge (if their credit terms have expired) with the explanation that you're simply passing on the cost of an overdraft that you have had to bear.

In addition, it's useful to examine the sales cycles of your various products, so that you can plot your cash-flow throughout the year. For example, if you have a lean period in the summer, you could start the sales process in January; the payments you receive six months later could therefore be used to carry you through the time when the shorter-term sales won't be there. In addition, there may be times when bills are high (particularly around tax deadlines), so you should forward-plan your cash-flow to have the money arrive just as you need it. In many cases, it may not be as simple as this, but if you don't have this information, you can't act on it.

Finally, it's important to think of ways to shorten your sales cycle. For example, a very simple action is to ensure that as soon as a job is done, the invoice is issued promptly. Same for cheque payments – lodge them as soon as possible. If there is a build-up of invoices that need to be issued, as well as payments that need to be processed, *you* are the cause of a lengthier sales cycle. Know, also, that it is four times easier to sell to people who have bought from you already: monitoring and growing retention in your customer base shortens the lead-in time, and makes it easier and less costly, because you don't have to start the sales process from scratch as you do with a new customer. We'll deal with this in much more detail later in the book.

2. *Is there profit within your revenue?*

Not all the money you're paid is actual profit – you need to factor in your costs, including your time. It is crucial that you end up with actual money in your account after everything else has been paid. It's also vital that you investigate this *before* you start; otherwise, you'll end up wondering what it was all for. You need to examine this methodically – check your profitability per unit, per customer and per activity.

Let's say that I'm going to approach my local community hall or gym to ask if I can start giving yoga sessions, and they agree, as long as I provide any additional equipment and promote the class myself. I'm going to charge €99 for a ten-week programme, and I'm aiming to have twenty people in each class. The first thing I'll need to do is work out all the costs in order to know what my gross and net profit levels are going to be.

I'll need to price some mats and props – everything that I'll physically need to deliver the class. I'm going to ask everybody to bring their own mats and buy ten of them myself, in the event that a couple of people forget theirs. If I take this from my expected revenue, I can work out my gross profit. I'll also need to consider any other costs, including insurance, printing of posters to put up in my local area, and accounting services. And I'll need to incorporate expected taxes. This will lead me to my net profit. Let's draft my profit-and-loss account:

Revenue (20 people × €99 per person)			€1,980
Less:			
Cost of sales			
Mats (€10 × 10)	€100		
Props	€100	€200	
Gross Profit			€1,780
Less:			
Insurance	€300		
Printing	€20		
Accounting	€100	*€420*	
Net Profit			€1,360
Less			
Tax (20%)		*€272*	
Final Profit			€1,088

Now I need to examine every input on this sheet to see if I can increase my revenue in some way or make my costs more efficient.

Next, based on the final profit, let's work out how much I'm making per hour. Let's say that each course takes an hour, but I actually spend another hour travelling to and from the venue, setting up, talking to people before and after the class, etc. In addition, I spend another ten hours printing posters, putting them up in my local area, processing paperwork for the insurance company and accountant, etc. If I take absolutely everything into consideration, I end up earning €36.26 per hour – that's the final profit figure of €1,088 divided by the 30 hours it takes to generate it.

The last part of this puzzle is to identify any other costs that you'll have to pay, those that aren't directly related to the delivery of the product or service. For example, in order to give the class, do I need to pay a babysitter and buy petrol to get to and from the venue? If so, I must take this off the final profit. Only now am I truly in a position to ask if this is worth it.

Many people may dismiss the time spent working through insurance quotes, etc., but this overlooked time is often what turns an activity into a loss. Remember, if you were to ask somebody else to do it, you would need to pay them. We have built a proprietary 'Find the profit within your revenue' calculator to help you out with this task on www.savvymoneyguide.com, so feel free to use that to help you with this exercise.

3. *Does the market replenish itself?*

A one-off idea can be great when it comes to bringing in those extra couple of pounds or euros. However, it's a much more beneficial exercise if, after you've built the infrastructure, the process can be repeated again and again without much extra work on your part. While negotiating a 3% raise might make for an uncomfortable conversation, and seem like it has a relatively small impact on your monthly salary, it has to happen only once for there to be a regular, permanent increase in your income.

In my own case, when I co-authored *Positive Economics*, an economics textbook for second-level schools, we knew the size of our market at the time and the potential, as well as the realistic, number of sales that we could make in one year. However, we also knew that every year, there would be a new cohort of students and hence our market would replenish itself. Of course we needed to take into account that after the initial couple of years, people would be able to buy the book second-hand, which would diminish sales, but the point remained that new customers would come along on an annual basis. As a result, the potential revenue that we could generate was much higher than if we had just taken the one-year static market into account.

In the case of the yoga class, could the teacher offer a more advanced class? A different type of class? Could they ask their students to refer friends? If your market doesn't have a regular need or desire for your product (e.g., home furniture and appliances), you'll have to figure a way around this: by widening your marketing reach to a larger audience; by complementing big sales with smaller ones; by increasing your profit margin; or by offering incentives for referrals. We will talk about exactly how to do each and every one of these activities in later chapters.

4. Could something go wrong and, if so, what's the worst that could happen?

If absolutely everything went wrong, what would be the consequences? Compare those against the potential gain and then ask yourself if the risk is worth it. Let's consider my yoga class idea. The local community hall or gym could say no, which would mean that I might be disheartened for an hour and they would miss out on the extra revenue. Or I might not get any people to sign up and it would have cost me €20 in printing and two hours of wearing shoe leather. That's really as bad as it could get. Now imagine if it went fantastically well and I was running three groups twice a year: my total final profit would be €6,528 ($3 \times €1,088 \times 2$). Imagine what I could do with this money – and the only risk is an initial €20 and perhaps a temporary dent in my pride. The question 'What's the worst that could happen?' is one of the most valuable business-planning tools around. It will allow you to plan for contingencies and still those panicky voices in your head.

This question can also stop you from venturing blindly into dangerous territory. For example, let's say that I'll have to pay €2,000 up front to take a franchise of a relatively unknown company. I'll have to back that up with stock worth €10,000, a €5,000 marketing spend, the salaries of two staff and possibly the sacrifice of no salary for myself in the first year. In addition, my wife is pregnant with our second baby, things are already tight and I'll need to get a top-up on the mortgage to bankroll the idea. If things were to go wrong, they could go very, very wrong for all of us. In this case, the stakes are too high, and the return is uncertain. Better to park this opportunity until a better risk/reward scenario comes along.

Having too many ideas can be as big a problem as having too few

Here I need to add a word of warning. Having a lot of ideas is great; but getting stuck at the idea-generating stage is not – it's an excuse to avoid action.

I once had coffee (yes, I have a lot of meetings over coffee!) with a man who was running a business in the healthcare industry. He was telling me that he had a real passion for healthy food and particularly wanted to play a part in turning back the tide of obesity in the country. I was listening intently as he went on to tell me how he was going to apply for funding to convert a room in a local community centre into a kitchen; he had drawn some scribbles of what his logo would look like, and he had ideas for a cookbook. He was very enthusiastic about this; people often sought out his recipes after dinner parties, and he'd been asked to give a cookery demonstration in his local rugby club. The bank had given his initial business plan a thumbs-up. Everything was going well so far.

Then it all started to go wrong. In the next breath, he told me that he was also going to set up a small gym at home and give personal training. He was going to create a series of workout videos. He was going to write personalized exercise plans for his clients. Just as I did in Step One, I asked him repeatedly, 'What's the dream? What's it all for?'

That's when he said, 'I don't want to be a millionaire. I just want to work my way into having enough money to do a three-day week.' Feeling it my duty to be 'cruel to be kind', I spent the next hour highlighting the gaping holes in his story. This is what I said to him:

- If the bank gets wind of the fact that you want to dedicate only a portion of your time to the project, as opposed to doing it full time, as stated in your business plan, it will get very cold feet.
- You can forget about having a family life, social life, personal life or indeed sleeping, if you try to do all that at the same time.
- If the actual objective is to work three days a week, you should evaluate all your options, focus on the most profitable, pour your efforts into that and build it up until some work can be outsourced to others.
- If you're going to try absolutely everything simultaneously, you won't give any one thing your undivided focus.
- If you were actually to picture a day with all these balls in the air, what would it look like? Be in the kitchen for 7 a.m., run to a personal training class at 11 a.m., record some footage at 3 p.m., go completely against your own principles by grabbing some carb-packed food on the go, hastily put

together an exercise plan for a client at 5.30 p.m., eat chocolate for a sugar boost, have another client at 7 p.m., prepare the kitchen at 9.30 p.m. and collapse into a stressed heap on the couch at 11 p.m. to start replying to e-mails. This would perhaps be a really good, productive day, but everything would be rushed, and nothing enjoyed.

When I asked him where he was going to get the time to think about marketing, accounts, strategy, going to key events, etc., his answer was 'Get up an hour earlier'; to which I replied, 'You haven't factored in time for meals as it is; now you're going to be chipping away at sleep too. Sorry, did you say that you were in the healthcare industry?'

Lots of ideas and lots of enthusiasm are wonderful . . . but in their place, at the brainstorming stage. You then need to compare them and grade them according to how practical they are, as well as by how much closer they bring you to the goal that you articulated in Step One. If you put effort into lots of different things, everything will just be mediocre. Don't spread yourself too thin.

Eventually you have to come out of product-development limbo

There is a fine line between going to market with a product when it is ready, and taking forever to get it ready. If you have a burning desire to create a new income stream, but you're scared, the fact is that most of us actually are. The way to progress is to start off with a series of small, easy-to-implement steps, in order to build confidence and gather momentum. However, it's only too easy to find a new sense of achievement once you've reached that place and stay there. We drag our heels at the thought of moving to the next stage: it's intimidating. But, ultimately, it's the only way to be effective.

I have asked many 'would-love-to-be' entrepreneurs over the years about their progress, only to hear 'We're currently working on the website' or 'We're working out the colours of the logo' or 'We're redesigning the look and feel.' Admittedly, these tasks have their place in business development and are important in their own right. However, if you don't have any customers and aren't (really) planning to go get them, nobody will care about the logo or the 'look and feel' of the website. Similarly, if you want to investigate the opportunities for creating more money in your workplace, it's very easy to convince yourself 'I will send that e-mail next week when things are less busy' or 'I will do an eight-week course on negotiation before speaking to my boss' – but the long finger doesn't point to any noticeable difference in your take-home pay.

I recently answered a message from an eLearning technology company serving the industry community, saying that it had a fantastic new product and that they were looking for 'beta testers'. This meant that we were 'privileged' to be the first people to use it. We could avail of the resource for free in exchange for reporting bugs and giving feedback. And of course they were happy for us to let everyone know about the new software. In essence, the company got:

- Free consultancy.
- Free market research.
- Some initial customers, since the 'beta testing' period was limited. Many of those who had initially found the software useful would choose to stay on as paying customers (and we were one of them).
- A buzz online: there were lots of people talking about the software's functionality, and the ease and speed with which it allowed us to develop innovative educational tools. As a result, the company got free advertising and highly effective testimonials, placed right in front of its target market.
- To implement an innovative retention technique. If you ask people for their input when building something, they feel it's partly their 'baby' too, and they will want the product to do well because of that emotional connection.

Needless to say, I'm still a customer and the product is making waves in the market. If you want to bridge the gap between sitting at home with something that's ready to go to market and actually issuing invoices, invite people to test it out to see if they like it; you can always work out an initial price deal for them. This is a 'softly-softly' approach to asking people to do you a favour in exchange for the use of your offering. If they don't find it useful, ask them why. This will yield some valuable data: maybe the market you thought you had isn't there and you need to adjust course. Maybe the clients didn't really have a need for it, and you must instead turn to solving a real problem or adding more value. Maybe the price that you wanted to charge was too high or too low. While initially this might be disheartening, it has brought you a big step closer to success. Starting again from this more informed place will stack the odds further in your favour.

To stave off procrastination, write a plan and pinpoint exactly how many stages away from a finished product you are; and add a timeline beside each step – make the plan SMART. Next, do the following:

- Write the steps in a calendar and look at it frequently to remind you how far along you are on your journey. If you happen to be dilly-dallying, you'll get a wake-up call.
- Ask a trusted friend/acquaintance/colleague to check in on you regularly. It's hard to ignore somebody who replies to your 'Well, I was just going to get around to it now' with disapproving silence on the other end of the line . . . especially if this happens on a regular basis.
- Find a mentor who has knowledge of the market and ask to hear their opinion of the product; if they know of ways you could improve it; and if there are any methods you could use to test it. Do your best to glean some of their marketing experience.

As a result, there will be plenty of mini-motivations to prevent that comfort zone becoming a permanent residence, and you can get some objective feedback to help you determine when you are really ready. It's a powerful combination that I use all the time.

Putting it all together with three KPIs

Have you heard of 'chocolate tasks'? These are the things that bring a lot of satisfaction but little, if any, value. I'm sure you won't be surprised when I tell you that I would be delighted to spend hour after hour scanning invoices, creating separate folders, building spread-sheets, colour-coding them, etc. But a different shade of purple for different customers is of no use at all.

When thinking about your talents and the things that you enjoy doing, of course you should let your imagination take hold – I encourage you to do this at first – but after that it's important to ensure that the figures stand up. For example, you might like to give people facials and other beauty treatments in your home. You're going to start off by charging €20 for an hour's treatment – after all, who could refuse? If you took care of ten people every Saturday, that would amount to €200 per day, and if you could slot in the odd one here and there during the week, you could actually make an extra €1,000 per month. How exciting!

At this point, I would invite you to consider the Realistic part of your SMART goal. Let's really think this through:

- ∿ Ten customers on a Saturday means ten hours' work – do you really think that people will come at 7 a.m. or 8 p.m. on a Saturday for their treatment?
- ∿ You'll need at least fifteen minutes between sessions to refresh the room, take their money, have that little chat about their skin type, etc. Also, what happens if somebody is late? You need to factor in 10 sessions × 15 minutes = 2.5 hours. At this stage, your working day is now 12.5 hours long.

- Are you willing to give up every single hour of every single Saturday?
- The price of €20 for an hour's facial will bring in lots of customers and certainly will undercut competitors, but how much profit is left after you've bought your supplies? You might get fewer customers at €60 per treatment, but you might find yourself with a larger amount of money in your pocket as a result. That's the objective, isn't it?
- If you have to buy lots of products upfront, order some soothing music CDs and decorate a room, how long will it take just to make back your money on this outlay alone? It's only after this point that you will start to earn anything at all. We haven't even brought up the prospect of your own salary yet . . .
- What are the regular expenses that you will have? How much will you need to spend to top up your supply of products? Will you have an increased electricity bill? Will you have to pay a bookkeeper or an accountant?

You might now be thinking, 'Oh my God, why bother starting at all?' However, my intention is not to put you off, but to help you see the pitfalls before you start, so that you can refine your plan to avoid them. A stitch in time will save you lots of nines!

Your head might be swimming from all the new information. Don't worry: this is exactly why we have Key Performance Indicators – to sum it all up and make it quantifiable. In short, to check whether your money-making idea has potential, sustainability and profit, you need to monitor these three KPIs:

- How long is the sales cycle? How long does it take from the very first step of reaching out to people to let them know about your offering, to the day when they become clients and the money is well and truly sitting in your bank account?
- What is the profit in this activity? Remember to compare the revenue with your gross and net profits. Not all the money

you make is 'take-home money': you need to factor in all your costs . . . and double-check that you haven't forgotten a cost somewhere. Your time is a cost; and if you want to grow your business at some point in the future, you may need to hire someone to replace you, someone who will want a wage. So know how much you are worth to your own business.

~ What is the retention potential? Can a customer buy from you again? How long before they buy from you again? Can they refer you to their friends?

I want to make this process as easy as possible for you. Therefore, I have developed an innovative spread-sheet with this very information, a step-by-step guide to filling it out and ideas on how to improve your results. You can download this at www.savvymoneyguide.com.

STEP THREE

Finding your market

7. The gap in the market and the market in the gap

Now that we know what you might sell, let's find out who might be interested in buying it. Market research is one of the pillars of your ability to make more money. You might come up with a genius idea, but if nobody is interested in purchasing it, no amount of marketing will save you. If you don't have a market, your idea, however brilliant, won't go anywhere.

If there really and truly isn't any extra work to be had at your place of employment, there isn't any point in asking about overtime. If the company isn't taking on new staff and hasn't done for the past five years, your idea of managing the induction process of new recruits won't get any attention whatsoever. If you're working in a European hotel, there isn't any point in trying to get people in Australia to pop over for a weekend break.

Why do you need market research? Exploring who might buy from you means honing in on the exact problem to be solved or the exact way you'll give pleasure – and what bothers one person might be a non-issue for somebody else. The problem you solve depends on who you solve it for. One more reason to do market research in depth is that it's absolutely essential to deal with competition. Market research is vital, and many money-making efforts flounder for not having taken this into account.

Market research is there to speed you up, not to slow you down

Which would you prefer? Reaching tens of thousands of people who don't want to buy from you? Or reaching one hundred people who all want to buy from you? If you'd rather look for a needle in a haystack, you're free to do as you please. As for me, I prefer to have my haystack packed to the gills with needles – and that is possible only with market research.

I was having a discussion one day with one of our US clients. They had identified a new territory they wanted to expand into, and I was tasked with investigating ways to reach out to that territory via the internet. The Head of Marketing made it quite simple: 'We can spend a dollar on a guy who won't even see our ad on a massive traffic site, as he'll be searching for general news, weather or something like that. Alternatively, we can spend a dollar on a guy who's clicked ten times to navigate his way to our ad and will be delighted to find that we have what he's looking for. All we got to do is find that guy.'

It would be so easy to just place an (expensive) ad in a large, national newspaper and assume that, because lots of people see it, the enquiries and bookings will just come rolling in. However, unless your product is suitable for a wide, general audience, this will have a limited effect. You need to have a much better idea of how to reach the people who want to buy the solution that you're offering. Where are they?

This has many implications. First, you can save money and time, and avoid losing confidence, by steering clear of people who have no interest in what you're offering or may even be quite negative towards it. It costs a lot more to buy an advertisement in a paper that sells a million copies than in a paper that sells 10,000. Similarly, it costs a whole lot less to buy 'pay per click' adwords that have 5,000 views per month than those that have 50,000. If you have targeted those 5,000 views, they are going to be far more interested in how you can solve their problem than the 50,000 people who don't recognize your offering as solving anything at all for them. Also, if your market is local (e.g., you're a plumber, or a gardener, or a local shop), the local paper is going to be far more effective and far less costly than its national counterpart. If you take this to its natural conclusion, it implies that the return on your investment, in a financial sense, is likely to be much better also.

Let's leave the money aside for a moment and get to the *heart* of the matter. In various roles throughout the years, I have been asked to work on a stand at general consumer shows. In those shows, the footfall was in the region of tens or hundreds of thousands of people, but only a tiny proportion of these people would actually fit our target customer range of characteristics. Can you imagine what it feels like to be rejected time and time and time and time again, simply because people have absolutely no interest in talking to you? If the event isn't totally targeted, it's highly likely that a significant proportion of people aren't going to be interested in the impact that you could make on their lives. It's an awfully demotivating feeling to be given that polite smile or dismissive expression as people (remember, tens or hundreds of thousands of them) walk past you. Talk about a blow to your confidence.

But I have also worked at shows where the footfall was average to poor, yet still everybody stopped to ask questions, sign up for the free takeaway and genuinely wanted to talk to me. That's the type of event where you're exhausted from trying to manage a crowd, as opposed to exhausted from trying to keep up your spirits and team morale.

Market research allows you to achieve your goals faster. If we re-examine our three KPIs, this becomes clear. A sales cycle opens with a conversation with a potential customer; develops into a 'lead'; converts into a 'prospect'; solidifies into a customer; and ends with the collection of money for services rendered. If you know what you're looking for in a customer, you'll be much sharper at identifying them. We're going to explore exactly how to do this later, in the next chapter.

If that person or company genuinely wants what you're offering, the conversion process is going to be much quicker and easier than in the case of somebody who is sceptical. The shorter lead-in time will translate into lower marketing costs and hence higher overall profit on a per-customer basis. Finally, a customer who appreciates what you have to offer will be much easier to maintain (and more likely to refer others to you) than somebody who feels they've been sold a commodity of limited use or impact.

Doing your market research simply means finding people who won't have to be persuaded that what you sell is worth more than their money, because they are eagerly waiting for just your product or service.

You notice a gap in the market – but is there a market in the gap?

Have you ever heard the phrase 'There may be a gap in the market, but there might not be a market in the gap'? This simply put expression means that just because a product or service is lacking (the gap in the market), doesn't mean that people (the 'market') are going to buy. Indeed, there may be lots and lots of things that you feel would solve a problem or create pleasure in your life . . . but you wouldn't necessarily pay for them.

A couple of months after the creation of my company, we had got past the first raft of challenges and successes. We were (and still are) offering financial training to companies, and things were going well. Only there was another challenge around the corner: we had plateaued. That's the thing in business: even though things might be fine at the moment, your KPIs will tell you if you're heading for troubled waters. In our case, I realized that, unless something essential changed, we would only be able to sustain our business at the level at which we already were, and we would never be able to go beyond it. As a trainer who delivers in-person tuition, I had to face the fact that there still were only twenty-four hours in the day, some of which were not billable (I still need to sleep).

We thought eLearning, courses delivered over the internet, would be the solution to our problem. And not just to our problem, but to the problem of other trainers like us. I realized there was a big opportunity: there were huge companies that served other huge companies and created eLearning modules for them. But small companies like ours were small fry in comparison with those behemoths. Why didn't we go to cater to that audience? If we could solve our own problem, we could solve it for other people too. We came up with a business model: trainers would pay us an upfront fee to transform their live courses into eLearning, which would cover the cost of development. Then, as their customers bought their training products, we would get a commission.

This was completely scalable for us (once the course had been developed, selling one more unit didn't require more effort); it kept the costs lower for the client; and we could make a margin from the product indefinitely. It sounded wonderful, and I was ready to spearhead the idea. I set about testing it and organized meetings with clients and contacts in order to pitch it to real, potential customers.

I started off by articulating the pressing problem that I could imagine they had, as it was my problem too. I showed them the fabulous interactions and graphics that can really engage a learner and outlined the financial benefits of adding this technological string to their bow. Everything was going swimmingly, until I mentioned the cost of development. There was a gulf between what they were willing to invest and what even the most conservative costs would be for authoring their content. If we were to sell our services where the 'market was at', our break-even point (the point where we would simply cover our expenses) would have been far too risky. In effect, we had identified a gap in the market, but there wasn't a market for us in this gap. This didn't happen at just one meeting; it happened at each and every one of them. My market research at this point was screaming a unanimous result at me, and I had to listen.

Why you need to adapt your idea to your market

I believe that as long as you know the broad parameters of what you want to sell, you should 'stop, look and listen'. For example, you might decide that you would like to:

~ Sell cakes.
~ Make money out of your love of cooking.

~ Give piano lessons.
~ Start an online business.
~ Approach your employer with a new idea.
~ Set up a travel agency.
~ Open your own salon.
~ Give golf lessons.
~ Commercialize research.
~ Become an affiliate for an information product.
~ Buy an existing business.
~ Take a franchise.
~ Develop an innovative new product from scratch.

Before you start to specialize or to refine the idea in major ways, I suggest that you focus completely on your customer. It's important to remember that market research is not a discrete task, with definite starting and ending points. It's not like you can tick a box and say, 'That's done.'

You have to consider in depth all the questions that I'm putting to you in this chapter. But there is a fine balance to strike: don't use market research as a way to procrastinate. Market research can become a very comfortable place if you let it. Make sure that, every time you note a major point about your target market, you go out there and be brave enough to test it. Brody Sweeney, the Irish entrepreneur who is building his second franchise model at the time of writing, has been quoted as saying, 'You can learn more from working at something than you can from all the planning in the world.'

There is a lot of information and learning waiting for you 'in the market'. You might think that you have reached the point where you have stalker-like knowledge of your customer. Then you speak with somebody who appears to fit that profile perfectly – only for you to discover something completely new and unforeseen. That's what makes the world go round. Your customer will grow, change and develop.

And remember that if you're employed, your customer is your employer, and you should still do your market research. You can improve and increase what you bring to the company, and grow your income and employability as a result. All the questions raised in this chapter can be asked about your boss and your company: 'How is the business changing? How can I grow my relevance? What new issues can I help with?' Also, it would be a good idea to figure out how much people doing your job in other companies are earning, before you negotiate your own conditions. This all falls in the realm of market research.

Expect the unexpected. Sometimes, what your market most needs from you isn't what you think. It is of course essential to be proficient at something in order to provide a high-quality offering. But there are other, sometimes 'softer' or 'lateral' skills you can leverage, and these have very little to do with sheer expertise. Who is the better maths tutor? The maths genius who can't communicate, or the person who used to struggle at maths themselves, and is subsequently patient and empathetic?

When I set up my own mentoring service to help people investing in the stock market, I needed to be able to show them how to set up an account, how to buy and sell shares, how to transfer share certs, bring down their costs, manage their currency transactions, understand tax implications, look up a dividend calendar, ask effective questions of a financial adviser, etc. What I didn't need to show them were the nuances of the credit default swap market or the latest details of the financial liberalization of the emerging markets. Much more important were my teaching skills, my flexibility in adapting to different learning styles, my willingness to explain jargon, and my ability to judge whether the client really understood, or just thought they did.

You need to be nimble to respond to changes in your market

Market research is vital because market conditions can change very quickly, so you need to have your ear to the ground, so to speak. I have a lot of respect for entrepreneurs and business people who show dexterity when reacting to fast-changing market conditions. I once met Mary McKenna, the Managing Director of Tour America, and asked the predictable question: 'How are you finding business at this time?' It was at the height of the recession, but I was greeted with a wave of positivity and energy: 'I see so much opportunity. We invested heavily in our brand, our marketing and our people. We all sat down together and said, there are not going to be pay cuts, but we have to find a way to build this company as a team.' They grew their market share and their revenue at a time when their competitors found it difficult even to survive.

However, this was not the first time she had dealt with threatening external conditions. As the name implies, Tour America specializes in trips to the US. On 11 September 2001, as the world watched the collapse of the Twin Towers, Mary instantly knew that much of her target market would now be thinking about different destinations for their travel. And different destinations were served by companies other than Tour America. Within three days, she had designed, developed and begun to execute a new plan: offering and specializing in cruise holidays, which the company continues to do to this day. She told me, 'I knew, the moment that I turned on the radio that morning, that something had changed. I couldn't avoid it and I had to act fast.'

In the summer of 2013 Ireland enjoyed a spell of amazing weather. You could smell the barbecues, feel the sun warming your skin and hear the shrieks of children playing outside. Summer had arrived. However, not everybody was in good spirits. I had a meeting with a client who also owned a restaurant. He told me glumly that the take was down €8k that week because people were choosing to dine al fresco in their back gardens. The following Sunday, Ardle and I went out for breakfast; as the owner of the café seated us, I asked her something along the same lines as what I had put to Mary McKenna and to my client: 'How is the weather affecting your business?' She beamed with enthusiasm. 'I'm only delighted with it. We started making packed lunches with sandwiches, snacks, pink lemonade, sweet treats and Prosecco for the mums and dads.

They're flying out the door and it's more than making up for the lost business. Long may it continue.'

Understanding how market research works

Over the years I've heard innumerable pitches – i.e., the answer to 'what do you do?' – that never mentioned who was being targeted by the business, and when I asked exactly *who* their customers might be, I received one of three disastrous responses:

- A blank stare.
- 'Well, anybody really.'
- 'People who are looking to buy the product we sell.'

Too many small businesses mistakenly think that market research is only what large companies do because of the apparent cost; you need expert staff, expensive reports, time-consuming focus groups and a twenty-page document as an output. Yes, companies like McDonald's were able to anticipate the changes in Western culture and brought salads into their restaurants before we knew we even wanted them; and, yes, they might employ people to project the path of sterling so that they can hedge their UK earnings two years hence. However, basic, telling, effective market research doesn't require a Ph.D., a million-dollar budget and four years. It's simply opening your eyes and ears, measuring what you observe and acting on it.

When you start out, it's natural to think that a euro from one customer is exactly the same as a euro from another customer. Therefore, why bother finding out all of this stuff about your poten-tial client, down to what they're planning for Christmas dinner next year? Come all ye who want to spend money. It's my belief that you don't need to go into infinitesimal detail to obtain some very useful data about your customer. But, for your money-making endeavour to have the best chance of working effectively and efficiently, you absolutely need to put some time into market research and to find out as much relevant information as you can about your target customer.

Let me reiterate: research doesn't have to be complicated. Large, expensive macroeconomic reports have their place. For example, they're great when you're presenting business plans to investors, a bank, a government official, a big new client, etc. It shows that you've done your homework, which in turn builds confidence that you understand the broader market place and that you've invested some time into reading about the industry. However, there is so much more to be said for going out and talking to your customers, or talking to people who talk to your customers, in order to find out what they're saying, thinking and feeling.

A client once asked me to deliver a workshop to retail investors in Switzerland. I knew the content of the workshop inside out, but I didn't feel that I 'knew' the Swiss investor. As a result, I took myself off to a market research library for three days, where I gained access to reports that could tell me everything I needed to know about them. I gained some very interesting insights (did you know the Swiss are the most insured nation in the world?), read about developing trends and gathered some macroeconomic data. The day before the workshop, I picked up a newspaper as I arrived at my hotel. So far as the actual presentation went, I would say that only about 1% of what I picked up in the market research library was of any use to me. On the other hand, the current news stories were what dominated the discussion. Admittedly, I didn't know everything about the nuances of their tax systems and the level of current account interest rates available and how that influenced their choices in investing, but they were delighted to tell me. In fact, asking questions about their financial environment was the perfect ice-breaker. They could clearly see that I had been interested enough to absorb local news and to think about how their economy fitted into the broader picture of European economics. This only goes to show: the high-level data can serve as background, but it's the micro detail that should be firmly in the foreground.

Let's take a case in point. I travelled through Chicago O'Hare International Airport yesterday; let's say that I'm considering opening a shop selling handmade chocolates in Terminal 3. Let's say that 100 million people go through that terminal building in one year. On average, they will spend two hours in the terminal from the moment they walk through the door – including check-in, security, leisure time and waiting at the gate – to the moment they step on the plane. In addition, let's say that I discover that they spend on average $30 on food, drinks and gifts. Therefore, using a 'back-of-an-envelope' calculation, the entire market is worth $3,000 million, and if I could capture 3% of that, I could make revenue worth $90 million.

I could go deeper and explore the trends of business people and wi-fi usage, time spent at the airline lounges and expenditure at various stores. I could investigate the plight of parents as they seek to entertain children during delays, the marketing ploys of restaurants to attract families, and the expenditure ratio of a corporate executive in relation to a family. This would all be very interesting reading, and I might take a specific piece of data and use it as the basis of some action. However, if I were to slice and dice the data significantly further and compare these results with those of all of the major airports across the world in colour-coded spread-sheets, how much actionable insight would I really get out of it?

It would be so much more useful to speak to the owners of the shops, restaurants and facilities to see what changes in the habits of their customers they've noticed: do the owners find that their customers' spending moves with the general economy, or are they a shielded group? Are they more inclined to spend when a flight is delayed? Do they come to premises solely through random footfall or has technology pointed them in the direction of a specific shop (e.g., TripAdvisor, Groupon)?

Then, with the chocolate shop still in mind, I would look at any competition that's already present in the Terminal and consider how I could offer something different, talk to similar companies in the other terminals (since they're not direct competition, it's likely that they may be very willing to talk to me) and learn from them. It

would be very worthwhile to speak to anyone who'd had a chocolate shop in that airport before, or who had operated in other
airports in the Midwest. It would also be helpful to immerse myself
in trade magazines, articles and case studies of other companies
that have successfully done what I set out to do. Finally, perhaps I
could obtain approval to run a survey: talk to people who actually
go through the Terminal over the course of a day and ask them
questions in exchange for inclusion in a free draw. Now I've got concrete, insightful, on-the-ground information that will really count.

Market research stops you wasting time

The right kind of market research will help you to avoid wasting
time selling to people who are not in your target market, to better
anticipate their objections, and to make your sales process more
effective. Market research will actually speed up the money-making
process, because it will eliminate non-ideal customers. I will refer
back to this point again and again and again throughout the book.

Let me tell you about the customer-that-shouldn't-be. You start
off in earnest; you're hungry to notch up successes in whatever
form they take. You spend an enormous amount of time on every
potential client, as though each one were a hot lead. Not a nook or
cranny of your market escapes you. Anyone with a pulse could be a
buyer. This enthusiasm is to be commended, and your motivation
will shield you when you suffer the rejection that will inevitably
come your way at some points on your journey.

However, let me warn you about customers who don't really
want, need or believe in what you're offering. Getting them to buy
from you could actually harm your money-making efforts. First, if
you're too aggressive with your selling, and they sign up just to get
rid of you, there may be repercussions in the future. They could
tarnish your reputation and describe you as pushy and intimidating
to their family and friends, which damages your selling potential to
other people. Alternatively, although they might initially agree to

pay a regular fee, there's nothing to stop them from cancelling this very soon afterwards. Now you have to start your sales cycle all over again. In a different scenario, they might call you up with lots of complaints and queries; the value of this customer service time would then wipe out the profit. Then there's the possibility that they could put other people off. If you hold promotional events, they might turn up just to try to catch you out. They can post unfavourable comments online and be much more influential than you think.

I'm not speaking ill of people who complain about unsatisfactory goods or services. We all have a right to do that, and collectively we bring up the aggregate quality of products by ensuring pressure is put on suppliers to give the best value and service to consumers.

But what I mean is that I have been in business and worked with clients long enough to know that sometimes people don't like or understand what you do and will make no effort to change that or to see your point of view. That's OK. Rather than expending a lot of energy on trying to change a person's opinion of your product, just because you feel that an attack on the product is like an attack on you, simply give a polite response and mentally put them in your non-core category. I have identified lots of these people over the years, and that's what makes the world a more interesting place.

Market research will eliminate the time wasted on developing difficult, unsustainable or unprofitable revenue streams. So how can you plan to boost your chances of success?

Getting started with your market research

If you've ever watched Champions League football or Lions rugby, you'll know that both teams have precise strategies. A manager doesn't walk into the changing room before a match and say, 'What's the plan gonna be today?' Similarly, we need to put a process in place to help you to execute your market research efficiently and effectively:

~ Step 1: Identify as many types of customer as you can imagine who won't buy from you.

~ Step 2: Of the remaining people, profile them demographically, if relevant.

~ Step 3: Of the remaining people, profile them geographically, if relevant.

~ Step 4: Of the remaining people, profile them psycho-graphically, if relevant.

~ Step 5: Research relevant competition.

Weeding out those who will never buy from you

As I have said, I have often heard people say 'Well, anybody, really . . .' is their target market. And it's not that they really think that 'anybody' will buy from them. What this really means is that they haven't given any thought to their target market at all. Harsh but, in my experience, invariably true.

Do you know of a product that is of interest to every single person on the planet . . . and one that they're willing to pay for? I don't. In fact, if your market truly was every single person in the whole world, you would be overwhelmed with business. It's also impossible for anyone to know 'anybody' in any meaningful way. Have you asked someone if they could tell 'anybody, really' about your services? They don't know Mr Anybody, Really. If you would like other people to tell their friends, neighbours, contacts and colleagues about you, you need to make it easy for them. What you need to do is to plant a seed in their minds, so that as soon as somebody says 'I could badly do with . . .', they reply with 'I know just the person that you need to talk to.'

I once met a B&B owner at an event in Nottingham. She stood up and began her pitch by saying that everybody was her target customer. The network leader bravely invited the attendees, in groups of two, to critique each person's introduction. The B&B owner was left on her own after everybody was paired up, so I went over to her. I started off the conversation by asking, 'Could you give me more specific characteristics of your typical customer, to help me think of people I could point in your direction?' She said, 'Well, anybody could be my customer, really.' I replied by saying, 'Well, let's start with people who absolutely aren't. What about newborn babies? What about the 80% of American citizens who don't have a passport? What about people who live outside of the UK who have a fear of flying? What about your next-door neighbour?' She dissolved into giggles and said, 'None of those people would have any need for my place at all.'

By the end of the conversation, we had sliced her market into two categories, and then sliced each category in half again. First, there were people in the domestic, as opposed to the international, market. In the case of the former, she was likely to attract people who were on a staycation, or attending an event in the area, or needed somewhere to stay while using local amenities. In the case of international visitors, they were likely to be on a trip visiting the UK or else visiting family and friends. Of course, there are other reasons why people might want to stay with her, but if she focused on attracting people who fitted into either of those groups and were looking to stay in Nottingham, she had a plan to work with.

Next, we split her market into new and previous guests. In the case of new visitors, she had to convince them from zero and had to compete against other properties in the area. Also, these guests were likely to be more price conscious, so it was necessary for her to stand out in some other way. In terms of attracting previous guests, she had to make sure to give them the same warm welcome that she had when they first stayed with her. And she needed to stay in contact with them periodically afterwards, to remind them that her B&B was still there to meet their needs as well as those of anybody else who was travelling to Nottingham to stay overnight. She would of course be delighted if they were to recommend her property.

Finally, she decided she was going to consider a type of loyalty scheme: people could earn extra benefits by staying with her in the future or by referring somebody who 'wanted a fun staycation in Nottingham, was attending a family wedding, or was a nature fanatic who might want to visit David Attenborough's Reserve'. We cracked it in fifteen minutes. She hadn't realized how much valuable market data was sitting in her reservation books over the years, and there wasn't one person there who was 'anybody'.

Of course, from a certain point of view, the people who buy from you are 'anybody'. You might not be targeting 'only' professionals, or 'only' women between twenty-five and thirty-five, or 'only' first-time home buyers. But you need to adopt a different point of view: all the 'anybodies' who buy from you have very specific characteristics in common. It's those characteristics you have to uncover. It's like going from being anonymous strangers to having a deep knowledge of someone.

Getting a firm picture of your best customer

Asking someone to describe their best customer is very different from asking them to describe their target market. The former really focuses the mind. May I suggest some clues? I'll revert to our defining KPIs in Step Two and suggest that the best customer that you can have is the person:

- who is besotted with your offering
- who buys your most profitable products
- who keeps coming back again and again and also tells everybody they know how wonderful you are

'Well, dream on there, Susan, but such a person doesn't exist,' you say. Let's think about that. I have a friend who goes to the same hairdresser month after month to get her hair done and buys lots of products while she's there. She spends much of Friday at work telling her colleagues that she is looking forward to going to the hairdresser and then posts on Facebook: 'Off to my second home today [*insert name of hairdresser*] and really looking forward to some fabulous pampering.' That's the type of ideal customer that I'm talking about. If a competitor was to offer her treatments for half the price, she wouldn't move.

Ask around you for recommendations and see how people react. The reaction you are looking for is when somebody praises a business in the highest terms, saying they go there every chance they get and that the experience is amazing. I'm sure you have heard somebody you know recommend a restaurant or another type of business like this. If you find a customer like that, treat them as your best salesperson . . . because that's what they are, and you don't even have to pay them a salary. Still, you should show how grateful you are every time you get a chance.

That ideal customer can also be an employer: the employer who loves and values the service that you provide. They are happy to pay you well and to give you a plethora of opportunities to develop as well as to increase your earning potential. They really want to hold on to you, which gives you job stability and the emotional validation of their regular appreciation of the work that you do. I have had employers like that, and I know many people who do too.

Solving a problem – a real one – or providing pleasure

There are times when people absolutely *love* handing over their hard-earned money to get a product or service. On those occasions, price doesn't even enter the discussion. It's just that the person has a very pressing problem, and it so happens that you can solve it; or they are after the exact kind of pleasure that your offer delivers. The consequences are that you'll have to overcome few, if any, objections from the customer before you make the sale. This means a fast sales cycle, a happy client and high levels of retention.

The following story demonstrates my point. I was due to be interviewed on Newstalk live one morning at 6.30 a.m., in the studio and – crucially – on webcam. I was parked in my car, drinking my takeaway coffee and listening to the conversation on that station at 6.10, when I heard something ping off the handbrake. I looked down and saw, to my horror, that a button had fallen off my shirt in exactly the wrong place, with the result that far too much was on show. Unless I wore my jacket backwards, it wouldn't cover what I needed it to. I ran about half a mile through Dublin, in my heels, to get to one of the few newsagent's open at that hour of the morning. They didn't have any safety pins. It was 6.23 a.m. so I had no choice but to go in, keep my arms crossed tightly and look absolutely ridiculous.

Now if somebody had magically appeared selling safety pins costing €15 each, I wouldn't have blinked. In the end somebody at the station was able to provide one, but I would gladly have paid for it – the 20c for the little piece of steel and the €14.80 for the humiliation limitation.

A solicitor once told me that what she sells is the sigh of relief she hears on the other end of a phone line when a customer rings her, frantic, and she's able to reassure them that she'll take care of their case, that they won't be sued because she can put together a watertight argument. Another example is the feeling you have of finally arriving in your hotel after your flight has been delayed, your train's been diverted, you're tired, you need a shower and crave that feeling of just settling somewhere. In each of the above, the service or product provider is solving a big problem that is really weighing heavily on the customer.

You can turn that on its head and look at situations where something can give that real, heightened, wonderful warm feeling when you close your eyes to savour the pleasure of every single moment. Ask a beauty salon owner to describe a mother who gets a facial during the first 'me-time' she's had since her baby was born three months ago. Have you ever been challenged to cut out meat for a month, and at the end of that month you get the smell of the juicy piece of fillet steak that's about to grace your plate? I remember the squeal of delight on the other end of the phone when I said yes to a neighbour who was having a babysitting emergency: she was leaving that day for a family wedding, her usual minder had called her to say she was sick, and every other single person who usually babysat for her wasn't available.

It's the same for employees. Who gets promoted and paid a higher salary to prevent them from moving on? Those who bring immense value through higher sales, higher staff motivation, good ideas, taking initiative on execution – the ones who anticipate and solve problems before they happen, making the company better, stronger, faster and more profitable.

In all these scenarios it's difficult, if not impossible, to attach a numerical value to the KPIs. How much value do you add to a person's life through solving a problem or giving pleasure? The first thing that you need to do is to work out the extreme scenario – describe the situation where your potential client is in extreme pain or in dire need of some pleasure. There aren't any barriers to the sale, apart from competition from a similar offering. The customer's value system is very powerful. Money is a secondary issue, if it's an issue at all, and so price may not be even questioned along the way. If you have the 'magic wand' to solve problems such as I have described, or are able to provide such pleasure as I have outlined, your normal ability to help somebody becomes almost supernatural.

I started to give grinds in exactly that kind of extreme situation. My uncle asked if I could help the son of a friend revise for his second-level exams. The exam wasn't for four months, but the boy was so worried and anxious that he couldn't sleep and was even vomiting from the stress. Of course he was completely unable to study in those conditions.

I sat down with him, and we calmly worked out exactly what he was worried about, what would be a good strategy for each fear (some were real, some imagined) and what would be a good study plan. As I worked with him over the following months, my ability to make subjects simple, to break concepts down into step-by-step processes, as well as my actual knowledge of the subjects themselves (I had taken the exam the year before), were viewed as a magical power, capable of turning a severely anxious household back into a harmonious one. It's easier to add value when the pain or the pleasure is really strong, and you can do something tangible to help.

8. *Encouraging people to realize that they value what you have to offer*

When all is said and done, you'll have a target market only if the people or companies within it actually identify themselves as such. *You may actually have to tell your target market that they are your target market.*

This is what I told the managers and owners of language schools at an industry conference earlier this year. I started with 'I won't tell you how to attract your target market, as you know how to do that already. Instead, I want to tell you about your hidden market.' They all wanted to know who I knew that they didn't.

Very often there is a group of people who have a problem that your offering can solve – only they don't know it. So you need to tell them. In the case of language schools, people who are lonely, looking for new interests or have just moved to a new area may not specifically be looking for an eight-week intermediate course in French. But if they saw an advertisement in the local paper that said, 'Looking to meet new people who share in your love of language? Check out our . . .', they may very well identify themselves as such.

Similarly, there are thousands of people who may be interested in changing direction in their career, seeking promotion opportunities or ways to strengthen their CV. They could tackle this in many different ways: studying a course, gaining experience in a different role, getting professional career advice, speaking to a recruitment company about CV optimization techniques. They might also be interested in learning a language. If they were to read an advertisement that said, 'Looking to boost your employability or to expand your career opportunities? Click here to find out how to turn your language skills into a larger paycheque', they would be much more able to identify the school's offering as a solution to their problem.

Language schools could also solve the problems of parents looking for summer activities for their children, and of companies which are working on expanding into another country. In each case, the customer has a need that could be filled by several service providers, but they are open to different solutions and a language school may be it.

In the example of the language school's target market, you might have noticed that different clients have different characteristics: people who want to learn a language for leisure versus for business, children, etc. One common characteristic would be that these people all need to be in the same area as the school, unless the tuition was delivered online, or they were intending to relocate. It's important to spell out those characteristics by drawing a 'robot portrait' of your ideal customer, in order to know who is likely to be a customer, and who is not. Let me start you off with a series of questions:

- Is your customer male or female?
- What age is your customer?
- What problems are they experiencing (which you may or may not be able to fix)?
- What are their personality traits?
- Where do they live?
- Where do they work?
- Where do they socialize?
- To whom do they outsource responsibility?

These defining traits fall into three broad categories: demographics, geography and psychographics. Let's tackle each one in order, while you keep in mind the following questions: 'How does my product or service fit within these scenarios? Where does my offering fit in the life of my customer?'

Demographics: at what stage of life is your customer?

We would normally associate the word 'demographic' with a specific age group, but it's more helpful to think of your customer's stage of life.

You can start by ruling out those broad age and gender groups which are totally out of your target market. Let's say you are left with the very broad category of women over thirty. That part is quite clear-cut, but the answers to the next two questions are far more meaningful, and they allow us to gain an insight into the pain and pleasure points of your customer.

At what stage are they in their career?

There are many stops on a professional journey, with a lot of emotions involved along the way. The person may be worried or excited about their future prospects. The person 'cutting their teeth' may feel overworked, undervalued and have idealistic goals and aspirations. The person on the 'rise and rise' may be time-poor, exhilarated and burned out sometimes. The person at the pinnacle may feel a huge sense of achievement and a simultaneous dread of unfamiliar territory ahead. The person who finds themself abruptly in freefall might be angry, lost and unsure of how to recover. The person approaching retirement may be looking forward to a slower pace of life and also be afraid of shedding what has become a part of their identity and sense of purpose. The person taking a break to raise a family may feel empowered that they have the opportunity, or might fear the loss of the structure and social life that their job gave them. As each new stage beckons, change is imminent and that person may or may not feel prepared. There will be changes in the amount of time they have for non-work-related activities. And there will be changes relating to the certainty of their money and its amount. If you (as a business or as an employee) consider organizations to be your target market, they too have a personality and a timeline. The larger the company, the larger the budget, but also the larger the number of constraints on it and the larger the number of people who have a say over it. If you're dealing with a business owner of a micro organization, often the rapport between you has an immense influence over the continuity of a business relationship. As the company grows, interpersonal relationships are challenged by process, procurement and the greater likelihood of changing personnel in changing roles. It can take longer to get things decided and done, but there is also the possibility of the order growing and hence the amount of money that you can make with that client. Like anybody, a company may have trouble adjusting to its new size. It may not have the capacity to service new business. It may not have the HR handbook in place. It may not be able to retain customers and staff who loved the company's previous personal touch. It may have lost productivity along the way or its previous investment in staff as some of them leave. Similarly, it may be ambitiously planning expansion and trebling the amount of business that it is doing with you. It may be winning awards and gaining prestige. It may be changing hands and undergoing a new form of leadership. It may be scaling back, rationalizing and 'right-sizing'. It may be becoming obsolete due to new technologies, new competition or internal problems.

As an employee, remember that your employer may well be trying to steer themselves as well as the company through separate or combined changes. In order for you to position yourself to be able to benefit them in the best way possible, you need to understand what's really going on. If you want to sell to a person or business, you'll be in a much stronger position to solve their problem or to help them on their way if you have knowledge of the important aspects we have just discussed.

At what stage are they in their personal life?

There are many happy and sad parts to a personal journey. They can present new opportunities for growth; enjoyment; a sense of 'moving on'; a yearning for the past; an inability to wait for the future; deep loss; powerlessness; excitement; anticipation; and a range of other emotions within the two extremes of depression and heart-racing exhilaration. The situations can range from leaving home, being in love, travelling, getting married, having children, watching your children leave home or emigrating, relationship breakdowns and bereavement.

We know these changes are inevitable and yet we can be taken by surprise when they happen. We can be both truly happy and heart-breakingly sad when some of these life events take place. We can feel powerless as other influences drive the people we love to make decisions that we don't agree with. We can feel excited and also petrified by the uncertain path before us. We can feel frustrated by our inability to adjust to the 'new normal' that life has thrust upon us as well as by a longing for the past. We can be in situations that are so wonderful that we pinch ourselves to make sure that we are not in a dream. We may also be at a place in our lives where we want to orchestrate personal change. Perhaps we want to lose weight, learn a new skill, meet new people, move into a new area, try something new, regain a sense of self, become healthier, find love, change our environment, let go of toxic situations, become happier, take part in something bigger than ourselves, spend more time on something that has grown in importance in our value system or tick something off our bucket list.

If you can help a person to solve a problem that keeps them awake at night, or bring a smile to somebody who has forgotten how to laugh, or enable someone to reach their goal, you can have an incredible role in somebody's life.

Think about it. Your boss wants to be able to spend more time at home with their family and you can take an additional hour off their workload each day, thus bringing them some precious play-time with their children. A bride-to-be wants to look perfect on her wedding day and you have just the facial to make her skin flawless. A parent is worried about their son's lack of direction in life and you have the life-coaching experience that can help him figure out his objectives. Doesn't this sound very different from 'I'm just wondering if there is any overtime available?' or 'I give facials at a 20% discount' or 'I'm a life coach'?

Don't for one moment think that I'm inviting you to manipulate people and emotionally blackmail them into buying from you. I'm simply inviting you to take a real interest in your customer's life. You will be able to create maximum benefit for them if you know exactly what's wrong or how to make a dream come true. The money will follow – and I mean *follow*. It will come only after you've done the hard work of truly solving a problem or providing pleasure for your customer.

Geography: where is your customer's attention directed?

It is crucial to find out where your customer is and, more importantly, where their concentration is focused. Only then will you have a means of reaching them. The internet makes it easier to reach your target market, but it has also given that opportunity to your competitors. You need to find out where your customer's attention is directed, and in order to do this successfully you must think about your client's typical day:

- Where do they live?
- Where do they work?
- Do they visit somewhere regularly?
- If so, what radio station do they listen to on the way?
- Where do they go to relax and unwind?
- Where do they go if they're stressed or worried?
- Where do they go to socialize?
- Where do they go to be entertained?
- Where do they go on holiday?
- Where do they go for personal development?
- Where do they go for professional development?
- What places do they pass on the way?

You will perhaps need to weed out any questions that are irrelevant to your specific offering. Also, as your customer grows and develops (refer back to demographics), the answers may change.

When I was studying Financial Maths and Economics in NUI Galway, I was a classic, clear-cut case. I lived in Galway city, went to college on campus, was a member of the Business Society, read the student newspaper, went to the stereotypical places that students went to socialize and took to the promenade in Salthill whenever I was worried or stressed. It would have been relatively easy to check my demographic and geographic characteristics.

In some cases, you'll need to answer only one of the questions above; all the others will be irrelevant. Sometimes the answer to this question alone will rule somebody in or out of a target market. For example, my personal answer to 'Where do they work?' is that I'm usually travelling internationally at least once a month, if not more. As a result, I'm not the likely candidate to sign up for a ten-week fitness course in my local community centre, as I would miss much of it.

Sometimes, although all of this information is very interesting, I need just one specific element of it. For example, if I wanted to position my offering to a specific sector, I could look into where they go for their continuing professional development and find the vast majority of them right there.

Often when people are stumped for ideas, they turn to the internet. Google's own statistics are that every day it answers over a billion questions from people in 181 countries and 146 languages. Now we have social media to refine information for us and also to be responsive to our personal questions. We can access individual blogs, forums, Facebook, Twitter and LinkedIn. People ask for other people's advice almost in real time on forums: 'Does anybody have any new ideas on potty training my daughter?', 'Does anybody know where I could get a Las Vegas style cake?', 'Could anybody recommend a great PR company for an event that I'm organizing?' While personally I'm not in the market for a ten-week fitness course in my local community centre, I'm a much more captive audience when engaged in a LinkedIn conversation about a London conference in my industry.

This information can be truly useful in identifying your market. If you have a locally delivered product or service, you can draw a circle on a map and contain your efforts within it. If your product is solely aimed at parents of pre-school children, you could narrow your reach to parenting blogs and parent-and-child groups. If you want to aim at the professional market, LinkedIn provides online access and tailored forums that will allow you to 'meet' them. If you can gather enough information on where people focus their attention during the course of their day, you're in a prime position to reach out to them via effective channels. This is going to be essential for your marketing strategy, as you will want your marketing to be where your target market is.

Psychographics: getting a picture of what's going on in your customer's head

The third category is a bit more elusive, as the term 'psychographics' refers to what your customer is thinking. But there are ways to figure out what that might be. We all have a primal instinct to avoid pain and pursue pleasure. However, the manner in which we do so is personal.

Some of us love to exercise. We love that feeling of putting on sports clothes, the increased heart rate, and the silent nod of approval we give ourselves every time we pass a mirror. We see exercise as a tool within our control and use it as a release valve for the day's overload. We use it to wake us up, to calm us down, to build our self-esteem. However, some of us hate it and will make every excuse not to leave the couch. We have a very unhealthy relationship with exercise and equate the timer on the treadmill with the only measure of success in our lives. As a result, while the dictionary defines exercise as 'activity requiring exertion or physical effort', our personal relationship with it is much more complex, and it's no surprise that an entire industry has been built on it. We all know how to run, how to lift weights, how to do a push-up and a jumping jack. What we are paying for is the necessary motivation; or for a faster means of getting a better, fitter, healthier body; or for the guarantee of results generated by accountability; or for the company . . .

If you want to give your customer the benefit of your product or service, you have to understand why they might want it. The key mistake that all of us can make is assuming that they want it because *we* think it's great. Similarly, if you approach your boss about getting additional benefits in the workplace, unless you can demonstrate the additional value that they will add, it's unlikely that you will be successful simply because you want them.

Ask these questions about your customer:

- What do they love?
- What do they hate?
- What drives them crazy?
- What do they crave?
- What excites them?
- What makes them feel loved?
- What makes them feel safe?
- What makes them feel relieved?
- What picks them up when they feel down?
- What do they fear?

Again, you don't need to have all of the answers, but you do need to know how your offering can change their lives. That's a dramatic statement, but each thing that we are willing to take our credit card out for has to have an impact on our current situation at that time – if it didn't, our wallets would remain closed. In the past week, I spent money on the following:

- Wi-fi in the airport: I wanted to use my time efficiently by working and fighting jet-lag.

~ Food-on-the-go: I wanted to spend time writing as opposed to cooking three meals a day, so I was willing to pay for the convenience.

~ Two beautifully decorated Irish coffee glasses: since I was the only Irish guest at a US wedding, I wanted to give my friend a quintessentially Irish gift.

~ Dinner at a restaurant: I wanted to say thank you for some wonderful hospitality.

~ Sports clothes: I always find that if I get up and put on sports clothes, I'm telling my brain that I'm going for a run, so that, like a satnav, it directs me out the door. Therefore, I bought the stimulus to ensure I stuck to my exercise plan.

~ A coffee and scone at a coffee shop: I wanted the ambience, the people watching and the background hum of an environment conducive to writing. (I was neither hungry nor thirsty.)

~ Subscription to a focused training website: I wanted to upskill myself when cooking at home by watching webinars simultaneously, hence I was looking for both more knowledge and more productivity.

From a psychographic perspective, I was willing to pay to avoid wasting time; I wanted to express appreciation; I wanted to educate myself; I wanted to find an enjoyable writing environment. These personal motivations resulted in money being spent.

Defining your niche

This is quite a lot of information to find out about your target market, and you might be thinking, 'But where on earth am I going to find all this?' Part of it is, indeed, about 'finding out'. But part of it is about 'coming up' with the characteristics. You can, and should, decide to cater to certain people at a certain stage in their life, and not to others.

I was having breakfast with a friend who has recently set up her own business. Self-employed for the first time, she was telling me how nervous she feels because there is so much to do, and yet a lot of uncertainty about how to do it. However, she is truly passionate about what she does and about bringing benefit to other people in doing so.

I asked her about her target market and her initial response was – you guessed it – 'Well, anybody, really.' I bristled. Going through the very same list of questions above, we whittled it down to certain characteristics. Next, I asked her, 'So how are you going to specialize?' Her eyes widened. 'What do you mean specialize? I just want to get started and hope that I can do as much business as possible. I don't want to be fussy.' This is a huge misconception – being 'fussy' is another way of saying tailored, targeted or specialized.

The market is a big place. If you're in business, there are billions of people with an insatiable desire for more products and services. If you're an employee, there are many tasks that you could take care of in your workplace in exchange for more money, or you could work another job or generate some new income outside of employment. Do you really want to chase it all?

I explained to her the need to educate her market to show them that they actually need or want what she has to offer. It becomes much easier when you state from the outset that you specialize in a particular group of people. This allows the customer to hear your message and immediately to say to themselves, 'That's me.' The more niche the description, the better: people who have to move for professional reasons such as job relocation; the parents of children learning to code; Facebook users who post status updates ten times per day; models with an hourglass figure; C-level executives in the pharmaceutical industry – you can tell each of those groups 'You are my target market' (but using different words of course . . . remember the hidden market of the language school?).

It's a good idea to look at various different segments of your market and identify which might be the most profitable. For example, if you were considering setting up a hairdressing salon, your 'market segments' might include men (many of whom typically have relatively little hair and pay less attention to it than their female counterparts), children (who generally don't have the money to pay for themselves), working-age women, post-retirement women and families. Having had numerous conversations with hairdressers about their business, I can tell you that they find their best customers to be women who are retired and return week after week. They don't have to spend any extra marketing money on them: these are loyal customers and they are more likely to get longer, more expensive treatments. In comparison, the busy professional is in and out for a quick blow-dry; the family makes a multiple spend while there, but it may not be very often and the man may be a small-ticket customer. Of course, there are ways and means to build a targeted, specialized service for each of these groups, but if one select group makes more financial sense than any of the others, perhaps that should become your speciality.

If your making-money goal is as much about enjoyment and fulfilment as it is about the rise in your current account, ask yourself which group you may enjoy serving the most? When I put that question to my friend, she told me she felt that she could be most helpful to people who procrastinate and who wanted to change that. That is the process you have to follow, in order to go from 'anybody' to your special customer.

9. *Enough about the theory, here's market research in practice*

There are loving people in our lives who will always try to save our feelings. They mean well, and we turn to them first at times when we're feeling delicate. They give us faith in ourselves when our own reserves are running low. If you ask one of these people if they would give you a raise or buy a product you're considering selling, they would probably tell you that they would of course. Sure, isn't it the proverbial best thing since sliced bread? I have had this happen to me on several occasions and I've learned to recognize that look from a loved one that says, 'I don't have a clue what she's talking about, but I haven't the heart to tell her', while they're telling me that they would definitely hand over whatever price I was thinking of charging.

While this is reassuring to hear, remember that your boss, or the person who you're sitting beside in a meeting, or the person who casually comes across your product on a shelf in a shop or online, won't have the same positive reaction just because it's you.

Your market research must extend beyond your immediate circle. You need to show your product or describe your service to your target market, and see what potential customers tell you. Depending on their reaction, you can now actively market your offering. Or you go back to the drawing board.

I recently told a business mentor about an idea that I was mulling over. She said, 'The best thing you could do is to send me a one-page business plan. Let me introduce you to two senior people in the industry and get them to tell you what they don't like.' In that short sentence, she outlined an ideal framework for doing market research:

- Articulate your offering in a short, concise way – if the person giving you feedback can't understand quickly what you're talking about, you've approached them too early, as you're not prepared enough and your offering isn't sufficiently clear.

- Find people who don't have any vested interest in your confidence – in this scenario, it literally pays to be cruel to be kind. Of course, your pride may take a bit of a battering, but when did you last have a human connection with the person who manufactured the washing powder, stapler or online gift card that you bought? If you weren't satisfied, did you stop to consider the feelings of the manufacturer before you criticized their product? No, because the product has to stand on its own.

- Elicit the views of people who have experience. Let's say that I've come up with a revolutionary type of nappy and then, as a board member of a charitable organization, I bring it to the next meeting and ask everybody around the table to give me feedback. They nervously glance at one another before one bravely tells me that none of them has children. Wouldn't that be a useful focus group? Alternatively, I could go to a local parent-and-toddler group and ask them, as people who potentially buy, use and dispose of nappies on a daily basis. I can watch for their reactions, listen to their comments and note their suggestions, as that group of people is totally representative of the kind of customer who scans a shop shelf for a quick solution to a crying child with wet padding.

- Listen out for and focus on the negatives – a tip that is so totally against my outlook that it troubles me even to write that sentence. But if there was ever a time for constructive criticism, it is now. You absolutely need to hear what is wrong. Why don't they like it? Why wouldn't they buy it? What would they change? Why would they choose the competition?

The business mentor could see my face falling when she said, 'Let them tell you what they don't like', and she smiled. She told me that one of the reasons for failure early on in any entrepreneurial journey is that the founder is too busy admiring their product, while the market sees it as below par. Ask, ask and ask again. You know that you have got to the end of the process when the 'negatives' that people point out are there by design. For example, one could say to someone who specializes in life coaching for female entrepreneurs that her offering doesn't sound like it would help her customers deal with bereavement. This is not something that she needs to change; it's simply recognition of the fact that she doesn't choose to specialize in that area.

How to ask the questions that will give you helpful answers

It's very easy to phrase a question to get the answer that you want. For example, you can ask questions like 'It's a great idea, isn't it?' or 'Imagine life if you could eliminate x or enjoy y.' This is sales language. Instead, what you need for effective market research are neutral questions that elicit honest answers. Listen carefully to the answers that you get to these four questions:

1. *Does this product solve* [insert problem] *or give* [insert pleasure element]?

Translation: do you see the benefit that I think you should? Is this product or service something that you might actually go in search of? Can you identify this product as the antidote to your problem or synonymous with the pleasure that you're seeking?

Do not say, 'So what do you think?', 'It's great, isn't it?', 'You probably think it's awful, but I'm still working on it.' The first of those statements is too broad: 'So what do you think?' doesn't help people to frame a useful answer. You need to find out (for better or for worse) if what you intend to bring to the market actually does what you intend it to do. The latter two questions put words into the user's mouth – let them come up with their own.

2. *How much would you pay?*

Translation: how much do you value the benefit derived from this product or service? If somebody recommended this product or service to you, at what stage would you recoil from buying it?

Do not say, 'I was thinking of charging €100 – what do you think?' Don't anchor their expectations by giving them a number either to agree or disagree with. They might think, 'Well, I would have paid €150 for it, but, yes, €100 is even better' – which would result in your underselling the offer by €50. This would be a serious loss in potential revenue, just for asking a question suboptimally. Their answer will most likely be different if it's their task to think about a number first. Also, if you suggest a number to them, you will bias their expectations. The person might have thought it was worth only €50 and been too embarrassed to tell you that they don't quite see how the extra €50 could be justified. They might say, 'Yes, I was thinking about the same myself', but, upon seeing the price in a shop, would actually drop it quickly and move away.

3. *What would you change?*

Translation: have I actually understood what the market needs or wants? Can you suggest ways that I could add value? What are your barriers to buying this product (and how can I overcome them)?

Do not say, 'Would you change anything?' Create an environment in which they feel free to criticize. Invite the person to really think about what would make them buy. It's easy to give an inert answer of 'No, I wouldn't.' However, if you ask them the question that I suggest, they'll be more likely to point out a negative.

4. Would you prefer to use a competitor's product and, if so, why?

Translation: how do I compare against the competition? What do they have that I don't? What don't they have that I do? If my product is set beside that of my competition, what would draw you to either of us? What elements differentiate the two?

Do not say, 'You wouldn't be bothered with anything else now, sure you wouldn't [*insert nervous laughter*]?' Again, remember that if somebody picks up your product from a shelf and then that of the competition, they are mentally comparing the two anyway.

Market research can give you crucial insights on pricing

If I say that my product sells for 'the lowest price', remember that I need to live up to that. If the only reason people do business with me is price, why would they continue to buy from me if they can find it cheaper elsewhere? Competing on price is often described as a 'race to the bottom', and it's true. If somebody undercuts me, I have to undercut them right back to live up to my marketing promise. They might retaliate in a similar way, and on and on we go, until one or both of us are out of business.

Few companies have executed this strategy continuously, grown market share and built a significant profit margin. The one that stands out is Ryanair – it truly does have the lowest fares. However, one needs to look below the surface to see how it can manage that. As it has grown, it has become more indispensable to airports and other suppliers, allowing it to lower the costs of its landing slots by negotiating discounts. Since it brings passengers to less-visited airports, it has been able to agree subsidies from the airports themselves. In addition, the company has gained a lot of press over the years for its charges for excess baggage, checking in late, printing a boarding pass, etc. Its 'Getaway Café' sells food, drink, electronic cigarettes, calendars, scratch cards, dentures, etc. (I'm joking about the dentures . . . but you never know). It also has joint-ventures with car-hire companies, parking facilities, local transport, hotels, luggage providers, etc. If you take a closer look, the low-cost airfare is simply a marketing tool used to get people on a flight; Ryanair actually makes its profits elsewhere. Once these people are on the plane, they are a captive audience for other sales messages.

There is a concept in economics called 'production and consumer surplus'. If you're willing to pay €10 but the product is priced at €5 (aka a bargain), you have received an extra €5 of value for free. This is called 'consumer surplus'. Similarly, if you intend to sell something for €5, but your customer is willing to pay €10, you have received €5 of 'production surplus'. Let me illustrate this.

I was charging €60 for an individual stock market training mentoring session a number of years ago. My explicit costs included travelling, meals 'on-the-go' and the time spent in actually training the mentee. The implicit cost was the time that I wasn't spending on bringing in new business while I was busy travelling to and from appointments and training people. I was really only starting out at the time and still in college. I didn't evaluate cost or profit or anything, I was just delighted to be generating an income. My boss told me one day that I should double the price; I told him he was mad. I felt that nobody would want to buy from me any more. He told me to run the numbers – even if I lost half my customers, I would still have a rise in profit, as my turnover would be the same (half the customers at double the price = the same amount in the end), and I would have a fall in costs. Afterwards, a regular client called me and I told him of the new pricing structure. He laughed and said, 'I was wondering when that was going to happen. You should have done that ages ago.' In fact, I saw a rise in the number of people requiring my services, because they interpreted my higher price as representing higher value. In this case, I was leaving €60 on the table at every session, and the customer was enjoying €60 of 'free' value, or 'consumer surplus'.

You may need to adjust your price from time to time to see what the market will bear – even when the economy is difficult. I suggest a soft approach of letting your clients know that you are introducing a price increase of x%. However, you value their custom and are willing to lock in their existing structure for the next six months. After that, they will roll over to the new rate. Gauge their reaction, and if you see evidence that you'll be able to preserve your profit, even if some clients fall off, then go for it. If you notice a huge negative reaction, you can follow up with 'We have reconsidered our new business model and are pleased to announce that there won't be any price increases for the next year.' Personally, I have found that it has been financially rewarding to test and see if there is some consumer surplus waiting for you to pick it up.

There are typically two ways to price a product:

- Add up all of your input costs, an estimation of the marketing cost per unit, the cost of your and/or your staff's time and then a profit margin.
- Examine the competition, ascertain ways to differentiate yourself and price accordingly.

Let's say I'm going to sell potted plants. The seeds, materials, pots and everything that I need are €2 per pot. I'm going to add 50c per pot for marketing. Therefore, if I sell the potted plants at €5 each, I have made a profit of €2.50. Right? Wrong. If I neglect to take into account my own time, then I'm overstating the margin. But, you say, 'I would be doing nothing else anyway.' I used to think like that too, and that's why I was leaving a consumer surplus of €60 on the table at every mentoring session. If you want to come up with a price on your own time, ask yourself a very simple question, 'How much would I have to pay somebody else to do it?', because that's exactly what your customers are doing. Before you think that it will only ever be you, as you don't ever have any intention of employing anybody else, think about what would happen if things go fantastically well.

Say, if the local community association decides that it's going to apply for the 'Tidy Towns' competition and they want to buy 200 potted plants from you because they would prefer to give the money to somebody in the area. Unless you stay up several nights in a row, you won't get this job done fast enough, so you ask two people to help. If you haven't factored your time (or somebody else's) into the price of the plants, by the time they're paid, you haven't made any profit at all on such a big order and you're exhausted.

If I had wanted to scale up my mentoring service by hiring other trainers, they would never have taken maybe five hours out of their day and travelled 100 kilometres for €60. They wouldn't have done it, and yet, because 'I would be doing nothing else anyway', I thought it was acceptable for me. So have a think about what you would need to pay somebody else to do the job that you're willing to do and let that be the price of your time.

As for pricing relative to the competition, you need to compare your offering to theirs. Why is it that Starbucks can charge four times the price that you pay in a petrol station, despite the fact that they sell a similar black liquid? After all, if I want a coffee to satisfy my thirst or to 'start my day', what's the difference? The thing is that people don't go to Starbucks because they're thirsty. They go because they want a comfortable ambience in which to meet a good friend or to have an informal meeting. They go because they want a high-quality soy latte with an extra shot, made with Fairtrade coffee, as opposed to what spits out of a machine at the back of a shop. They go because they have gained familiarity with the branding, the green theme and the logo standing out on the high street. Starbucks have taken a coffee bean and made an experience out of it, one that we associate with convenience, quality, good conversation, settling into the day, consistency and ten different ways to describe how we want our caffeine. If you're doing some pricing market research, identify whether you're adding or taking away from the competition's offering and then price accordingly.

Why market research is essential in dealing with competition

Very often when people say that they 'don't have an idea' for a business, they actually mean that they have yet to come up with something completely original that nobody has thought of before.

I hear this all the time. But there is a big problem here: in business jargon, 'competition validates the market'.

If other people are already making good money at something, it means there is a market for this thing. Inventing a completely new product or a completely new way of doing things means you are adding a whole extra step to your sales process. You will need to, first, educate your market about why they need your product; then make your market understand that they are actually your market; and then sell to them.

People often quote Facebook, Amazon, Apple and companies that came up with completely new ideas and then made billions. But are these ideas really new? Facebook came long after Bebo, MySpace and Friendster. Amazon, initially, was simply a mail-order bookshop. The process of selling books has been around since Caxton; Amazon simply conceived an innovative way to do it. Apple only makes computers, mobiles and music-playing devices. Is that so very revolutionary? Again, it's the dexterity, style and brand of the product that they changed. And then I often wonder whether the people who celebrate these innovators consider how many start-ups sink before we ever hear of them, because they couldn't convince their potential market that they were solving a real problem. In fact, if you read the stories of any large multinational that 'disrupted the market', it didn't happen overnight, smoothly or easily.

Of course, it's understandable that you would want zero competition: if people hand over money to the competition, they're not giving it to you. However, the very fact that people are spending money in exchange for the way in which the competition is solving their problem or giving them pleasure means there is a valid market. In other words, consumers feel that the offering is valuable enough to spend money on.

But competition has a bright side that you can use to your advantage: they actually make your market research easier (by proving that there is a 'market in the gap'), and they give you a basis to build on. Instead of starting from scratch, you can now simply think, 'How is my offering different from Acme Corp's?'

I can walk a mile through Dublin and pass about thirty different coffee shops. I know where I want to go and always make a beeline for a boutique place tucked into a corner of Stephen's Green. Why do I bother walking a whole mile, when I could just stop at any other coffee place on the way? After all, I'm simply looking for a place to sit and write while sipping an Americano.

I have visited thousands, if not tens of thousands, of coffee shops over the years. Yet the majority of them have been bland and functional. In many cases, they did fulfil a need for the people who walked in. They wanted to get a takeaway coffee, to have breakfast, needed a break on a shopping trip, etc. I could probably count on two hands the number of places all over the world where I make a distinct effort to walk right through a city so that I can find my coveted spot.

Often when I ask people what makes them different, they squirm and say, 'I don't know. Hasn't everybody done everything by now?' The thing is that everybody hasn't, and anyway you're unique as a person, therefore you're different for the simple reason that you exist. All that you need to do to separate yourself from the competition is to consider in what way you are different, and then to describe this difference. Personally, I love a coffee shop with a good atmosphere. This can be created by the warm attitude of the owner and staff, or by a tasteful decor that shows a lot of thought has gone into it, or by good, unobtrusive music. I will make a point of visiting certain places whenever I travel if they have particularly good, imaginative food. Do you know how many chicken curries, chicken tikka paninis and fruit scones that I have no choice but to eat when I'm on the go? I will make it my business to go somewhere that has a healthy, delicious salad or an authentic Indian curry or a mouth-watering omelette. My cousins with kids have different requirements: they like places that will give them some pencils and colouring paper. My friend loves a busy spot where we can catch up and have a great natter. My previous colleagues always used to choose a place that had good parking and reliable wi-fi. There are lots and lots of ways to be different – you just need to figure out what they are and then tell the world.

I used to have a regular Friday-morning slot on Irish radio, with Gareth O'Callaghan. In his introduction one morning, Gareth announced, 'And here is our positive economist, Susan Hayes, to speak to us about . . .' Later on that day, I was laughing as I told my fiancé about the way Gareth had described me. His reaction was immediate: 'Why don't you secure the domain name? Buy www.thepositiveeconomist.com.' That's how the name stuck. Over time I became known as somebody who focuses on the positives – what's in your control, what you can positively influence within your own economy.

One day I got a call from the lunchtime show at Newstalk (where I had my button catastrophe in the previous chapter). The producer said to me, 'We've spent the entire show today telling the nation that unemployment is up, the bond yield is down, reported GDP is worse than projected, and so forth. Will you please come in tomorrow and tell us if there is anything to be positive about at all?' I have had lots and lots of calls like this one, simply because I made the effort to look for what made me different. I didn't spend hours and thousands of pounds with a consultancy company to figure out why I was different, because all I had to do was to listen to how other people described me.

I'm sure you've heard of the 'elevator pitch': you step into a lift, start a conversation with a stranger who asks what you do, and before they reach their floor you've explained your offering, your target market and why somebody might buy from you. An elevator pitch is useful to answer the ubiquitous 'So what do you do?' The goal is to be precise and to the point, to avoid boring or confusing your lift-sharer, and to give them an opportunity to decide if you could help them solve a problem either for themselves or for somebody else. The elevator pitch is, in fact, part of your marketing strategy.

A good formula for a short, concise, punchy elevator pitch is: We solve this problem [*insert benefit*] for this group of people [*insert market*], but we do it this way [*insert differentiator*]. You might like to check us out at [*insert contact detail, e.g., website address*].

For example, the elevator pitch for *Positive Economics*, the textbook that I co-authored, depending on the audience, would be: 'The book helps students to prepare in the best possible way for their economics exam; it helps teachers to reduce their preparation workload. Our text brought the syllabus right up to date with recent events, is completely exam-focused and is complemented with a suite of eLearning. You might like to check it out at www.edcodigital.com.'

The elevator pitch for *The Savvy Woman's Guide to Financial Freedom* would be: 'With this book, I help women to reach financial freedom by highlighting a clear, actionable, practical path. It's different from other personal finance books because it gets to the true *heart* of why people haven't achieved their financial goals yet. I wrote the book as if I was sitting with a friend who wanted to move forward financially but wasn't sure how. It's actually complemented with a 22-week e-mail course so that I can go the distance with them – you might like to take a look at that at www.savvywomen online.com.'

In both of those cases, I indirectly referred to an abstract 'general competitor' by describing what is worth noting about the product (the book or textbook) – if a feature is worth telling about, it's because others don't offer it, or do so in a different way.

Very often, the problem that people have in constructing their elevator pitch is expressing what they do in a non-technical way, without any jargon, particularly if you're involved in technology or manufacturing or any high-end industry. To start with, always focus on the problem you solve and who you solve it for. People don't need to know all the details of your product; they need to know where it fits into their life. It can be helpful to refer to a famous company that does something similar. I met the owner of www.whohasit.com and he described it as 'We are the eBay for spare parts.' The secret to a great elevator pitch is simplicity. Apple did a fantastic job of explaining what an iPod was by describing it as 'a thousand songs in your pocket' – notice how there is no mention of however many gigabytes of memory, or the AAC encoder technology they use. Similarly, Realex cleanly describes its own service in fewer than ten words:

'Enabling thousands of websites to sell online'. Test yours on a number of people and when you move from the polite nod to a genuine 'Oh, I see', you know you've cracked it.

Knowing how to interpret your market research

Having asked, it is very important to listen to what the market tells you. It is also important to see the bigger picture and not get side-tracked by the small stuff. If one person tells you that they don't like what you're suggesting, don't write it off completely. On the other hand, if ten out of ten people in your target market tell you they would all reject your product or service, you know that you've got to go back to the drawing board.

I saw the Magic Whiteboard pitch on *Dragons' Den* UK. As a financial trainer, I thought it sounded like a great idea to be able to take an erasable sheet of polypropylene paper and stick it on to any flat surface. However, the first Dragon absolutely rubbished the idea and said, 'It would never work.' The remaining four investors fought tooth and nail to get a piece of the action, as they saw unlimited possibility. If you take a look at the Magic Whiteboard story today, it has grown in leaps and bounds, and the founders proudly note on their website, 'We are now Theo Paphitis's most successful *Dragons' Den* investment of all time.' Since they were in the Den, they had four other opinions to bravely wait upon before the session was finished . . . but imagine if they hadn't. Imagine if they had asked that one person what he thought, left it at that and wrote off the product. Look at all that wouldn't have happened.

It's a fine line between having enough tunnel vision to see your project through to completion, and being stubbornly unwilling to read the writing on the wall. I told you earlier of my own experience when I went to several of our customers and potential leads about our new eLearning pitch for the individual trainer. However, I got rejected at every turn. I couldn't ignore that. I had to listen to what people were telling me.

Many people asked me what this second book was going to be about and whether it would be along a similar theme as the previous one. I found it very easy to pick the title, because that's what the market told me it wanted. As I did interviews and wrote pieces to promote *The Savvy Woman's Guide to Financial Freedom*, I was being continuously asked, 'Tell us how to make more money.' There were lots and lots of people on the airwaves and the small screen offering money-saving tips in ways that were highly effective and useful. However, there were very, very few people talking about how to find tiny, small, medium and large income streams. As I sat down with the publishing team a couple of months after my first book launch, I told them that I wanted to write exactly what you, the public, told me that you were looking for.

To gather useful opinions and feedback, I suggest that you do these four things:

- Ask people for help in understanding how to process market research. There are thousands of people who have done it before you – leverage their experience. You could contact your local enterprise centre, people that you already know in business, online forums and mentors. Remember that by asking people for help, you're giving them the satisfaction of being of help.

- Check in with hard, cold numbers and with a timeline. Let's say that you've given yourself a month to look into various avenues to see which ones might work. Four months later you wake up one morning and you say to yourself, 'I should really start doing something.' You have just lost three months' money. Remember the Timely element of a SMART goal in Step One. Also, if people report to you that they would like three bells and two whistles more than what you originally had in mind, go back to your original KPIs in Step Two and examine profit in particular. Does this addition fit in with your original objectives?

∼ Be open-minded to change and refinement – your idea comes from your heart *and* your mind. If somebody criticizes it, it may feel like they are criticizing you directly. It's important to separate the two. If you let this hold you back from truly examining the offering, you could go into the market place too early and get a much bigger ego attack. There is money hiding in your idea – let other people's views, experiences and thoughts draw it out.

∼ At the point you've stopped learning anything new, stop asking questions. There will come a time when you'll start to hear the same objections, the same likes and dislikes and effectively the same feedback. When this happens, you know enough to make those changes and to react accordingly. Market research can stretch out forever and become a very comfortable place – one you don't want to leave . . . Make sure you take action on the main points and then get going.

The next step

While all this may sound overwhelming, it boils down to this . . .

First, take some time to think about your target market and explore their demographic, geographic and psychographic characteristics.

Next, ask questions of those who fit this target market; elicit feedback from them using the four questions that I suggested earlier. You can do this by speaking with them directly, sending out a survey, asking questions on social media, informally bringing it up in conversation, etc. Feedback on your specific question can also be found on forum threads, interviews or any other material where the topic has been discussed and documented.

If, at this point, you find that your target market has different needs or wants or even characteristics than you thought, congratulate yourself on a job well done. Don't berate yourself for 'not having thought of it earlier'. If we were omniscient, we wouldn't need to do market research. But we are not, and this is why market research is so absolutely crucial when you embark on an endeavour to make more money.

And if you find that the market does, says and acts exactly as you thought it would, it's still a job well done. You have an accurate understanding of your customer and are ready to proceed to the next step.

STEP FOUR

Understanding the different roles of those in your market

10. *The four faces of your customer*

As a child, I played with jigsaws. As an adult, I play with cooking utensils. I absolutely love any type of gadget that feeds into my love of cooking: a garlic slicer, adjustable spoons, stencils for designing messages on cakes, a decorative grater plate that allows me to turn nutmeg into the smell of Christmas. I love them. If you can get me into the homewares section of a department store, you have a seriously captive customer. And I'm not the only one: research shows that women are responsible for buying 80% of household goods.

So how do you reach me and, more importantly, my wallet?

Perhaps you don't actually need to get to me personally. I make no secret about my love of all things kitchen-related, and, as a result, those who want to get me a present at some stage often consider the failsafe option of buying me something to do with cookery. Did you know that in the US 10% of the entire retail market is dedicated to gift-giving? The average consumer spent $2,062 on gifts in 2006, 60% on holiday gifts and 40% on other occasions throughout the year.

Let's say that my brother wants to find a gift for me for Christmas. In this hugely lucrative world of presents, there are two characters in the sales process: there is the buyer (my brother) and the user (me). What are we both actually looking for? In my case, the value proposition is clear. I actually want to enjoy the experience of using a mixer, a juicer, a Lazy Susan (and, yes, I have heard all of the jokes). However, my brother is looking for something totally different. He wants to see my smile on Christmas morning. And he doesn't want to have to walk to ten more shops before he gets his gift. He wants me to enjoy my present. He is concerned about two things: my reaction, and his own finite time as he slots gift-buying into his busy day.

Second, my circle of family and friends knows that I'm getting married this year. If my fiancé and I were to go to a homewares store, create a wedding list and send it out with our invitations, we would personally have done the marketing for the store. By targeting us, the shop can reach all of our guests too. They simply need us to look through their selection, pick out what we want and then give our wedding guests the choice to buy their gifts there. If we were to do that, the motivations are totally distinct: my fiancé and I want products for our home, but our guests (the buyers) want a quick route to finding a present and the assurance that we'll be happy with it.

Let's go one step further. Imagine that somebody wants to buy a gift for me and they don't know what to get. However, they know that they can't go wrong by buying a gift voucher in a department store. The shop itself would be absolutely delighted with this, as 27% of recipients never use the gift card, and of these 55% have more than one unused card. Essentially, these purchases turn into interest-free loans of which almost a third are never called in: $2 billion is left unspent on gift cards each year. On top of that, 66% of people who use gift vouchers end up spending more than the value of the card. And if I, as the recipient of the gift, have never been to that shop before, the gift-giver has helped the shop to expand its customer base.

As you can see, if you sell homewares there are many potential customers for your product arising out of my love of cooking. Thinking laterally about your product or service and who might buy it is crucially important. Do you really – *really* – know who buys from you?

You might say: it's my employer, the guests who stay in my hotel, the kids who come to my dance class. Take toys. If you sell toys, you might say: 'Easy. My target market is young parents with children aged between four and eight years old.'

Wait a minute. You sell toys, yet your target market is parents? Who are you selling to, the children or the parents?

'Well,' you say, 'the children use the toys but the parents buy them, of course. The children don't have any money . . .'

I see. So, in fact, your 'customer' consists of at least two people – the end user and the buyer. Who do you market to? The end user? Or the buyer? Does your advertisement appeal to children, who will then ask their parents to buy the toy (throwing a tantrum if necessary)? Or do you show parents how your educational toys are good for the development of their children?

In fact, the persona of the 'customer' can be broken down into four components or roles. These four roles might be embodied in one person, but, equally, they might be spread across four people. The roles are buyer, influencer, user and budget provider.

Understanding the multiple personalities of your customer

I witnessed the following argument unfolding in a friend's sitting room one day. Her husband bounded in the door with a tablet computer and was showing it to the kids, who were delightedly planning all of the apps that they were going to download. She, on the other hand, wasn't so enthusiastic. 'That looks great. How much was it?' He sheepishly replied, 'It was €600, but it was on special offer, so I got it for €500.' He bought it without mentioning it to her first, because he knew only too well she wouldn't agree. After a little while, she came around and all was well again, until he proceeded to say that he was going to supplement this piece of technology with a laptop. She said, 'So you're planning to take €1,500 in total out of our personal savings and then when I told you that I was going on a spa weekend last month with the girls, you told me that I was wasting money.' He countered that with 'Ah, but this is for work.'

When you're selling electronic gadgets and spa weekends, you have to be aware of the people around the buyer who might object to what they perceive to be indulgence. But the salesperson would have had to follow my friend's husband home from work that day to know about her criticism. On the other hand, if my friend had been in the shop with her husband, the sale of the tablet might never have happened. Influencers are all around us, and they weigh heavily in any buying decision. They are in our homes, on the internet, in the workplace and in just about every place that we look and listen. They may not be a buyer or a user of a particular product, but they can have a huge impact on the sales process. Let me give you three examples of who might be influencing you at this moment in time.

Children have buying power worth $1.2 trillion per year, and the impact of the money that they spend themselves is dwarfed by the effect that they have on their parents' and guardians' spending behaviour. Nobody wants their child to stick out like a sore thumb because they don't have a themed schoolbag. Few have the patience to listen to an hour of wailing in the supermarket because their tween wants a specific type of cereal. Children pick what to eat 85% of the time during fast-food visits. As I was growing up, the 'Pat the Baker' advertisement had a great cartoon storyline and a 'stick-in-your-head' theme tune. It was clearly aimed at children, and it worked. On many a Saturday, as kids accompanied their parents on the weekly shop, they would spot the branding on the 'Pat the Baker' bread and start singing the tune; undoubtedly they had a voice in the buying decision at that moment. So how can brands reach our children? It's very easy. The average American child is estimated to watch between 25,000 and 40,000 television commercials per year and their UK counterparts consume approximately 10,000 TV ads annually. Let me contextualize that. According to the *Journal of the American Medical Association*, children between the ages of two and seventeen watch an annual average of 15,000 to 18,000 hours of television, in comparison with the 12,000 hours spent per year in school. Many might argue that our patience with advertisements is dwindling with the onset of Netflix, TV players and box sets. However, the advertising world caught on to that years ago. There are so many other ways to reach your kids: brand licencing, product placement, schools, banner ads on websites, stealth marketing, viral marketing, DVDs, games, social media, etc. For a company, it is very worthwhile to influence children, who in turn influence adults into buying or not buying certain products.

There is often a lot of hype around the eye-watering amounts of money that celebrities get to endorse a certain product or brand. If we see a sports star drinking a particular sports drink, the product itself becomes synonymous with their achievements. This familiarity can often influence our choice when we are faced with this or another drink in a grocery shop. The decision happens in a split second, but it has been influenced.

Let's say that I'm driving for an hour on a Sunday and I'm listening to the radio. One of the guests starts a sentence with 'Well, I was in Hotel X last week and I have to say that we really enjoyed it. The customer service was fantastic, there was lots to do and it was just wonderful to get away for a couple of days', before they launch into a debate about work/life balance. At the same time, I may just have been thinking that I have visitors coming from Australia for the wedding. They mentioned that they would like to see a bit of Ireland, since they were coming so far, and a thought pops into my mind that maybe that hotel would be a nice place for them to spend some time. As a result, the guest on the media has (quite likely) unintentionally led me to choose one accommodation option over the others in the area.

Finally, we often seek out other people's opinions deliberately. I called my travel agent, as I needed accommodation near an airport in New York because my connecting flights were a day apart. She said, 'Sure, that's no problem. Hotel Y is coming up as the cheapest here. One minute now . . . No, actually, I don't like what they say on TripAdvisor. I don't want to send you there. Let me have another look . . .' The effect of social media is immense. Have you ever decided to go (or not to go) to see a movie because of a review? Have you ever been looking through Amazon and bought a specific book because the reviews were more favourable? Have you ever engaged with a supplier solely because you asked for and received a recommendation from your friends on Facebook or someone you follow on Twitter or a group on LinkedIn? I know that I have.

If you can identify and win over an influencer, it can make such an impact. I was giving a presentation to a group of business owners on this very topic recently and afterwards a nightclub owner approached me. He told me that during the week, the market of students in the city was significant, but they all went where their friends went. His team sat down one day and wanted to figure out how they could identify the leaders. Who actually decided where their group would end up socializing on a Monday night? They soon cracked it. The committee members of the university societies were the decision-makers. As a language club finished its meeting, for example, committee members announced to the group that they were all going to a specific pub or nightclub. Straight away, the phones were out as the attendees texted their friends to let them know where they were going to be. Their friends then texted their own friends, etc. The nightclub owner approached eight societies (two for each week night) and offered them free passes into the club for their members only. This act alone changed the social scene. I don't need to say it, but I will anyway: the committee members were not buying all the rounds in the nightclub. They were simply influencing the market to follow them . . . and very effectively so.

'Buying' decisions also happen in the workplace, and those decisions have their own influencers. I recently met up with a friend whom I hadn't seen in a while. He told me how frustrated he had felt at work. He'd wanted to move up in the company, but didn't see any immediate opportunities, and was beginning to feel taken for granted now, as he had been there for some time. He had approached HR about ways in which he could progress, and they'd had a polite, civilized discussion with him. They emphasized his valuable contribution, showed their appreciation for his flexibility and highlighted many of his positive points. In essence, he knew that they wanted him, but were just assuming that he would stay due to the difficult economy at the time. While this conversation was pleasing to his ego, it didn't really advance him in any way. His 'buyer' wasn't biting. There wasn't any point in approaching the actual budget provider because the finance department didn't know him by name: he was only a payslip to them. He decided to start talking to some influencers.

A couple of days later at the office water-cooler he casually asked the person known as the office gossip if she had heard that a direct competitor was hiring. She said, 'No, I didn't hear. I wouldn't be interested anyway . . . why? You're not thinking of leaving, are you?'

'I've been here a while, you know. I have a lot to offer, but I have a lot more to learn. Perhaps it's time for new opportunities. Anyway, I've a deadline for tomorrow, so I better get back.'

Within two hours, he received an e-mail from HR. They had just heard of a promotion recently decided at board level and wanted to have a preliminary discussion with him.

But the four roles are even more clearly defined in the case of the textbook *Positive Economics* I wrote with Trudie Murray and Brian O'Connor a couple of years ago. When the three of us decided to work on the textbook, the first thing that we needed to do was to approach a publisher with a proposal. We deliberated about the best way to do that.

We knew that there were several categories of people we had to take into account. The students were obviously the user. We needed to make sure that the product itself served them well. We knew that it was important for the book to be exam-friendly, colourful, full of scenarios that were relevant to their stage in life and easy to follow.

Now who was our buyer? No, not the parent. The parent is usually only following instructions and buying the book that the teacher puts on the list. Therefore, while the parent provided the budget for the book itself, the teacher was the actual buyer and it was the teacher we needed to convince. We needed to design the book in such a way as to minimize the amount of work for the teacher, so we provided a solid structure based around the teaching calendar, contextualized the current lessons with up-to-date examples, suggested other resources that could be useful in the classroom, and included a bank of questions as homework as well as extra exercises and their solutions – all to make life as easy, productive and time efficient as possible for the teacher. If the teacher didn't buy *into* the book, the parent would never even hear of it.

But we couldn't stop there. There is one other party in the

process. We, as authors, were not going to be in a position to go to each school and educate the teachers about the benefits of this new resource in their classroom. However, the sales reps who worked with the editorial team would be meeting the teachers and would hear any objections to the book. Hence, the sales reps were a key influencer in the process. We needed to share our passion for our book with them, pointing out all of its benefits and how our book was different from others in the market. When the sales reps played devil's advocate and started to list the objections they were likely to face, we needed to enable them to prove the textbook's worth.

How can you tell who is who, and how do you handle them?

It is important to make a reliable, quality product that offers a great experience to the user. In some cases you need to ensure that you sell to the actual buyer, while arming the influencer to represent you in the best way. In others you need to give the buyer arguments to win over a reluctant influencer (see the example of my friend and her tablet-loving husband). And sometimes, ironically, as in the case of my friend who was finding it difficult to progress in his job, the budget provider doesn't need to be considered at all, as they are not the person standing in the way of a 'sale'.

But how can you influence the influencer? Your detailed market research will come in handy at this point, because you will need to have walked a mile in your customer's shoes. This was brilliantly demonstrated to me a few years ago. I was working with a company that had a stand at an expo. The show was called 'Toys 4 Big Boys', and with a title like that it was quite clear who made up the target market. However, the event organizers were pretty sharp. The mid-twenties-to-mid-sixties-aged 'boy' they were looking for was potentially going to have a 'girl' who might influence their plans on that day. If a woman gets to see her 'big boy' at the weekend only, or would really appreciate time together after a hard week at work, she might object to going to a testosterone-fuelled event where said boy's attention would be on motorbikes and such. Imagine the conversation: 'Sweetheart, what are your plans for the weekend? We might go to Toys 4 Big Boys? Doesn't that sound great?'

The stroke of genius on the part of the organizers was that they had identified this possibility and come up with a clever strategy. They took a whole section of the venue and invited beauty therapists, masseuses, stylists, tarot card readers and a company that was currently promoting the latest girly drink to exhibit in a separate female pampering section. As a result, a couple could go their separate ways and be happily entertained for a few hours before contentedly meeting up afterwards. This was a clear case of inviting one person to buy, but making a focused effort on winning over the influencer, thus eradicating a barrier to purchase before it even arose.

If you can identify who exactly the buyer is and sell to them what they're actually looking for, you will have greater sales. Let's go back to the example of my brother in the homewares section of a department store, idly lifting the lid off a rice cooker and reading the box. Imagine he is approached by a salesperson. If she begins listing the fabulous benefits of the rice cooker he's looking at, she is wasting her time. All he wants to do is buy a present for his sister. How is the salesperson going to figure that out? She needs to ask a couple of initial questions.

SALES REP: 'If you want any help with the different brands, just let me know.'

MY BROTHER: 'Well, actually, I'm not sure which one to choose.'

Scenario 1

SALES REP: 'Well, the rice cooker that you have in your hand can be used in the microwave, is dishwasher friendly and has a twelve-month guarantee. We have another one that costs about €30 more and is electric. It will cook the rice perfectly and keep it warm for as long as it's plugged in. It's actually very popular with people who love to cook. I have one myself and I use it all the time.'

Scenario 2

SALES REP: 'Do you cook rice often yourself? It depends on your usage really.'

The difference between the two is that in the first scenario, the sales rep jumps right in and gives a comprehensive comparison of the benefits of the product, which would have been very effective if she had been speaking to me, the user. However, this is not at all relevant for my brother. He might be happy to learn of the benefits at a later point in the sales process, because he will then be able to repeat them to me, to show how thoughtfully he chose the present. Jumping right in with the benefits, though, is not the best strategy, as it's too much irrelevant information at that stage in the sale: the buyer is likely to run away from the information overload.

In the second scenario, the sales rep poses an unassuming, yet open question as to who is actually going to use the rice cooker. Upon finding out that this is a gift, she should change the discussion to the suitability of the product as a present. The buyer *first* wants to make sure they are making the right choice for a present – and then they will perhaps be open to listening to the features of the rice cooker. This one question alone could be the difference between making a sale and satisfying a customer . . . or not.

In addition, if you sell to the buyer, as opposed to any other participant in the process, you're more likely to achieve targeted marketing. Recall my earlier example of the couple set to wed. If a department store devises a strategy to attract couples planning their wedding gift list, their effort is more likely to result in a greater spend, more efficiently achieved. Instead of going after all the different people who will be attending the wedding, for an average spend of €100 each, their marketing money and effort would be better spent approaching two people only, the bride and bridegroom. The couple will attract many multiples of €100 without the shop having to expend any additional energy.

As for the influencer, do not underestimate their power; ignore it at your peril. When I was organizing my book launch last year, I asked the person at the venue if she had any recommendations for a caterer. She suggested one company that they used and with which they were very happy. I was really busy at the time, so I had a quick look at the website, asked the caterer for a quote and the deal was done. From the point of view of the caterer, this was an ideal transaction, quick and easy – but only because they had a satisfied customer who had turned into my influencer. On the other hand, when I was thinking about going to see a new show a couple of months ago, I looked at some reviews online before booking the tickets. The reviews said things like 'wasn't fully thought out', 'funny in predictable ways', 'average' and 'expected better from this gifted artist'. I did not proceed with the booking.

Influencers can be your best salespeople. Let's say that we meet at an event and I tell you that my book is the only blueprint that you'll ever need on your journey to making money, it's better than anything else that you have ever read, and it's *just* fan*tastic*. Now compare this with your trusted friend calling you up to say, 'I got a book last week and it truly gave me food for thought. I reviewed my financial goals for the year, put some of her suggestions into prac- tice, am using words like "KPIs" and have actually started to make more money already. Maybe you should look out for it?' In the first case, the language I use to describe my own product is much stronger and more enthusiastic. However, in the second case, some- body that you trust has endorsed the book and highlighted how it has already worked for her. You're far more likely to listen to her than to me.

It's important to arm your influencers with all of the information that they need to sell on your behalf. This will result in greater sales, happier customers and a higher return on your efforts. Listen to the concerns that they have. Make every effort to answer them pro- foundly and exceed their expectations. If they say that they require the signoff, help or approval of other people, do your utmost to assist them. Find out what the third party is really looking for or wants to avoid. Can you make this happen? If so, tell your influencer all that they need to know, and be genuine about it. If you can't do it, tell them and let the truth surface before they put their name to an initiative that is destined to fail. They will respect you for it, and that's the type of ethics that wins satisfied, loyal customers for life.

How do you identify and satisfy each party you're selling to?

How do you find out who is who? And how do you satisfy them? Let's start with the end user. It's very important to design a great product or service for them, for a number of reasons. If you negotiate better terms in your workplace in exchange for better productivity or ownership of a new task and then you don't actually do anything, it won't take long for an employer to feel short-changed and aggrieved. If you open your home to paying guests for bed and breakfast accommodation, and then serve lukewarm sausages, out-of-date eggs and instant coffee, the number of your guests will quickly dwindle. If you claim that your product or service does x . . . and then it does it badly, or not at all, you'll quickly find there isn't a market willing to pay money for it. In addition, the end user often becomes the most powerful influencer. A restaurant can die a quick, painful death if the restaurant reviewers have only bad things to say when interviewed on radio or in their Sunday paper columns. There can be a surge in business for a particular tourist attraction if it rises to the top five as voted by TripAdvisor members. A website can experience a huge wave in traffic if a celebrity or thought leader in a certain industry endorses it as their 'must read' for the week.

Buyers usually identify themselves as the main motivator behind the purchase. They actually want to go on the training course, get somebody a present, go to a certain venue for the Christmas party, etc. They have a particular problem or pleasure point that is important to ascertain and then solve or satisfy, as we discussed at length in Step Three. However, very often an influencer will have a say in the buyer's decision. Your sale and the amount of money in your bank account will depend on whether you can win them over. In order to find out who they are, you just need to open your ears. I'm sure that if my friend had been with her husband in the computer shop while he was checking out the laptop he wanted to get (which she was swiftly going to put a stop to), he would have said to the sales assistant, 'I would love to buy it, but it's my wife that you need to convince (nervous laughter)' or something to that effect. It would be up to the person selling to him to come up with ways that the computer could actually benefit the household, as opposed to just him. For example, he could be more productive at work and hence wouldn't need to stay late two evenings in the week; the children could use it to do their homework in years to come; they could download movies and solve arguments about who wanted to watch what; my friend could use it herself for [*insert reason*]. In this way, my friend's husband would have had a far better chance of putting the case to her. And of course I'm not encouraging anybody to manipulate anybody into buying anything. I would only ever pursue a sale if I felt that the product or service would actually add value to the buyer. My friend who wanted a promotion only went to HR, and subsequently to the office gossip, because he truly believed that there were better ways that he could serve the company. The textbook sales reps were genuinely convinced that our book would be of immense benefit in the classroom, and this is why they accepted the challenge of representing it to teachers.

I was having lunch with a business woman in London one day. We were both thinking of attending an event the next week. There was a relatively high price attached to this, and we were casually chatting about whether it was worth it. She then said to me, 'Well, I'm just wondering if my four colleagues want to go too, because then it's big enough to cause me a headache with my finance department.' In this scenario, while highlighting that she was a buyer, she identified the finance department as a key influencer: her problem was the admin – getting management to sign off on a purchase order and to complete the related documentation afterwards. The question that the event organizer would have needed to answer was how could they make this as easy as possible for her?

I was sitting with the head of the education department in an organization in Manchester one day. She was deliberating whether to book a certain training programme with us or not. They had identified a need, liked our offering and had the budget to spend accordingly. However, as I tried to move the conversation along to the stage where we decided on a date and the logistics of the training, I found she wasn't going there. I thought to myself, 'There is something wrong here and I need to find out what it is.' I judged that the best way to draw out the issue was to face it head on and I gently asked, 'Do you think that you might face any obstacles in implementing this programme?' 'Yes, I do. The main problem is actually freeing sixty staff for two days in one block.' She was envisioning going to the team managers and asking them to release their staff for two whole days – and meeting with significant opposition. I immediately suggested breaking the training day into three parts and the teams into three groups and to run it twice. As a result, the attendees could choose a time for the modules that suited them; and, from the managers' perspective, only a third of the staff would need to be released at any one time. She breathed a sigh of relief and we agreed the deal.

Reputation is also an important factor: it reassures the buyer and makes the influencer's job easier. Credibility indicators are one way to build reputation: we give references when applying for a job, provide testimonials from previous clients, point out good reviews on online forums, etc. If you notice somebody criticizing your product or service, address it fast. This shows that you react to your customers and also that those who buy from you get good service and are important to you. Look up managers' responses to bad reviews on TripAdvisor and you'll quickly learn the dos and don'ts.

To identify who is who, you need to listen to objections to the sale along the way, or include pointed questions in your market research and then, most importantly, make sure that you take care of them.

Your mission at the end of this chapter is to go back to your market research and identify each of the four 'roles' in your target market. Who is the buyer, who is the user, who is the influencer and who is the budget provider? Are they one and the same person, or different people? Are there several users? Several influencers?

Then, consider what each of these people is concerned about – what is their specific problem, and how will you solve it? You need to sell to the buyer – or you need to enable the buyer to make a case to the influencer (my friend and her husband). Or, alternatively, you need to enable the influencer to make a case to the buyer (the person who recommended the caterer for my book launch). And you need to make sure that the user is happy with the experience of using your product or service.

Reaching out for help to make your dream a reality

II. *Letting go of the fantasy of going it alone*

We so often hear the stories of legendary entrepreneurs who spent years toiling away secretly in their garage, withstanding unthinkable setbacks and difficulties before making it big, that we end up thinking that that's what it takes to succeed in business. But, remember, these are stories, full of what makes a story worth telling: drama and conflict. Of course the hero *has* to be the underdog, the journey *has* to be long and arduous, and he *has* to overcome terrible odds and conniving adversaries – and he usually has to do this all on his own because he has a vision that nobody shares. The famous stories are worth telling because they do indeed have a dramatic element to them, but they are stripped of inconvenient detail that might make them more complex and less one dimensional. After all, you wouldn't buy a book or go to a movie to learn about someone who'd had it relatively easy, with lots of foreseeable ups and downs, but no major setback along the way.

When it comes to your dream of making more money – whether it's a modest amount to help the family budget, or the start of a business you hope will grow and become a serious player in your sector – the fantasy of 'going it alone' is not helpful, and it's one you should let go of. Indeed, when I look back at my life, the times when I felt most alone and under pressure were those when I was least able to pursue my dreams.

Let's go back to the beginning. You're just getting started and you're not quite sure what the next step is. Perhaps you're in a tight spot right now and it looks like things will never get better. I know the feeling well. There was a lonely summer when I was in college when many of my classmates had gone to far-flung destinations around the world, and by my own choice I had stayed at home. I felt that everybody around me was busy with their own lives and that I really didn't fit in anywhere. I didn't have the confidence to ask anyone if they wanted to go somewhere or do something, as I just felt they probably had their own plans and didn't want to be spending the day with a lonely desperado. I was at that awkward stage when my teens were well and truly over and yet I didn't quite know how to be the early-twenty-something enjoying the best years of her life (as people were telling me that I should be).

Or early in my working life, when I was still carrying a huge amount of student debt. There were times when, on opening my phone bill, I knew that it would hoover up the better part of my salary for that month . . . and I had only got paid the day before. My short-term debt was such that I lived on my overdraft and I couldn't see a way out. It was a whole month before another pay packet would come and that seemed an awfully long time away.

I had a similar feeling when I first set up the business. I was sitting in a tiny room that I had made into an office, and I could see nothing but the street in front of me through the blinds on the window. Nobody knew about the business, as it had only just been set up, so the phone wasn't exactly ringing off the hook. I had put a load into the washing machine, washed the dishes and hoovered the stairs, so I couldn't distract myself with a household task to give me even a tiny sense of achievement. I sat there thinking, 'How will I ever, ever, *ever* get from here to being the glamorous business woman that I want to be? Maybe I won't. Maybe this is it, and it's only the likes of the people that I read about in the paper who actually get the floor-to-ceiling glass offices and win prestigious awards and have a need for an HR department. Maybe this is as far as I'll get. This isn't what I signed up for. Maybe I've made a mistake.'

I came through each one of those situations. In my personal life I feel nourished, content and enjoy a wonderful sense of purpose within my relationships with other people. I honestly can't remember the last time that I used my credit card. Every coffee that I didn't buy, every 'eating out' experience that I turned down, every euro that I found under the bed or behind the couch went into getting rid of that expensive, threatening piece of plastic. And the company has now reached several milestones. In each case, I clawed my way out of the situation that I was in.

My pivotal moment of getting through my lonely time at college happened when I was sitting in a late-night coffee shop opposite a nightclub. I had a great seat for people watching and was observing the usual shenanigans that go on outside these places. The girls who are unable to walk properly in shoes that looked great in the shop. The lads who are getting braver with every pint. The security guards who are trying to decipher who's telling the truth about their age. I sat there telling myself that this was the liveliest my social life had been for a while, even though I was sitting on my own nursing a pot of tea. That night, I wrote a list of things in a notebook that I could do on my own without feeling that I was imposing on anyone. I could go to Toastmasters, join a class, volunteer, go on tour in another country, visit family . . . As the list got longer, I felt that I could somehow take control of the situation. The funny thing is that I never actually needed to look at that list again. The minute my attitude shifted towards looking at the positive things I could do in my life, the situation started to turn around.

In the case of the business, I needed to get out of my state of inertia and helplessness by engaging with other people. I went to networking groups and met others who were also in start-up situations. I looked through online forums, helped people out on questions if I could and submitted comments on topics.

I also made sure that I developed other interests outside of my 'job'. If you work from home, there isn't any clear division between work and the rest of your life (i.e., the journey between your office and your home is the width of the doorframe), and any negativity in the former can spill into the latter. To get rid of that sense of claustrophobia, I wrote down a list of every opportunity (or even a whiff of one) and put it up on a notice board in the office. I reported any tiny development to prove to myself that I was moving forward.

I also have to give credit to my then boyfriend (now fiancé), who surprised me with a present of a three-day business course, because he knew that I felt like I was stuck in a rut. In addition, I made a weekly coffee date with myself, in which I would go out to reflect on those goals that I had decided upon. I would write down every action that I had taken to bring myself closer to them, and make a list of tasks for the following week. Little by little, I got back on my feet.

Embarking on a new challenge can't be horrible all the time. Otherwise, why on earth would anyone do it? Yes, there are low points and sometimes the going gets tough, but on the whole it is an immensely enjoyable process. More often the obstacles you'll meet along the way are of the kind that makes you excited to work at overcoming them; but, when they're too big and threatening, you'll need to reach out for help. In most cases, you'll look back and identify a key learning point in the experience.

My secret technique for keeping up morale

One night I stayed in an airport hotel in Eindhoven, Netherlands. Airport hotels can be notoriously bland places, with the same decor and the same busy travellers the world over. I had been giving training that morning in Amsterdam and was travelling by train. I worked on my e-mails throughout the journey, and by the time I arrived I'd had enough of the laptop. Tired and bored, I went to the hotel restaurant for dinner on my own. I always take pen and paper with me on these occasions, to brainstorm and strategize. For some reason, on that night I took my diary.

I started to flick back through the pages. I smiled as I recalled a funny meeting. I sighed as I remembered the stresses of a particular day. I fondly remembered some experiences. Then . . . I started to fill in the blanks. With the benefit of hindsight, I could trace back developments that were now bearing fruit to a phone call, a chance meeting, a long-shot e-mail, a coffee with a like-minded person. There had been days that had seemed banal when I lived them; I had dismissed them as 'just another day in the office' or maybe I didn't notice them at all. Still, their slow accumulation had brought me to a better place. Other days had entries for big, memorable events – signing the contract for the book, the day my brother got his dream job, my friend's wedding.

By the time dessert arrived, I felt so much more grateful for the little things that had snowballed into big ones: our company's healthy accounts, a colourfully stamped passport and memories to last me a lifetime. So why, I asked myself, did it take exhaustion and boredom combined for me just to open my diary and go back over the previous months?

I decided that night that I would write every achievement of the day in red pen at the top of my diary. The rule was that I couldn't let the day go by without noting an achievement. Some days, you can note the big things: win a new client, publish a book, get engaged, receive a wonderful testimonial for a job that you did, see a new city, have a heart-to-heart with a friend, be nominated for an award, etc. These are all fantastic, obvious achievements and certainly worthy of the red pen.

And there are days when you tried something that you were previously too afraid of, when you were so tired and yet kept going, when simply making it through the day was an achievement in itself; days when you just felt happy, days when you made a decision with honest conviction to change a behaviour, that you stood up for yourself, that you did the right thing. Like me that night, you may not notice that a seed's been planted – but the red pen will remind you when you reflect back.

I find that lots of people go into reminiscing mode on New Year's Eve: everybody comments on the speed at which time passes and questions what they really did with that year. I have a 'New Year's Eve' feeling regularly, and I don't need to rely on my memory to come up with a few significant events, when really it's the accumulation of the tiny things that made the big things happen. The red pen works wonders.

So that's my secret, and if you adopt the practice you'll realize that making progress is more a matter of a slow accumulation of rather small achievements and less a climactic battle between the lone hero and all the odds that are stacked against him. No, it doesn't have the same romantic ring to it. But if you make sure to notice your achievements, however small, you'll be able to follow your rise to stardom. Nobody is an overnight success – it's just that, until you are a success, nobody will pay attention to the small things. Then it will look like you burst on to the scene from nowhere. But only you will know the amount of effort you put into it.

Surround yourself with positive people and a positive atmosphere

You have to create around you the conditions in which your endeavour will flourish. At the moment my company has an office at Dublin City University, along with other companies, some of which are much bigger than mine. In this incubation centre, the atmosphere is very conducive to focused business efforts. Simply by virtue of having an office there, I am able to frequently interact with ambitious and positive people, whose objectives are similar to mine.

And even if I don't necessarily talk to other people on any given day at DCU, there's an atmosphere of business success that lifts me and gives me energy. Have you heard the phrase 'Fake it until you make it!'? I have come up with a slightly different – more positive – version of this saying: 'Act like it will happen . . . and it likely will!'

One day I printed off 'Susan Hayes, Managing Director' in large letters on to an A4 sheet that I could fold over and stand up on my desk at home in Cork. My cousin walked in and incredulously asked me what was I doing with my name on the desk? I told her that it was a temporary fixture until the gold-plated one was ready for my office at the top of a building in the future. I have often tricked my brain into believing something was going to happen and then worked off the assumption that it would. It has rarely caught me out. I think atmosphere is very important. It has to be conducive to whatever you're doing at the time.

I often ask my clients if I can travel to their offices and work there for a day or two on the specific project that we are contracted to do, to get a feel for their environment, understand who does what and have those conversations at the printer that let you really identify the DNA of a company – the sort of thing that a website can't ever tell you. For instance, a couple of years ago, I moved to Malta for a month when we first started to work with some Maltese clients. One might say that you don't 'move' somewhere for a month, but by virtue of living there, I could absorb a little of the Maltese way of doing things. I read the paper there every day. I shopped for bread and milk, as opposed to postcards and fridge magnets. I went to Mass in the local church. I learned of the places that locals went. I had a keen interest in their culture and way of life. While this is an extreme example – and mightn't be something you could do as readily as I could at that particular stage in life – the lesson is useful. I power through these projects because I immerse myself in my customer's environment and make an effort to leave my own presumptions at the door and become part of their team, if only for a little while.

Asking for help is an essential part of learning to make more money

In this book I recommend a lot of things that might be outside of your comfort zone, possibly triggering a feeling of *How on earth am I supposed to do that?* One part of the answer is to keep going back to your trusty Key Performance Indicators and to continue taking one step after the other. Push through, persist, and the needle will move. The other part of the answer is to ask for help. Find somebody to whom you can say out loud 'I want to learn how to do *x*' and get useful feedback, be it expertise or reassurance.

The good news is that there is an abundance of resources out there. Help is available every step of the way. You can benefit from other people's advice, other people's experience, other people's time, other people's money. There are different kinds of helpers as well: accountability partners; mentors; specialists who have a certain kind of specific deep knowledge; state agencies; grants and awards. Not to forget cheerleaders and devil's advocates – remember that one of the most helpful business questions you can address is 'What's the worst that could happen?'

If you share the same claustrophobic feeling that I felt when I first started out, and if you're afraid of imposing, why not start online? Google doesn't judge. You can get help by searching for information, and you can also provide help (and get practice at offering and articulating the solution you want to sell down the line) on forums, LinkedIn groups, etc.

'I don't want to ask for help because I don't want to be seen as weak' may be a common self-deprecating thought. But wanting to single-handedly conquer everything is an ego problem that can thwart your money-making efforts. Especially as accepting help is a wonderful way to establish a meaningful connection with others.

And asking for help means you'll have to jumpstart your own progress, because it forces you to do a certain amount of work. If you want to ask for help with your business plan, you're going to have to come up with a business plan to show the person who has agreed to help you. In order to ask for help, you have to do the work in order to have good questions to ask – you can't just say 'I need help – please solve my problem for me'; you need to articulate the problem you're having and show that you've tried to solve it. In addition, by articulating your issue in a way that somebody else can understand, you're actually starting to solve the problem yourself by beginning to work on it. So don't for one moment think that there isn't any merit in asking for help.

By asking for help, you're also bringing value to others. Remember the discussion of role models: you might be under the impression that a certain role model is totally out of your reach. But you'd be amazed how a simple e-mail saying, 'You inspire me when you do x; I have followed your advice on y and got z result; I particularly appreciate your take on a, b and c topics; if d is part of your plans, I would love to hear your thoughts on it.' This is immensely valuable feedback: people whom you think of as 'more advanced' than you will appreciate knowing that their own efforts are having a positive impact on yours. You're giving them a positive testimonial, as well as the proof that what they recommend is of value to you (and possibly to many other people), and that it actually works. 'I implemented your advice on x and it worked, and this is the result that I achieved.' You're offering confirmation, validation and encouragement.

You might think that your idols have it all figured out and don't need your encouragement, but you'd be surprised how rare it is to hear from the people that you try to help with your endeavours, and how wonderful it feels. I wrote my first book because I wanted to share all the systems that make my finances a worry-free part of my life. I dearly hoped that others would be helped. I knew only too well the constricted feeling in the chest that comes when you're afraid of running out of money, when you don't have enough to pay the bills, or when you have to deny yourself yet another nice thing. Although the book was highly practical, I shared my knowledge from a very emotional place.

Every time I get an e-mail, a tweet or any other kind of message from a reader who says 'Thank you for lightening my load, thank you for showing me the light at the end of the tunnel, thank you for showing me how to add €$xxxx$ to my bottom line', it makes my week. It is a sign that I'm doing things right, and that what I do is useful to others. Without readers' feedback, I might now be wondering was it all in vain and am I just crying out in the wilderness. I'm always interested in hearing how things work out for others.

Just because you don't yet know how to do something, this doesn't mean you can't add value to the person who is helping you. Asking for help is wonderful for so many reasons. You'll realize how much help is available, and how much simpler things actually are than you might previously have thought. Of course there will be things that are difficult; simple does not mean easy. But, at the same time, you'll come to find all the resources that you need in order to go forward. Asking for help is a very important part of making more money: other people have done it before you, and state agencies are set up for this very purpose. Asking for help could cut months, if not years, from your learning curve, and could save you thousands in the long run.

So just how do you ask for help?

The short answer is that you simply call people and make appointments. Really, it's that simple! Let me show you how it works. Earlier in the book, I told you my story of getting started in Malta. I spoke about the delegation that came to Dublin, the Enterprise Europe Network that facilitated the communication, FinanceMalta, which set up meetings for me, Malta Enterprise, which provided me with a driver, Ryanair, which sold me a great value fare, the travel agent who got me a good deal at a hotel, and then all of the meetings that I had with businesses, organizations, state-funded bodies and the universities there. Look at the number of people involved. I had enlisted the help of lots and lots of willing 'volunteers', paid and unpaid (or not paid by me directly), in both countries.

There are a couple of points that I would like to make about this. First of all, I didn't go out to Malta as an initial step: I met the delegation in November, and it wasn't until a few months later that I actually went to the country. During those months, I was able to interact with all of my 'helpers' from the comfort of my own office and to build the confidence that I needed to go out there. I built the contacts that I needed, and I made myself known to them, one at a time. Only then did I start to believe that my dream of having an international business had any sort of realistic chance whatsoever.

Preparation is the key to laying the groundwork for success. It will help you to get the knowledge that you need; your perspective will change, and you'll come to realize that what you want is actually possible and in the process of becoming a reality. If you don't feel that you have the confidence to go directly to your employer or to initiate a sales conversation or to start a small business on the side right away, start organizing with a view to dealing at a later date with the things that you don't yet feel ready for.

Second, think about everybody who helped me along the way: their own interests were aligned with mine. That I was making a trip to Malta after meeting that delegation was a direct result of their visit and was a measurable output: the delegation had succeeded in its objective of sparking business interest in Malta. The Enterprise Europe Network is a body funded by the European Commission to help companies export. My visit to Malta was another measurable output for the organization, validating it: thanks to its help, an Irish company extended its business reach to another European country. It's easier for such an organization to justify and increase the amount of funding it receives if it can prove that the money is being put to good, measurable use. FinanceMalta is responsible for promoting the interests of the financial services industry. I was in a position to add value to that sector by offering specialized financial training, by providing a link with Dublin (a fund domicile and servicing hub of Europe) and by facilitating new introductions between the two nations. Malta Enterprise's *raison d'être* is to grow inbound foreign development investment and outbound trade. If I provide information to other Irish companies about doing business in Malta (which I have done over and over and over again by now), I'm helping their cause. I also added to the sales of Ryanair and the travel agent. In the case of the meetings I attended, people are only ever going to engage if one or both parties can add value to the other, so it was up to each of us to find a way to do that. So, while I was asking for help, I was also helping each person who was helping me.

Third, I had got quite used to corresponding with everybody at that stage, and I was looking forward to meeting them when I did get off the flight in mid-January. Also, by then, I had built up a lot of excitement about seeing this new place. I had read a lot about it, been speaking to people from there, had 'Google Mapped' it, and now I was going to see it all. The sense of uncertainty and impossibility had morphed into a sense of adventure. However, that didn't stop a white fear running through me on the first morning, as I looked up the imposing marble staircase that I had to climb to the office where I was due to have my first ever international meeting. At the top, my host welcomed me and asked me to tell him about our business. Suddenly I was back in familiar territory – that's all it took to surmount what I had previously believed to be insurmountable.

It is so important to just get going. At the very beginning, it's best to concentrate on something that is really easy to do: sending e-mails, looking for information, researching different opportunities on the internet and making appointments with helpful agencies. However, it's vital that you follow through. Once you've built up a little momentum, once you feel more confident that you can navigate new territory, you have to take the leap for the real results to show.

12. *A world of experts just waiting for your call*

When somebody I knew told me that she didn't think she was going to spend a day applying for a €30,000 grant, as she probably wouldn't make the cut, I asked her, 'How long would you spend working on a proposal for a client that could garner €30,000 worth of business?' She replied, 'I would spend weeks.' I pointed out the obvious: 'Well, then, why wouldn't you spend just one day applying for the same amount of funding?' She applied, got the money and told me afterwards that, by highlighting the simple mathematics involved in the decision, I had taken away the emotional uncertainty. Suddenly she had a much more rational way of looking at the opportunity. Without it, she really wouldn't have gone for it. So many people make the same mistake as my friend nearly made. You don't want to be one of them.

When people think of getting help, they usually think of their friends and family, or reaching out to an acquaintance who might have the information they need, or mustering up the courage to e-mail somebody they admire. But there are institutions, organizations and agencies that are devoted to helping you make more money. I have used their services a lot myself, and a constant refrain I hear from them is that they're under-utilized, that not enough people come to them.

We have created a directory of supports on our website (www.savvymoneyguide.com), so that you can click straight through to the organization that you might be looking for. But to get you started, here is a breakdown of the help that is out there.

1. *State agencies that provide financial and non-financial support*

In several countries, there are organizations that are funded by their governments to help people set up and grow businesses. They may provide grant aid for feasibility studies, expansion, trade show visits and some forms of consultancy. They may act as a lender or a guarantor of money and may also buy an equity stake in the company. In addition, they may offer training, mentoring, market research, information, workspace and introductions. I have mentioned earlier the help that our company has received from Enterprise Ireland, Malta Enterprise, FinanceMalta, UKTI, etc.

2. *Networks*

There are lots of organizations that set up with a view to giving their members an opportunity to meet each other. They can be geographical, industry specific or based on a common thread among people. For example, I'm a member of the Irish International Business Network, and I attend their events in Dublin, London and New York to meet other Irish people in business. In addition, I'm a member of the eLearning Guild, which has built up an online community of eLearning practitioners and which holds events in San José, Orlando and Las Vegas. I'm a member of the CFA (Chartered Financial Analyst) Institute, as it's the professional body with which I chose to study. In each case, I find like-minded people and businesses. I have developed an immense pool of contacts, a body of knowledge and a calendar of events through these three groups alone. It's also highly beneficial to attend events to develop knowledge, discover opportunities and meet people in similar situations.

3. *Chambers of Commerce, professional institutes and learning centres*

There is another type of organization, one that doesn't concentrate solely on events and networking, but rather on other business needs, including education, representation, personal development, engagement with the academic community, etc. For example, our company is a member of the local Chamber of Commerce, which organizes trade missions to new territories, provides member-to-member discounts and networking opportunities, and holds educational events. I'm a member of the Institute of Directors, as it has a significant information portal on the roles, responsibilities, opportunities and challenges of being a director. It offers discounts (which I use regularly), educational events both on-and offline and networking events. Also, our company is a member of the Learnovate Centre, which harnesses Ireland's eLearning capability by bringing together smaller industry companies, larger multinationals and the research community, with a view to furthering their international competitiveness.

4. Recruitment companies

Recruitment companies have one primary goal in mind: matching candidate to company to form productive, satisfied employment, in order to make a profit. They are a great way of finding a good position for you in the labour market by pairing you with a suitable employer. In addition, many offer CV advice, interviewing skills, information on salary levels and employment conditions, and various other valuable services. I went to Edinburgh for a summer in college and arrived in that beautiful city without knowing anybody at all. I interviewed with a number of recruitment companies and told them the nature of the job that I was looking for at the time. They placed me for the full time that I lived there and were immensely helpful.

5. Incubation centres

Incubation centres are larger buildings that house tens of start-up companies at a time. It depends on the centre itself, but their benefits can include workspace, internet, parking, catering and printing facilities, a company address, a place to hold meetings, training programmes and guest speakers. Our company migrated from my home office to an incubation centre within the first month. We have all of the aforementioned benefits, as well as many additional ones from our relationship with Dublin City University, where the centre is based. Our incubation centre has several 'Resident Experts', i.e., larger professional services firms that give us some time for free or at a very low cost, depending on the ask. Once we were doing business with a client who required us to sign an agreement with some potentially unfavourable terms. I felt it was a little out of our depth, so I approached the Resident Expert legal firm, Arthur Cox. A senior member of staff reviewed the contract, pointed out the possible pitfalls and armed me with the right questions to ask. Finally, it's fantastic to be surrounded by other people getting started in business. I love to sit in the café and watch everybody buzzing around the place, catching snippets of their conversations about their latest deals, trials and tribulations. It's a hive of activity. Judging by my experience, becoming part of an incubation centre is a super way to start up in business.

6. Online resources

There is an abundance of information on the internet. LinkedIn is a vast, deep and incredibly useful source of information, discussion, recommendations, activities, etc. It's a great idea to set up a profile and build your own virtual network. Also, you can learn a lot from participating in as well as reading the conversations on LinkedIn Groups. There are innumerable forums where participants discuss various topics and blogs where people write their own articles. Social media is an immediately responsive tool that enables users to get answers, market research, opinions and thoughts very quickly from those who are of interest to them.

7. European funding

There is a supranational European agenda across the EU that supports international trade, transfer of innovation, cross-border visits, cultural integrations, sharing of best practice, etc. Billions of euros are available for the pursuit of these objectives, and there are often people employed to help applicants figure out which programmes are for them, navigate the process and ultimately put the money to work. For example, I referred earlier to my fantastic experience with the Enterprise Europe Network.

8. Intellectual property (IP)

Our generation has produced thousands of inventors, innovators and explorers. It's very important to protect intellectual property through trademarks, patents and copyrights. This can be a complicated world, and you let your eyes glaze over when dealing with it at your peril: loose legal shelter can be extremely dangerous. There are several bodies, including the World Intellectual Property Organization (WIPO), that help people and companies identify, retain and shield their IP.

9. Personal finance portals and help lines

Many governments have procured, developed and expanded state-funded organizations to educate their citizens about various personal finance issues including budgeting, pensions, making a complaint, insurance, bank accounts, loans, money saving and investment. Often people don't know that they have resources, help lines, tools, information and lists of useful contact details available to them, and yet all this work to help them manage their money optimally is provided by their taxes.

10. Online information portals

The biggest information site in the world, at the time of writing, is YouTube. It is a tagged video directory with content on just about any topic that you could possibly imagine, and it is of course totally free. There are also streamlined education websites that operate on a subscription-based model where you mould your own educational journey. For example, I use www.lynda.com to upskill myself on various forms of technology and software. In addition, iTunes have lots of free business podcasts on various topics.

11. Equity/angel/private investment

If you set up a company, you can sell part of that company to an investor. We have become accustomed to watching these transactions play out on *Dragons' Den*. There are lots of organizations that match investors to businesses.

12. Corporate Social Responsibility (CSR)

There are thousands of large companies that have a policy on Corporate Social Responsibility, which is the giving of time, money and people towards efforts to further a better world. In some cases, those activities are based around helping a start-up, perhaps by giving them access to their resources.

13. Free events

In the majority of the above cases, the various organizations hold live events either online (called webinars) or in bricks-and-mortar locations. If you would like to try them out, it's a very reasonable request to ask to attend one of their events for free before joining or paying a membership. On some occasions, they'll want to cast their net wider and encourage new people to come along to a specific event to showcase one's offering. In the case of paid online portals, they often offer a very low-cost or free trial for a period of time. If the group is a state-funded agency, they frequently have events and resources that are available without any cost.

14. Libraries

There are shelves full of books in a library filled with information about making money and the skills required to do so. In addition, they can have copies of business magazines, market research reports, free access to the internet, subscriptions to news providers and librarians who can help you navigate your way through. In preparation for presentations, I often spend an afternoon in a market research library to bring me right up to date using information that isn't freely 'googleable' for all the reasons that I mentioned in Step Three.

On top of all of this, you can apply for awards. They're a fantastic resource – awards and grants are a way to earn recognition and publicity, and very often to receive a significant prize to help your business. Yet they're woefully under-applied for. Why do so many people act as if awards are unworthy of their time? I have spoken to many award organizers over the years, and they often throw their eyes to heaven as they speak of their struggle to get people to submit an application. In many cases, we don't think that we're good enough, experienced enough or have enough of a chance to win and therefore we don't try. However, there are lots and lots of people who also think the same and leave it to others to walk through that open door. If you actually apply, you have already set yourself apart from all those who haven't.

Our class in college was told about a plethora of awards, scholarships and exemptions that were available to us. Only a tiny fraction of students went forward for any of them, but those that did all benefited, either financially or otherwise. I joined the CFA Institute when I initially enrolled for their Level 1 exam. I paid for the exam myself and began to study in preparation. A couple of months later, I received an e-mail to say that the Institute was offering scholarships to those who had paid out of their own pockets. I thought that I hadn't anything to lose and so filled out the short form. Lo and behold, but didn't I win it? When I'm presenting to entrepreneurial groups, I often ask how many people have ever nominated themselves for specific accolades, and I rarely get an enthusiastic burst of hands in the air. Believe me, you have less competition than you imagine. Also, if you're looking for a point of differentiation on a CV, for a testimonial from an authoritative body or kudos within your industry, an achievement recognized by a third party in the form of an award can be the perfect answer.

Lots of funding is available for many different purposes. There is funding for people who want to set up their own business, run a feasibility study, expand their organization, get work experience abroad, revitalize disadvantaged areas, preserve the length of time that older people can live independently, research, and so many other reasons. There are even people employed in various agencies whose role it is to help you navigate your way through the criteria, identify exactly what you're looking for, fill out the forms and respond to any queries. For example, my company is a client of Enterprise Ireland, a government-funded body with the objective of cultivating Irish entrepreneurship and growing exports and employment. We applied for, and received, feasibility funding to develop an eLearning competency within our business. We were assigned a 'Development Adviser', who helped us every single step of the way and has been a fantastic sounding board.

It's also important to look at the non-financial supports that are available. These may come in the form of training, mentoring, information, support groups, resource banks, etc. Education is often high on a government's agenda, and there can be a whole range of state-funded or subsidized training on every skill that one might need to grow one's money-making ability: negotiation, interview techniques, sales, time management, leadership, team dynamics, bookkeeping, etc. Again, if you search for these terms and register on the website of various associations, you may be amazed at what you find. I have done lots of this training both when I was in employment, as it added value to the workplace through my increased productivity, and when I set up my own business, as I needed to build my skills base.

One day I received an e-mail from a comprehensive holistic pro-gramme that was putting out a call for applicants. It looked interesting and I thought it might be worth a phone call to find out more. I filled out the form, which included searching questions like 'What are your current barriers to growth?', 'What is your USP [*unique selling point*]?', 'What are your personal goals within the business?' At this stage, many people can't be bothered to take the time to really think about these questions and compose an answer. Many organizations that provide funding use this subtle criterion as a barrier to keep out people who aren't serious and don't want to put in the effort. After being accepted for the initial stage, I had a short interview. I got a call within the day to say that I had been given a place on the programme called 'New Frontiers': three days' training a month for seven months, and we had to set milestones for which we would be held accountable. The group synergy was won-derful, and I met some great like-minded people. We were each given a mentor and an executive coach as well as a €1,500 grant. In my case, I used the money to attend a hugely beneficial conference in Orlando, where I made fantastic contacts, gained a lot of industry insight and got a glimpse into the future of eLearning. I used part of our feasibility funding from Enterprise Ireland to subsidize the flights and expenses to the US. Imagine that: this huge bonus was just there for the taking, simply because I put in the work necessary to fill out a form.

13. 'Now that I have this information, direction and advice, what do I do?'

It's important to educate yourself, but don't feel that you've achieved something hugely significant simply because you've enrolled on a course or because you've spent money. Your KPIs will tell you when you need to ramp up the action. Studying doesn't move the needle on KPIs. Going out there and applying your new-found knowledge to real situations does.

You don't need to spend too much money at first. Remember, you need to think about your profit. Investing in yourself is all very well, but your KPIs will tell you whether it's worthwhile to spend the money on a form of education, or to attend an expensive networking event, or to go to a conference. There are so many free resources: start there, apply what you learn, and build on this foundation.

Another currency that you need to be attentive to is time: learning is great, but you need to put a cap on the time you spend learning. Going out there and doing things is the best way to learn and internalize new knowledge. So don't put off taking action until after you've studied some more – studying is a great excuse to delay the moment when the rubber hits the road.

How to make sure you stay on track – making yourself accountable

As I finished school and then college, I used to often hear 'You have your whole life ahead of you' – and I used to wonder: at what point does that actually change? When is the tipping point? It's easy when you're seventeen to say, 'I'm going to be a millionaire when I'm thirty.' But it's not so easy when you're twenty-eight. Later on, a sudden mid-life panic or a tragic dose of reality will jolt us awake – where has all that time gone? What have we done with our life? If you make plans for 'someday', remember that 'someday' is not a day of the week. To reach the results you want, you have to engineer it so that your 'someday' becomes a reality.

I once attended a personal development course and the presenter asked us to take out a blank sheet of paper. We had to draw six columns and write one of our uppermost priorities at the top of each. He then asked us to take ten minutes to think about where we would like to be in five years' time, in relation to each of these highly important areas in our lives.

As soon as this was done, he instructed us to repeat the exercise, but this time to look three years into the future and to write down what we should have achieved by then to put us on track to hit our five-year goal. He asked us to do the same for how life would look just one year from now in order to be on course for our three-year goal. You could feel everybody getting a little shifty in their seats at this stage. The presenter spotted somebody crossing everything out and stopped her right in her tracks. 'Hey, hey, hey, what are you doing?' he said. She replied, 'This is ridiculous. There is no way that I can ever get to where I want to be within five years . . . or even fifteen years for that matter. If I'm going to do this exercise properly, I may as well do so realistically.'

He told us all to put down our pens and apologized to the woman in advance for making her life an emotional case study for the class. He said, 'You have two choices at this juncture in your life. You can rip up that sheet of paper and your dreams with it, but, if you do, be very conscious of what you're doing. If it's the right thing to do, be fully aware that you may have been berating yourself for a long time about not getting to a place that, in fact, wasn't a realistic objective.' (The woman's lip started to wobble at this point.) 'It's like writing a to-do list that assumes 26-hour days and trying to pack it all into a waking day. On the other hand, maybe you're giving up too easily. Maybe you have the time to do whatever you want in five years. If the issue is time, what if you found a way to clear just one hour every day? If the issue is people, there are lots of people who work in various different organizations to help you. If the issue is your confidence, you're the only person who can solve that, and it's not an elusive secret as to where to find that. It's right inside you, waiting to unfold. Now, before you tear up your ideas, in more ways than one, really think about what you're doing.'

He took the attention off her by asking us to repeat the exercise, only looking six months ahead, i.e., what would need to have happened by then for the one-year goal to be a realistic proposition. He pushed us a step further and asked us what we would need to do just in the next month for our six-month dream to take shape. You could hear people making the sound of air leaving a tyre as they knew this was the answer . . . but it wasn't comfortable. He then came along with the killer blow: write down what you need to do in the next week to put yourself on to the trajectory to your five-year goal. 'You have now broken what seems the absolute, maximum achievement that you can imagine at this time right down to six individual actions that you need to do in the next week. That's all,' he said. 'You can leave here today and live your lives the way that you have been. Or you can change course to become the person that you want to become. If you don't, I want you to see, feel and hear yourself saying to yourself and your future self that you're rejecting those dreams. If you roll over in your bed and press "snooze" that morning when you've set the clock an hour earlier, I want you to say to yourself, "I'm willingly rejecting my five-year ambition." If you come back here next week with that list complete, to be quite honest, you have immensely increased the odds of reaching that five-year "impossible dream". You choose.'

This was an incredible lesson: short-term goals are vital. So ask yourself: what will you have done by this day next month? The diary can be a very powerful ally. You can also set up meetings with an accountability partner. An accountability partner is someone you can sit down with at regular intervals to share goals, report on progress and plan the next set of targets. It could be a friend, someone you have met through work or your partner; indeed, you might have different accountability partners for different aspects of your life. It's something that you do for each other. Accountability partners are a wonderful way to help you stay on track and make sure you don't procrastinate: they gently but firmly make you scrutinize your actions – or inactions – on an ongoing basis (I tackled this technique in detail in my first book). Be accountable by choosing dates for having achieved or at least tried certain things. Your accountability partner will be the one you don't want to disappoint too many times in a row when they ask 'So what have you achieved since we met last time?'

One such accountability partnership is the aforementioned Friday night 'board meeting' I have with my fiancé and business partner. While I love the grand name, it really is a weekly discussion over dinner and a bottle of wine. The agenda is clear: we talk about everything that's going on in the business and everything to which we think we need to devote more time and energy. I see it as one of the ultimate business practices that has driven me personally as well as our company forward, and is my favourite time of the week. I get to spend quality time with the man I love talking about a topic I love. However, it's not just because it's 'nice' that we have kept up this tradition.

First, the best and widest-ranging decisions that we have ever taken have been at board meetings. We have decided on changes in the strategic direction of the company, the appointment of new staff members, new avenues that we would try and ways in which we would solve problems. This happened because we gave ourselves the opportunity to stop and actually think. It is a time outside of general office hours; and it's the beginning of the weekend – we can actually unwind while still in a gentle work mode. We aren't in a rush, and if something takes an hour to discuss, we have that time to give to it. We aren't running out the door to a meeting, or having to cut a phone call short due to another incoming call or watching the clock as we need to be somewhere afterwards. This is when we give the business and each other our full, undivided, unhurried attention.

Second, we're willing to hold each other accountable from one week to the next. If we write something down to be done by the week after, we know that it's going to come up in conversation the next week. If it was left undone, we need to address why. I often find myself saying throughout the week, 'I better find time to do that before Friday night.' If there wasn't that meeting, there wouldn't be a soft deadline and procrastination could kick in. I truly believe that the progress we have made is because we have integrated KPIs and held each other accountable on those measures.

Finally, it has given us both the time and the opportunity to learn about each other's points of view, opinions and outlooks, well in advance of any issue cropping up. As new opportunities and challenges come along, it's important to focus on them without having the additional pressure of suddenly finding out that we have opposite opinions on a fundamental issue. I have learned a lot about him, as well as about myself, during those discussions on a Friday night. I feel that both as a management unit and as a couple, we are stronger for this wonderful environment that we have set up for good, solid and thoroughly enjoyable communication.

In addition, I often have these sessions with myself. I find that any time that I'm out of my normal routine or if I'm on holiday or feeling stuck or highly energized, I can think more clearly about what needs to change. I go to a stimulating place with lots of activity. This could be in the café in my office building, a coffee shop that is one of my 'places', or one of my favourite spots. My aunt's house is a wonderfully warm place; the garden has a wall that I used to sit on as a child and daydream. As an adult, sitting on that wall brings back that youthful blue-sky thinking and I can drift into a fantasy. As I come back to earth, I find that I've separated from the constraints of what actually is and developed some strategies to make that fantasy what-could-be into a reality.

I also use the diary or regular meetings to hold myself accountable. If I go to a quarterly event, I decide on three things that I would like to achieve by the next time somebody meets me there and says, 'How are you getting on these days, Susan?' In some cases, if it is a structured training programme, the organizer will specifically ask me to outline what I've been doing in the last three months. It's incredibly satisfying to list the different 'boxes' that have been ticked. As we hop from one day to the next, focusing on the e-mails that we need to send, the family event that we need to get to and the shopping on the way home, little incremental actions don't get acknowledged. If you think that you haven't really done anything in the last few weeks or months, look at your red pen comments at the top of the pages in your diary for a very effective refresher.

Alternatively, I pick a (realistic) time in the diary and note down that I will have achieved a certain milestone by then. Using the SMART goal technique, I break down what I need to do and how I'm going to get there. As the day and the hour roll around, the diary entry pops up. At this stage, you either feel that 'YES!' feeling or else you have that thud in the bottom of your stomach that says, 'Another month gone and yet no development.' It's important to place reminders in front of you, to stave off or minimize procrastination, to reinvigorate your enthusiasm and refocus your efforts.

Should you seek out mentors?

Although I'm a great advocate of asking mentors for help, some can be unintentionally unhelpful. I asked a woman who had done what I really wanted to do to meet for coffee one day. I was truly in awe of her business and the level of success she had achieved, and I had so many questions to ask. I was curious about the decisions that she made when she was at my stage. She had been faced with my dilemmas earlier in her life, and it appeared to me that she taken a pathway that I couldn't see from where I was. I was so excited to meet her.

Perhaps I was naive, but I genuinely thought that I would walk away armed with all of the information that I'd need to make the right choice. I was ready to listen hard and soak it all up. However, from the moment that I sat down in the chair I felt uneasy. While talking to her, I felt junior and intimidated. She began by listing her achievements, starting from the setting up of her business, upon which I sincerely congratulated her. I asked her how it had all happened and would have been willing to sit and listen agog for the next hour. Her answer was curt: 'It's simple . . . I work 364 days a year.'

My heart sank. I had every intention of working hard back then, just as much as I do today. However, in my opinion, there is a lot more to life than being enclosed, metaphorically and physically, within four walls while the rest of the world gets on with their balanced life. She went on to tell me how she never really got to see her mother and used to get up at 3 a.m. to fly all over the world twice a week. Some phrases kept coming back: 'hard slog', 'arduous' and 'get on with it'.

She was clearly a highly accomplished person, and I learned a lot about the industry and her career progression in speaking to her. I disregarded my initial feelings and was willing to let first impressions not count. I went ahead to tell her of my own ideas and dreams. She said, 'I think you're going to find that hard' and left it at that. I felt as if she knew something that I didn't, but wouldn't tell me. To be quite honest, I left the meeting feeling quite unnerved. That's the thing about speaking to anybody about their dreams: handle them with care.

However, in spite of all this, I did manage to ask: 'Have you enjoyed any of this?' This was the only time that her face broke into a smile. She said, 'Of course, it's great to talk to inspiring people five days of the week. It's been fantastic.' At least we agreed on something . . .

The lesson of this episode is that if somebody discourages you from trying, take their opinion with a pinch of salt. They're not you. Maybe they were having an off day. Maybe they had a chance to show off to an admiring audience and wanted to paint the 'blood, sweat and tears' picture (but, if you asked, they would do it all over again in a heartbeat). Maybe they didn't know that you had set them up in your head as a mentor and that they weren't living up to the character that you had created. Surely you shouldn't discard your ambitions because one person has no idea of the role they are supposed to play.

The important thing to remember is that everybody has been through hard times. The main thing is that they're happy and working on their own KPIs. This book is about making more money, but in line with your own choice of lifestyle. The woman whom I met that day was happy to be submerged in her work in a one-dimensional world. I absolutely commend her. However, her way is not the only way to success. We often read admirable stories of superhero business people pulling an enterprise from the jaws of defeat and turning it into a money-making machine. As I said earlier, that makes a compelling story and gripping TV. But we often can't identify with these larger-than-life characters and think that if we're not jumping out of our skin to toil tirelessly at revolutionizing a company, we can't achieve our financial dreams. I utterly disagree.

If empowerment to you is to be able to comfortably be a stay-at-home mother until the kids are at a certain age, let's figure out a way of doing that. If your ambition is to build the next multinational, let's get started. If your desire is to make that little extra money to go on vacation, let's do it. You don't have to abandon your personality and become a power-hungry hot-shot exec. I once read a wise woman's quote in an interview: 'If you let other people choose the game you play, even if you win, you won't really be happy.' All you need to do is to figure out a plan for *your* dream and, above all, enjoy it.

A couple of years later, somebody approached me to meet for lunch. She told me that she felt stuck where she was at the time and had so much ambition without any particular place to direct it that she felt like a pressure cooker. I listened to her talk about her journey so far, what was working for her, what wasn't, where her demand came from, where her profit came from, etc. My plate cleared while hers remained untouched. I then told her everything I thought about what she had just told me. I outlined each of the avenues where I thought she could develop. I spoke about the ways in which I had travelled down those avenues myself, how I had succeeded or failed (both are equally valuable from a learning perspective) and the questions that I felt she needed to ask of herself.

At the end, she was beaming: 'You've answered it all for me. You've hit the nail on the head and now I know what to do.' I stared at her blankly. I didn't know what I had said or, indeed, if I had added value in any way. It's just that I hadn't held back. She bounced out of the coffee shop and on to pursue her destiny. Bewildered, I went back to the office feeling delighted that I had been able to give her some insights that she found helpful.

Nobody has the capacity truly to appreciate how many experiences, life lessons and nuggets of learning they have accumulated over the years. You know far more than you could possibly imagine. You have so much to give to the world, simply by passing on what's already in your head right now. Likewise, other people have the answers to every single question about life's journey. I love this Chinese proverb: 'If you want to know the road ahead, ask those who are coming back.' It's so true. While your path through life might be unique, no matter how good or how bad, at least one person (although it's more likely to be one million) has been there already. You may feel like you're alone today, but somebody else has stood in that very same spot before. Of course, you have everything that you need to figure the way forward yourself, but it's longer, lonelier and more resource-intensive if you don't give others the joy of helping you.

Connecting with people who have your new money

14. *Talking to your market so that your customers will listen*

I bristle when I hear that marketing is just a buzzword and consists of nothing but jargon. Marketing is about finding the best way to communicate with the people in your market. Like market research, marketing is neither inaccessible, nor mysterious. It is the step that comes before sales – and nobody would ever say, 'Ah, sales, that's just a buzzword, it's only a catchphrase.'

We have grown accustomed to talking about marketing only in relation to business. Yet, throughout our lives, we are all involved in marketing. Say you want to meet new people in your local city. By choosing to go to a busy bar or joining a class, you're effectively putting yourself in the best environment to make that ambition a reality. You are marketing yourself by putting yourself in front of your target audience of new friends. During my time in college, I went to several careers fairs that the Careers Department had organized. I used to walk around the stands picking up some brochures; I spoke to the companies and universities exhibiting, gave them my contact details, etc. This was a very clear form of marketing on my part. I went to a place where lots of future clients (aka employers) were interested in hearing my message (aka my CV).

In many cases, we do it so naturally that we don't realize we are doing it at all. That's because marketing is not just a catchphrase but the child of common sense: you have to make sure a client, or an employer, knows about your offering, and that they are aware of the ways it can benefit them. Marketing is putting your product or service in front of your target audience, and telling them that your offering is the answer to the problem that they are actively trying to solve.

But unless we have defined a strategy for it, marketing can easily expand to take up most of the day; without a strategy, it can also become a reactive activity, where I'm forever responding and never initiating an interaction on my own terms. For example, I come across an online forum where I contribute some nugget of advice; then I get an e-mail about an event, sign up to go to that tomorrow; I get a call from a potential customer, spend an hour doing an e-mail for them; I write an article, send it to a couple of magazines and some blogs in an effort to get it published; I send out three tweets; I spend two hours reading updates; I price some advertising space in the local paper. It's now 5 p.m. and I haven't started doing any of the follow-up calls that might actually have generated sales.

The reason that I espouse KPIs as strongly as I do is because they keep us focused on what can really make a difference. I could get twenty different articles written and featured in various different magazines, newspapers, blogs and e-zines. What a result. Unfortunately this might have a low impact if the magazines have a readership that I can't really give a value to; if the newspapers are distributed in a part of the world that doesn't have access to my offering; if the blog has zero hits; or if the e-zine editor forgets to mention that I'm the author of the piece, which means the reader has no idea that I wrote it and has no means of contacting me. With the right marketing approach, I could have saved myself much fruitless effort, as my articles would have reached the people who needed to hear from me.

Making marketing manageable – and effective

Set both a time budget and a money budget for marketing. Rather than let your time be directed by people who organize events, by advertising salespeople and by the endless, time-consuming waltz of social media, why don't you set the agenda? Dedicate a set period of time to focusing on marketing activities. They will get done, and all without hijacking your whole day. Similarly, keep an eye on how much marketing money you're spending and, more importantly, the return that you're making on this investment.

Take care to preserve your motivation and belief as well: you're at the stage where some not so successful experiences can eat away at both. You might mistakenly think that you 'can't' do it and that all your efforts have been wasted, when it's just that your message might be ineffectively worded and directed at the wrong market.

Imagine that I'm reviewing my career options. I'm going to strategize about what to do next, and I'm committed to working hard to get some employment. I sit and think and eventually come up with a list of five things that I'm going to do:

- Write a CV and include a bullet-point list of every single job, bit of education and hobby that I have ever had.
- Print off 100 copies and drop one into every business in the area.
- Upload the CV to lots of free advertising websites.
- Stick up a couple of posters in the local community hall, the local shop and the church, advertising that I'm looking for work.
- Go through the Chamber of Commerce directory, phone all of the businesses there and ask if they might have a job for me.

This truly would be 'hard work'. Now surely, after all that effort, I'll get something, somewhere, from somebody. However, this is the equivalent of throwing spaghetti at a wall and hoping that some of it sticks. If I were to apply a marketing strategy to this approach, here is what I would do differently:

- Learn some CV-writing techniques, craft a well-articulated, one-page summary of what I have to offer to a company and include a personalized section for 'role-specific information'.
- Plan each day as if I had working hours when I would be at my 'office' (that is, my computer in the sitting room) by

9 a.m. Spend the morning following up on any correspondence from the day before, answering e-mails, supplying extra information, updating profiles, tweaking my CV for specific roles, reminding companies of our previous contact, setting up appointments, participating in online forums, etc. Stop for an hour for lunch at 1 p.m. Take two hours in the afternoon to 'open leads' (applying for new jobs) until 4 p.m. Plan the next day's strategy until 5 p.m. and then close the laptop, go for a walk and switch off until tomorrow.

~ Approach some recruitment agencies to apply for suitable jobs, gain some current industry information, practise my interview techniques and glean some tips from those who professionally match people with employers.

~ Comb through the internet looking for jobs that would be suitable and start off by applying for those that are as senior and as well paid as possible. If my applications aren't being accepted because (and only because) I don't have the experience, then scale down progressively to a more junior role.

~ Engage in LinkedIn Groups and other social media outlets where the hidden job market can be found. Post helpful comments, actionable suggestions and make pointed contact with people and companies that are in a position to help me.

The second method is far more effective, structured and likely to result in a better paid, more suitable and more rewarding job. In the second scenario, I'm working smarter, not harder. In fact, it would probably take a lot less time than the former approach, where I'd just be wearing actual and metaphorical shoe leather. That's what marketing is all about: taking a well-articulated message and conveying it effectively to your market, where they're eager to listen to you.

SMART *thinking applied to* The Savvy Guide's Marketing Framework©

Marketing is mostly about choosing what not to do. Rule out everything that you can't do, won't do and wouldn't fit your message or your target market, and you'll be left with just a few avenues. Then apply SMART thinking to the ideas that made the cut. Let me show you what I mean.

Eighteen months ago, I spoke at a conference in London; it was one of the best events that I ever participated in. The organizers did an amazing job, and the room was full of fantastic people. But it was my responsibility to turn the event from an enjoyable day into a super marketing opportunity. I went with a strategic focus and applied my SMART approach.

SPECIFIC:

~ [*Medium*] This symposium was a networking platform.

~ [*Message*] My 'elevator pitch' was going to be about one part of my offering: being a keynote speaker on economics.

~ [*Call to action*] I was only getting started in the UK at the time, so I simply wanted to expand my network by meeting with as many people as would be worthwhile, find out about various networks and go to events to support this aim. My call to action was to meet for a coffee after the conference.

MEASURABLE:

~ I created a spread-sheet afterwards and noted every single opportunity that I had come across that day including:

  ~ Everybody who had agreed to meet me for coffee.

  ~ People who had offered me the opportunity to speak at their events.

  ~ Promotion opportunities: other attendees offering to introduce me to a certain media outlet, or to feature a guest article or a piece in their internal newsletter about *The Savvy Woman's Guide to Financial Freedom.*

∼ Each introduction that people were willing to make: some were within their own company, some were to other people in their network, some were to other network organizers with a view to letting me know about future events.

∼ I reviewed the spread-sheet regularly and noted:

∼ What the discussion at the various different coffees had produced.

∼ The results of the speaking opportunities at subsequent events.

∼ The outcomes of the follow-on promotion opportunities.

∼ What each of the introductions led to.

As far as I could, I tried to put a value on the quantifiable revenue generated from the day and the related follow-ups as well as the intangible benefits, and I compared this with the costs of the conference: time, flights and accommodation. This would enable me to quantify the 'return on investment'.

ATTAINABLE:

With such a strategy, I had made everything I wanted to do attainable: I was going to embrace every single opportunity that offered itself, I wasn't going to leave a single stone unturned, allowing me to make the most out of this day and enjoy myself immensely in the process.

REALISTIC:

To be quite honest, I had no idea what was realistic. I set out that morning to make it a day to remember and one that would count in the life of the business. I didn't know what I would come away with, except for zero energy in the tank, as I wanted to leave it all at the venue.

However, the day was only going to be a success if I made sure to follow up on those meetings – and that had to be planned realistically. I already had some idea of when I would be back in

London, so when I met people at the conference and was asking them for a coffee, I had already thought through the next step. I wasn't asking them for coffee at some undetermined, far-off time; instead I was asking them whether they were free on a specific day and at a specific location. I made it clear that I was serious about this market.

TIMELY:

~ I promised myself that I would take a half-day the next day (a Saturday) to create that spread-sheet and send every follow-up e-mail. I knew that it would be in their inbox before they arrived in to work on Monday, and I wanted to build on the momentum of the day itself. After the conference, I got to bed around midnight. I could get only two hours' sleep, as I had to get a bus to Luton Airport, and a flight to Malta at 6 a.m. When I got there around noon, I needed all the willpower I could muster to resist the siren song of the fluffy pillows on my hotel bed. Instead, I refused to give in to my fatigue until every single follow-up was done. I devoted thirty minutes every day for the next week answering e-mails, sending reminders, setting up calls and confirming meetings.

~ I put the review of the event on the agenda for the board meeting when I got home from Malta two weeks later.

~ I have returned to London every month since to build upon that foundation and my spread-sheet is blooming!

All this might strike you as terribly time-consuming. And perhaps in the beginning, or when you need money yesterday, you might take a ready-aim-fire approach. In the long run, though, if you want your money-making efforts to be sustainable and your results substantial, you need to take the time to make your marketing 'data-minable'.

As a service, our company will oversee an entire webinar campaign for another company. This means that we can help them to do, or completely take control of, the following: managing the technology, promoting their online events, and creating and delivering the content of the webinar.

On one occasion, a company asked us to work with them on a series of webinars to attract new clients. Together we decided to use LinkedIn advertising as the primary means of marketing. Now suppose we had drawn up an advertisement that said, 'We would like you to buy our product and make money from you. Please sign up to our webinar and have your credit card details ready'; then we had held a webinar that hit our audience over the head with all of the technical aspects of the offering, complete with an in-depth discussion of nano-this, mega-that and kilo-the-other; and then we had just flatly asked people to sign up and buy it. When it came time afterwards to see how much money we had made, I think I can accurately predict that the amount after the dollar sign would have been a pretty little zero.

Instead, we worded a short, snappy, yet comprehensive LinkedIn advertisement that had 'Free Webinar' as the title and invited people to register through the link provided at the end (this was our 'call to action'). We developed a forty-minute session giving people five valuable key information points; we took questions for another twenty minutes; and then we described three ways that this product could enhance their lives. We invited them to take a month's free trial and provided an automatic rollover facility to a paid membership when the free month was up (and they could of course stop the membership at any time).

We measured each and every one of the following:

- The number of people who registered for the webinar, as a percentage of those who had seen the ad (i.e., the number of impressions).
- The number of people who tuned in to the webinar, as a percentage of those who had registered.
- The number of people who stayed throughout the webinar to the sales pitch at the end, as a percentage of those who had tuned in to the webinar.

~ The number of people who took a trial of the offering, as a percentage of those who had stayed for the entire webinar.

~ The number of people who rolled over to the paid offering, as a percentage of those who had taken out a free trial.

Time-consuming this may have been, but we now had the following information:

~ Out of every 1,000 hits on the LinkedIn ad, we knew how many people had signed up for the webinar, the trial and the paid offering.

~ The attention level on the webinar, as a proxy for the interest of our audience in the content that we were providing.

~ The profit on the exercise, as we could compare the total revenue generated by the paid offering, less the cost of the LinkedIn advertising and the cost of the time spent by the people executing this marketing plan.

~ The return on investment of the marketing plan: the total amount generated, compared with the cost. For example, if we spent $1 on marketing and it generated $1.50, we could extrapolate that spending $1,000 on marketing would generate $1,500 in sales.

With this information, we needed to ask ourselves:

~ Was LinkedIn an effective platform for us to reach our target market? We needed to look at the number of people who registered for the webinar, versus the number of hits that the ad received. If we were to do the same with advertising on a website or Google Adwords, we now had a set of data to compare against.

~ Was our ad effective enough? Could we have increased the number of registrants for the webinar by wording the text of the ad differently? As it happens, we tried five different variations and two gained much better traction than the rest. Of course, this had a positive effect on every other measure, as more people turned up for the webinar, took the trial and rolled over to the paid offering as a result of this tweaking.

- Was our webinar content of interest to people? If people were tuning in and then exiting early, we needed to examine why. Perhaps some were called to an emergency or another task. But they might have been bored, found our content to be irrelevant or too basic for them. If people were staying the course, asking lots of questions, sending us positive feedback and looking for the video recording of the webinar afterwards, we knew that our customers had a hunger for this knowledge and wanted more.

- Was the sales pitch at the end effective? Did we wait too long before introducing the sales message? Did we try too hard? Did we not make it obvious enough that the product was available to try? Did we give a good enough 'webinar attendee only' deal, which incentivized people to sign up there and then?

- Were the product and the trial experience of a sufficiently high quality for people to pay in order to continue enjoying the benefit? Did we follow up quickly enough and often enough? Did we inadvertently give them any misconceptions about what the product would do that disappointed them afterwards? Did we build on the momentum of the webinar with appropriate customer service? Did we make it easy enough to buy afterwards?

Now consider the discussion that we had after that first webinar when sitting down with the client. We had lots to talk about and several key, measurable, identifiable ways that we could change, build, review, grow and develop with the company and their customers. Yes, this is time-consuming, but look at all that we were able to discover. This is time truly well spent.

In addition, if this company were to engage in any other marketing activity, they now have a comprehensive set of data against which to compare its effectiveness. In one glance at a spread-sheet, they now knew what worked, what didn't and the questions that they needed to ask to increase the return on their investment. This information would save them a fortune in time, resources and money, and it was highly valuable market research in and of itself, allowing them to better position their messages as well as better allocate their efforts, time and resources in the future. This is the type of situation that marketing, finance and management depart-ments of companies dream of.

This example concerns a big marketing campaign for a big com-pany. But even if you're freelancing from your living room, the underlying principles will continue to apply: put your marketing where the attention of your target market can usually be found (remember the 'geographic' component of market research) and make sure that what you put in front of them is not just noise but a demonstration of your expertise and the value of what you have to offer.

It's crucial that you measure whether your marketing is actually effective. Of course you wouldn't put a poster on a wall in a dark corner of a building where nobody ever goes; this sounds obvious, and yet so many businesses advertise in metaphorical dark corners, and then complain that nobody is buying. Begin with making absolutely sure that people will actually come across your market-ing message and then measure everything that's useful. How many people click on the link or call the number? How many end up buy-ing, compared with the number of people who came across your poster?

The 'message in a bottle' marketing approach, which lacks any measurable, quantifiable element, is too often seen with Google Adwords and social media – Facebook, Twitter, and the dozens of new sites that are created almost daily. So don't fall into that trap and keep a close eye on your KPIs, as always. Good, targeted, effect-ive connection with your customers takes time, yes, but not nearly as much time as haphazard hit-and-miss marketing.

My marketing mix: networking, joint-ventures and PR

I have chosen to concentrate on networking, joint-ventures and PR to promote my business, as these are the avenues that have repeatedly offered the best return on my time and money. I'd like to discuss networking in particular, because it's such a double-edged sword: it can deliver fantastic results as long as you find the right network, are specific in what you want to get out of it, follow up effectively and are strategic about it. But it's also very easy to fall into a packed calendar of events, coffees, lunches and travelling between them all – and I'm speaking from experience here.

The examples of CorkMEET and the conference I attended in London gave you frameworks that can be used to establish SMART goals for a networking event. I have employed networking for many reasons, among which are:

1. To find buyers (as distinct from selling). Once you know who your target market is, you can be quite clear about who you want to meet. If you know that they're going to be at a specific event or industry conference, you can make yourself known to them, get their cards and initiate contact. This is not selling: this is the start of establishing a relationship.

2. To meet with influencers – as you know from Step Four, influencers have an important role to play. There are lots of people who are in a position to help you, and not just buyers: those willing to give a recommendation, to introduce you to somebody in their network, to give you an audience, to share valuable insights and opinions, etc. A neutral place like a networking event is a great opportunity to walk up to them and get your point across concisely, but think about how you can give them something too.

3. To get me out of the house or office so that I meet people – yes, this is a selfishly sociable reason, but I have to admit that I have done it. However, sometimes we need to be around

people who are doing the things that we want to do as if they are on autopilot, while we're still struggling a bit. If you're just getting started, if things are slow, or if you've hit a lull, it's very easy to wallow in self-pity. At least when you have an appointment in your diary, it gives you a sense of purpose and get-up-and-go for the day. That's all that you might need to take action to get past that short-term business block.

4. To listen to a certain speaker. Sometimes I have an interest in the topic (business development and financial markets) and in other cases I have respect for a particular person and I want to hear their point of view and meet them.

5. To perform some of my own market research. As I'm delivering an 'elevator pitch', I observe people's reactions. Do their questions betray that they haven't a clue about what I do? In that case I need to work some more both on refining my offering and on clarifying my elevator pitch. Do their eyes glaze over and they give me that polite nod and smile? Do they reinterpret it in their own words and say, 'So basically, you . . .'? As I talk to people in my target market, I'm always listening out for mentions of the issues that they're having (which we may be able to solve); or how they answer questions that start with 'Wouldn't it be just fantastic if . . .'; or how they express their opinion on an industry development.

6. As I have often alluded to throughout the book, I regularly go on training courses, as I believe that it's very important to continually upskill myself both in general business and in my own sector. Often on such courses you can meet people whose businesses complement yours, who may be scouting for initiative-taking partners or who could be potential clients. An opportunity to network doesn't explicitly need to be a networking event.

7. I always try to consider who else would benefit from attending a presentation or a breakfast or a webinar or any other

event. As a result, I can help others, as others have helped me by thinking of me for an invitation. I know what it's like to organize an event and how helpful it can be when people bring somebody else along. It also gives me an opportunity to give value to a client outside of our training and eLearning offering; to offer something to a prospect before or after putting a proposal to them; or to thank somebody in a meaningful way.

15. *Building your own marketing plan*

This is where the homework you have done after reading earlier chapters will pay off. In devising a marketing plan, the work that you do in understanding your customer at market research stage will stand you in great stead. If you know exactly what their pain point is and / or how to give them meaningful pleasure, you can concentrate on articulating this as effectively as possible in the best place to gain their attention. However, if you get to the marketing stage and have skipped doing your market research, you could spend a lot of money finding out that your customer doesn't actually listen to a certain radio station. Or that they don't really care if you can solve a problem they didn't really know that they had. Or you could drive 100 kilometres to realize that your potential clients don't go to the events that you thought they did. Trial and error is expensive and time-consuming.

Don't pick a random marketing strategy 'just because'. Make sure it fits your target market, your type of offering, and the time and money you have available. I love networking, as it fits my personality, my target market and what I can offer to it. It also has good synergy with the other two avenues I chose, joint-ventures and PR. But you can use *The Savvy Guide's Marketing Framework*© to strategize about any type of marketing.

The Savvy Guide's Marketing Framework©

There are six stages that each and every marketing activity should have:

1. Medium
2. Message

3. Call to action
4. Follow-up
5. Measurement
6. Review

1. Medium

There's a plethora of marketing campaigns and platforms available, but I'm going to outline ten broad categories below:

DIRECT CONTACT

You can approach people or organizations directly, if they are relatively few in number or if you have a relatively cost-efficient method of reaching a mass market. However, it can also be very time-consuming and expensive, if your market is less than enthusiastic about hearing from you. Personally, I have used this form of marketing in several ways over the years, including any time that I applied for a job or the time that my two co-authors and I approached a publisher about our economics textbook proposal.

Examples of direct contact:

- A job application sent to one specific company with a vacancy.
- Calling a particular company or person to set up a meeting.
- Sending an e-mail to a mailing list.
- Handing out flyers at a shopping centre.
- Posting vouchers to homes.

PUBLIC EXPO OR TRADE SHOWS

These are large-scale events aimed at specific targets and with a view to attracting a significant number of people. They are particularly good for reaching a large group of people all at the same time when you have either a low-cost item to sell at the stand (one that would be of interest to the attendees, of course) or for collecting names and e-mail addresses to target afterwards. However, if the organizer hasn't promoted the event enough and in the right way, you can run the risk of low footfall or lots of uninterested people. In our case, we exhibited at the 'Women Outside the Box' festival in Bristol, as we felt it was a good fit with *The Savvy Woman's Guide to Financial Freedom*.

Examples of targeted exhibitions:

- 'The Family Show'
- 'Day of the Investor'
- 'Ploughing Championships'
- eLearning Guild's 'Learning Solutions'
- 'Be Fit'
- 'The Money Show'

JOINT-VENTURE

If you can pair up with another supplier who offers a product or service that complements yours, it can be a powerful combination. In this case, two (or more) different businesses can come together and offer a combined package for a certain price. If they both let their respective audiences know of the collective benefit of the offering, they can increase sales for each other. However, you need to make sure that you stand to gain as much as you give. This was a particularly useful method for us when the company began, as we didn't have clients or a track record. We joined forces with a couple of other companies, e.g., executive education providers, to add to what they could offer their existing customers, and we gained a lot of business, testimonials and experience.

Examples of complementary joint-ventures:

- Wedding or [*insert occasion*] package – hair and make-up.
- Photographer, graphic designer and printer.
- Training agency and several different trainers.
- Gym, nutritionist and personal trainer.
- Dentist, orthodontist and teeth-whitening specialist.

PUBLIC RELATIONS (PR)

PR consists of informing your audience about you and your product or service via traditional media channels. In this case, your audience would be interested in hearing what you've got to say about a certain topic or what advice you've got to give or what experiences you can share. The sales message in this medium is much more subtle than the short, sharp, simple message of an advert. PR can act as 'free' advertising and contains the unspoken endorsement of the medium in which you appear. However, you need to ensure that your message is actually reaching your target audience. It's easy to get caught up in the initial excitement of 'I'm on the TV', but PR is a marketing activity only if it brings some tangible benefit to you and your initiative. I did a lot of promotion via traditional and online media last year to let the world know about *The Savvy Woman's Guide to Financial Freedom*.

Examples of PR:

- An interview on TV.
- Participate as part of a panel on radio.
- An article in a newspaper.
- A feature in a magazine.

ORGANIC ONLINE MARKETING

If you don't spend money on advertising, but work at attracting people to your site, this is said to be 'organic' marketing. This happens if you convey a message that people want to hear and that they deliberately navigate their way through the web to see. Also, if your content (e.g., article, copy on your website, YouTube video, social media posts, etc.) corresponds to the terms that people are searching for online, it can rise through the 'Search Engine Optimization' ranks. This means that, when people are searching for a certain term or phrase via a search engine like Google or Yahoo, they will be directed to your content if it contains the term or phrase they used, and if it has been recognized as reliable by the search engines. This is a highly cost-effective way to build traction and trust with your market. However, it can also be a painfully slow, labour-intensive method when used on its own. I write a blog on www.thepositiveeconomist.com, I write guest articles and pieces for other websites, and I often contribute to social media discussions.

Examples of organic online marketing:

~ Researching terms related to your product or service that have a high number of searches and then including them in the copy on your website – this is another way of listening to your target market (or observing their 'clicking') and knowing which words they use to describe their problem or their desired outcome.

~ Writing a regular blog about a specific topic.

~ Creating text, video and audio (podcast) content and uploading it to your website.

~ Being a guest contributor on a high-traffic site that links back to your website or social media page.

SPONSORSHIP

Companies create brand awareness by associating their name with an event that provides multiple opportunities for putting their brand in front of customers. Their logo, name and message can be seen and remembered by the audience of the event. Sponsorship is a useful way to build brand familiarity with a large group of people. If the media provide coverage, the effect can be magnified. It's very important to document exactly what you are set to receive in exchange for sponsorship, as 'brand awareness' is difficult to measure. We have sponsored charitable organizations' events in the past with a view to supporting the work of the charities themselves and bringing our brand into the spotlight of our target market.

Examples of sponsorship:

~ The name of a company and its logo on the sports jersey of a popular team.

- A company's marketing materials being put into the guest pack of each attendee at an expo.
- A radio newsreader saying at the end of each bulletin, 'This is brought to you by [*company name*].'
- A company's name on the tickets to a music concert and their branding all over the venue.

NETWORKING

This involves going to events and conferences, and attending the gatherings of groups, associations and other business people, to meet with your target market, and with people who can introduce you to new customers and help you in various ways in your business. Also, there are several online networking opportunities including forums, blogs, social media and discussion groups. Finally, you can ask the people within your network to help you with a marketing activity. This is a particularly useful medium if your customers also go to networking events, thus enabling you to meet several people at once and increasing the return on your investment of time. As I mentioned earlier, it's easy to fill a calendar (and your calorie count) to bursting point with breakfasts, coffees, dinners, lunches, phone calls, meetings and follow-ups. You need to be strategic with your time and efforts, and focus on what will actually make an impact on your bank balance. I have been involved in networking groups at home and abroad, online and offline, regularly and through one-offs, during my entire time in business – far too many to mention.

Examples of networking:

- Joining a group that meets regularly to hear guest speakers, introduce people to each other and facilitate discounts between members.
- Attending an industry-specific conference where the attendees are in your target market.
- Participating in a LinkedIn Group where you are providing expertise and value to a group of people who could potentially be your customers and/or influencers.

◠ Sending a message to your network to invite them to come along and bring a friend to an event that you're organizing.

ADVERTISING

This is when you would place an eye-catching, effective, direct sales message right in front of your target market, either on- or offline. If you have identified people who are actively looking for a solution to a problem and you can provide that solution, or as having a desire to enjoy the pleasure that you can offer, they may already be interested in your type of offering. This can be a very effective way of getting across your sales message to a high volume of 'qualified' (already interested) potential customers. It's absolutely crucial to develop a well-thought-out plan as to how you will measure, capitalize upon and ultimately benefit from an advertising campaign: being in front of your customer doesn't automatically equate with sales. I have overseen several advertising campaigns for companies, and I wrote in detail earlier in the chapter about the LinkedIn campaign that I designed and executed.

Examples of advertising:

◠ A 4 cm x 4 cm advert in a classified section of a newspaper saying 'Window cleaners available'.

◠ A TV ad featuring happy, active kids and laughing parents, enticing viewers to enjoy the unforgettable experience of visiting a famous theme park.

◠ A poster in a local coffee shop showing a perfectly toned body and giving details of a ten-week Pilates course that will result in a 'bikini bod'.

◠ An ad on Facebook saying 'Wedding Dresses for under €500' that appears when somebody changes their status to 'engaged'.

◠ Paying for your flower shop to be the first result on a Google results page when somebody searches for 'Where could I get blue chrysanthemums in Edinburgh?'

EVENT-DRIVEN MARKETING

You invite people to a free or paid event with a view to educating them about your product or service and then inviting them to buy what you have to offer. This can be a great way literally to listen to your market, as you can hear them first-hand, answer objections if and when they arise, focus their attention on you for a period of time and narrow down your sales outreach to those who are truly interested (i.e., the people who do turn up). However, events can also be an expensive (if you need to hire a venue and provide catering) and risky (if very few people show up) activity, unless they are planned and executed well. We organized two book launches for *The Savvy Woman's Guide to Financial Freedom*, and I have worked with hundreds of organizations in promoting events at which I've been a speaker.

Examples of event-driven marketing:

~ Free workshop on 'Social Media Advertising'.
~ A free webinar on 'How to earn a million dollars in a year'.
~ An open viewing for a house between 2 p.m. and 5 p.m. every day this week.
~ A book launch.

WORD-OF-MOUTH

This is probably the most potent of them all. If one trusted friend recommends a provider to another, the friend is far more likely to request their services and to go on to buy from them. This is a fantastic way to do business. It's crucial to remind people to tell their friends and colleagues about what you do. Remember that it can also work against you if you leave a negative impression on a client. I have often asked for, and received, the support of others in recommending our products and services to other people.

Examples of word-of-mouth marketing:

~ A previous boss recommending or writing a reference for a member of staff to another employer.

- One neighbour telling another about a company that they used to service their boiler.
- A customer's tweet about the experience they had with a company.
- A recommendation on LinkedIn.

2. Message

Now that you've found a way to communicate with your market, what are you going to tell them? It's important to be humble in this scenario – people are drowning in thousands of bits of information every day, each vying for their limited attention. Some will slip by unnoticed, some will creep in subliminally, some will conform to their value system, some will distract them, some will be interesting, some will be grotesquely fascinating, some will be memorable, some will be quickly forgotten – and a few will actually make an impact. So how can you make that grade?

KEEP IT SIMPLE AND SINGULAR

What is the one, and only one, not more than one, just one, isolated one, key one, individual one point that you want to get across? Are you getting my *one* message here? Don't confuse your already swamped customer with multiple things to which you want them to react. For example, compare the effectiveness of these two pieces of text on a quarter-page ad in a newspaper:

Today we are introducing our new revolutionary product, holding a discount sale on our existing stock, changing our opening hours, opening new premises and holding our one-year anniversary party. Come to our new shop, old shop, our party in the local town hall, our website and call us on our new hotline too.

For one day only, we have a one-off sale with 30% off selected stock. Come to our store today on Main Street between 9 a.m. and 5 p.m. for these exclusive, not-to-be-missed, great-value deals.

In the first case, the reader doesn't know where to go or what to do, and has already lost interest in my ad. They've very probably decided to move on in the blink of an eye. In the second case, a potential customer may raise their eyebrows with interest, mentally check their diary and try to pack in a trip to the shop before the day is out, as my language has clearly highlighted that there is the possibility of bagging a bargain, but that possibility is time-limited. The parameters of my offering are crystal clear, and I have told the customer exactly where, when and why they should look for the product.

SELL WHAT THEY'RE ACTUALLY INTERESTED IN BUYING FROM YOU

You may recall from Step Three that people don't buy food at a restaurant because they're hungry; they buy an evening with their girlfriend, the prestige attached to taking a client to the best place in town, the convenience of not having to cook themselves, or a means of expressing gratitude to somebody who has done them a favour. People don't buy concert tickets to hear the music of their favourite artists – they buy the experience of creating memories with loved ones, the atmosphere, the glimpse of the person who makes the cover of an album come to life. Make sure to incorporate the real benefit into your marketing. For example:

- Save money by switching to our new, low-cost, value-packed plan.
- Make money today by referring our tried and trusted product to your family and friends.
- Eliminate stress by letting us take care of your travel plans.
- Grow your productivity by an hour a day by following these three simple steps.
- Boost staff morale with our team-building programme this month.
- Impress your clients and set your business apart with personalized, branded stationery.

- Increase your earning power by building your CV with this gold-standard qualification.
- Get peace of mind with our life insurance policies.
- Find friendship with like-minded people at our golf club.
- Lose weight with our intensive, 30-minute exercise plan.
- Get fitter and have fun at our salsa slim eight-week course.
- Surmount that fear and grow your confidence with others at our public-speaking masterclass.
- You deserve some 'me-time' – relax in our luxurious, waterside spa.
- Rejuvenate and improve your well-being at our award-winning retreat centre.
- Boost your energy levels with our health supplements.
- Stave off coughs and colds with our nourishing, vitamin-packed bread for all the family.

3. Call to action

Now that you've found your audience and told them about the impact that you can make on their life, what exactly do you want them to do? The answer to this question should start with a verb: *call, text, register, tweet, attend, visit*, etc.

While of course you want them to take money out of their pocket and give it to you, there may be an additional couple of steps before that happens. For example, let's say that I'm going to start giving Pilates lessons in my local community centre and I print off a couple of posters to put up in shops, cafés and the library. Let's actually think of the process that a potential customer will go through before I get the cash into my account:

- Look at my poster.
- Call or text my number to get more information.
- Decide whether they can trust me to be a qualified instructor.
- Decide if the time/price/programme is right for them and reserve their place.

∼ Turn up at the beginning of the course.
∼ Pay the money.

Now compare the difference between these two calls to action on my poster:

Arrive on the night and bring €99 with you!
or
Call today to get more information!

In the first case, I'm not giving the potential client the opportunity to ask any questions or to contact me to make sure that I'm actually real, and I'm blatantly asking for money. I also haven't given myself the opportunity to gather any market information. I don't know how many people are interested, how many people wrongfully discarded my offering because they didn't think it was for them, and I can't draw out the objections that I could have answered and tackled. I'm also relying solely on their memory and motivation to guide them on to the Pilates mat, as I don't have any way of contacting them, and they don't have any way of contacting me.

In the second case, I'm not asking for a financial commitment, I'm simply inviting the customer to make themselves known to me and to ask about anything that they would like to find out. If somebody worries that it will go over an hour, which would put them in a tricky situation with babysitters, I can assure them of punctuality. If somebody is worried that they will find themselves in a room full of perfectly flat stomachs and elastically flexible bodies, while they're still shifting the Christmas pounds, I can tell them that people of all 'shapes and sizes' are welcome and encouraged. I can develop a rapport with them on the phone and invite them to put their name down while having the conversation. I can have a significant influence on their decision to reserve their place at that moment in time.

In addition, if I take their name and number, I can send out a reminder text a week, then a day, in advance of the class to everybody who expressed an interest. This has the impact of putting my offer to build strength, lose stomach inches and tone muscles right back in their minds, as undoubtedly lots of other things will have competed for their attention since they saw my poster. This gives me a much more powerful effect on their decision to move from a name on my list to a person in the queue on the evening. If they are there, they are very likely to have brought the money with them.

Look at the impact that one line on a poster can make.

Thinking the whole process through to completion is crucial. Including a 'call to action' simply means telling your prospect in no uncertain terms what they need to do to be brought closer to you. Let's examine a suitable call to action for each marketing platform:

DIRECT CONTACT

- [*An e-mail to somebody that you know*] Would you be interested in meeting for a coffee?
- [*An e-mail to a list of people*] Register through the link provided to sign up for the webinar.
- [*A postal mailshot*] Come into our store to redeem this voucher.

PUBLIC EXPO

- [*Free draw*] Sign up today for a free draw.
- [*Demonstration*] Come along to our demonstration today at 2 p.m.
- [*Show offer*] Buy one, get one free – Exclusive Show Offer.

JOINT-VENTURE

A joint-venture is a two-stage marketing strategy. First, you need to engage with the joint-venture partner, so you need to make direct contact with them. Second, you decide which, among each other's products and/or services, you're going to market, and how. The call to action is thus a combination of the other marketing routes.

ADVERTISING AND PR

When somebody comes across a piece of promotional material about you and your offering, you could have the following calls to action:

- Register for your free trial pack today at . . .
- Text [*insert word*] to [*insert number*] and a member of our team will call you within twenty-four hours.
- Call [*insert number*] and quote [*insert identifying word*] to get your 10% discount.
- Tweet us your thoughts at # [*insert Twitter hashtag*].
- Visit [*insert website*] for more details.

ORGANIC ONLINE MARKETING

This marketing approach has two facets to it:

- Writing guest posts on other people's forums, blogs, websites, etc., with a clickable link to bring them back to your own site. You might have the following calls to action:
  - Click here to read more valuable insights.
  - Click here to download this free report and gain access to others.
  - Claim your free 'Three Steps to Success' at [*address of website*].
- Attracting the search engines to your site. As people search for a topic like 'lose weight fast', 'getting my baby to sleep' and 'money-saving tips', the technology behind the engines scours the internet trying to find the most relevant content. If your site has lots of references to the 'keywords' in these terms, your site address and a short description will show up higher in the search results. As a result, using the words that

your target market is searching for makes it more likely that the search engines will act on your behalf. The technical term for this process, as mentioned earlier, is called 'Search Engine Optimization'.

SPONSORSHIP

This is a very broad area, so you need to speak directly to the people behind the sponsorship deal to see what's on offer. In many cases, this effort is about giving your business, your logo and your slogan visibility. You need to make use of that in the best way. For example:

∼ If you gave your leaflet to each person who attends a sponsored event, you'd be using the call to action mentioned in the advertising and PR section above.
∼ If you're showing a visual to an audience, you can invite them to tweet their messages with a hashtag.
∼ If you sponsor a prize, you can request that people do something to enter: fill out a short form; text their name and an answer to a question to a number; or scan a QR code and then leave their e-mail address on the 'landing page'. In addition, you could ask to present the prize, introduce yourself as a representative of your company and announce the winner.

NETWORKING

Networking is a similarly broad forum. You need to be clear what you're looking for: introductions to people within your target market, meetings with potential buyers, meeting new people to expand your network? For example, in these three cases, as you speak to people at events, you might ask them:

∼ Would you feel comfortable introducing me to [*insert name*]?
∼ Would you like to meet for a coffee at some stage in the next fortnight to see if there are ways that we could be of benefit to each other?

∼ Do you have a business card so I can send you an invite on LinkedIn?

If people have come out of their homes or driven to a hotel after work to hear you or somebody else speak, or if they have made time in their diary to listen to or to view a webinar online, they have already shown a strong interest. People's time is precious, it has lots of claims on it, and you have proved that your offering is worthy of that. (Don't disappoint.) You need to have an action plan to turn this interest into custom, and this requires two things:

∼ Spelling out the offering and then giving attendees an easy way to buy from you:

  ∼ Offline: 'To enjoy the benefits of what you have seen here today, simply go to the back of the room and speak to [*insert name*], who will process your order.'

  ∼ Online: 'To gain access to this exclusive members' area, simply click on the link in the chat pod and fill out the short form, which will take about thirty seconds.'

∼ Giving a special offer for that event – it's very easy for somebody to walk away with the genuine intention of calling you/signing up online/looking into your offering again afterwards. However, they will no sooner have left your event than they have to answer a voice-mail, look at a text, think about picking up the kids, stop to get something for dinner on the way home, etc. If you give a special offer for an event, you focus the customer's mind on buying there and then, so that they can start enjoying the benefit of your product or service right away. Also, it rewards them for taking time out of their day to spend an hour with you; you have an opportunity to hear their questions, objections, comments and can develop a rapport with them. For example, you could include:

- Online: A 20% discount is in place for the next twenty-four hours if you call this number and quote [*identifying word*].
- Online: For everybody who signs up tonight, you get fourteen months' access for the price of twelve.
- Offline: If you place your order at this event, we will also give you a book and a €20 complimentary voucher.
- Offline: We have a special offer this evening: if you decide to reserve your place, you can invite a friend to come along for 50% of the price.

WORD-OF-MOUTH

Word-of-mouth isn't something that happens only if you're lucky. There are people who, when they have received an exemplary product or service, will want to tell everybody about their experience and refer their friends and family. I love to tweet about good experiences that I've had with companies, hotels, restaurants, etc. However, there are also lots of people who would be delighted to do the same, but they just don't think to do so. It's your job to help them. Remember that an endorsement from them to a friend who trusts them is far more effective than your telling said friend about your wonderful product or service. This form of marketing is actually your customers acting as your sales team. If you come across somebody who wants to do this, treat them like royalty.

There are several prompts that you can drop into conversation to remind them of how grateful you would be if they would refer you to other people:

- Do you know of anybody else who could benefit from my [*insert offering*]?
- [*After they tell you about somebody else who has the same problem or is in need of the pleasure that you can give*] I would be delighted if you could introduce me to them?

209

- Would you mind [*putting a comment on my Facebook page/ review on TripAdvisor/retweeting my tweet*]?
- We actually have a referral scheme where we give people [*a month's free access/a 10% commission/a voucher for a meal*] if they introduce new customers to us. Would you be interested?

4. Follow-up

Unfortunately, if you've done absolutely everything right up until now and then stop, it will have a rather limited effect. This is the killer step. This is where the magic happens – where a passing interest can turn into monetary commitment. The reverse is also true: unless you undertake the steps to get to here, this step will be a lonely place, as there won't be anybody to follow up on.

If somebody has already invested in you, through their time, attention span or initiating contact, do give them due respect and respond with value. From experience, I also know that we may have a genuine intention of doing this, but sometimes things get in the way – tiredness, lack of resources or an emergency of some sort.

I have worked on several different stands at expos, and they are truly exhausting. At the end of the last day, you pack up and dream of your pyjamas and a pillow. You have a box full of interested leads and smile happily to yourself that you gleaned a lot of benefit from the event. However, you're only about 10% of the way there. The real work starts now. You decide you're going to just take the day off tomorrow to recuperate and then get started. Next thing you know, it's Tuesday morning and you have an inbox full of e-mails to deal with, a job that has to be done, a couple of phone calls to be returned and then it's 7 p.m. Definitely, tomorrow. A week later, you finally start phoning the people who left their details with you that day. The thing is that a lot has happened in their lives too since their five-minute meeting with you (and the other fifty exhibitors they spoke to), so your impact has weakened considerably by now.

There is only one remedy for this. Plan ahead. In the same way that you factor in the two days that you will actually exhibit at the show, put a full day into your diary to follow up. Don't plan any meetings on that day, put an auto-responder on your e-mail to say that you're out of the office today and will reply tomorrow, let your voice-mail collect your calls and *focus*. I would say the same for absolutely every other marketing plan.

Following up involves two actions on your part: having a method and then scheduling in the time to do it. Let's consider how to do this depending on your call to action:

- You have a meeting with a recruitment agency tomorrow at 2 p.m. and you make sure that you're free from 9 a.m. until 10 a.m. the next day to do any follow-ups after the meeting. During the discussion, they ask you to send them three references and a copy of a qualification, and to add in three lines about your career break in your CV.
  - You follow up with an immediate e-mail to thank them for their time, saying that you're going to gather the information and that you're looking forward to working with them in the future. You contact three previous employers via e-mail, scan the copy of the qualification and give some thought to describing your career break. In addition, you send the recruitment agency two bullet points of how you could tailor your CV to the jobs that you discussed with them.
- You have invited people on a mailing list to sign up for a webinar or a physical event next Tuesday:
  - Schedule the Wednesday beforehand to design the content, develop any materials (PowerPoint slides, etc.), think about the special offer that you'll give attendees and do a complete dress rehearsal, which you record and listen back.
  - Compose and set up the system so that it automatically sends out a reminder to everybody who has registered on the Thursday before, the Monday before and the hour before.

~ Ask a colleague to listen to the recording and suggest ways that you can improve.

~ [*Webinar*] Create a special 'webinar link' to click in order to avail of the deal and then ensure that this process is as easy, simple and uncomplicated as possible. Compose an e-mail that goes to attendees, thanking them for their time and including the link to the recording and a reminder of the special webinar offer. Compose a separate e-mail that goes to people who were absent from the webinar, saying that it's a pity that they couldn't attend, giving them the link to the recording and details of how to register for the next webinar.

~ [*Physical event*] Make sure you have another person with you to take orders after the event itself. Ensure that you have the capability to take payments (e.g., process credit card details securely, etc.), if you tell people that they can pay using this method. Print off order forms that are clear, comprehensive and easy to fill out. The following week, call everybody who attended to ask them if they're happy with their purchase (if they bought) and ask for feedback on the event (if they didn't). Compose an e-mail to people who registered but didn't turn up, with details of the next event and the link to secure their place.

~ You're sending out a mailshot inviting people to claim their voucher at your shop, and the week before the vouchers go in the post, you spend a day doing the following:

~ Creating a setting on your till to incorporate the discount into the receipt.

~ Explaining to your staff how to deal with the voucher in the transaction.

~ Setting up a process where, if the voucher is used, staff will put a red cross on it and put it into a dedicated box underneath the till so that somebody can't walk out the door with it and use it again.

∽ You've collected the 300 names and e-mail addresses of those who entered the free draw at an exhibition. You block out every morning of the week after to:

  ∽ Input the details into a spread-sheet, e-mail responder or 'Customer Relationship Management' (CRM) system.

  ∽ Contact everybody with a call to action (which loops us back into the direct-contact platform): attend a workshop, visit your website or avail of a show offer for a limited period.

∽ You have invited people to come along to a demonstration at 2 p.m. at an expo:

  ∽ Ensure that everyone working on the stand is back from a break at this point and ready to field questions or process transactions.

  ∽ At the end of the demonstration, give a clear call to action:

    • Buy today at our special show price of €10.
    • Try it out for yourself for just €19 for six weeks – simply talk to the friendly, knowledgeable staff at our stand and you can enjoy the benefits right away.

∽ You have a coffee with a potential joint-venture partner, client or networking contact at 10 a.m. You're not going to be back at your office until 3 p.m. and have to make some calls. You need to go home and spend time with the kids before bedtime. You block out 9 a.m. to 11 a.m. the next morning to:

  ∽ Send an e-mail thanking them for their time.

  ∽ Compose a tailored proposal.

  ∽ Introduce them to somebody who could be a client of theirs in turn.

  ∽ Tell them about an event that's coming up soon that may be of interest to them.

∽ You have placed an advert in a sector-specific magazine and invited people to register for a free-trial pack today at your website. You clear your diary for the day before the ad is published in order to:

~ Ensure that the link is working and put through a test request.

~ Ensure you have enough stock ordered to deal with the anticipated demand.

~ Ensure you have freed yourself up (or somebody else) for three hours every day for a week after the ad has been placed, to ship the materials.

~ You have run a radio ad inviting people to text a certain number with a certain word and a member of your team will call them back within twenty-four hours. You take a day out to brainstorm with your team and then you clear enough time during the ad's two-week run to call those listeners. You need to:

~ Test out the text connection to ensure that it's working perfectly.

~ Arrange that you or your team have capacity to call those who respond.

~ Plan what you're going to speak about when you do call them and what the objective of the call is (which loops back into the direct-contact marketing step).

~ You write a press release about the introduction of your new service and the local paper agrees to print it or you write a guest blog post for a high-traffic site. The piece invites readers to visit your website. You spend an hour preparing your site the day before publication, and then you devote two hours on publication day and an hour every day for the next week following up on results.

~ On the day before publication, you take another look at your website and make any changes that you think might be beneficial: mentioning that your new service is going to be detailed in the paper this week.

~ On the day of publication, you promote the article (and the link, if available) through all of your social media channels and respond promptly to any engagement.

~ On the days following the release, you have the time in your diary to reply to e-mails, answer phone queries, follow up with initial interest, etc.

5. Measurement

I wouldn't blame you for thinking at this point that there is so much that you could do . . . and so much time that it could take . . . and so much money that it could eat up . . . and with limited time and money resources, what should you do?

I have worked with companies with hundreds of employees in a support role, highly proficient, experienced people in marketing and seven-figure advertising budgets – and they ask themselves the same question. They answer it with the very discussion that follows.

Let's say that you need to get milk to put in your coffee and have just popped to the shop. You don't care about packaging, your familiarity with the brand or the nutritional value. The decision is only about price. There are two identical one-litre cartons on the shelf – one is €1 and the other is €7.50. Which do you choose? I would imagine that you would spend the smaller amount of money, since that would be a much more efficient spend. I suggest that you apply the very same logic to the time, money and energy that you invest in your marketing.

However, you will be able to do this only if you can measure your results – it's easier to choose between identical cartons of milk because they clearly look the same. It takes a little extra effort to identify whether two marketing strategies are in fact identical (which can be spotted if they're producing identical results). Sometimes the relationship between a marketing campaign and revenue is very clear-cut and easily documented. In other cases, it requires you to be focused on what you get out of an activity. The impact of some efforts can't be measured with numbers or a ruler or a spread-sheet, and, if this is the case, you need to be aware of this before you initiate them.

Let's now take a look at how we might analyse the various marketing platforms:

DIRECT CONTACT AND NETWORKING

~ A spread-sheet of every direct-contact meeting that you have had, listing:

  ~ If, and how much, revenue has come from each one.

  ~ Other benefits from those meetings, e.g., building up confidence from an interview, introductions to new people, nuggets of wisdom from the other person, market research garnered.

  ~ The number of contact points (e.g., meetings, calls, e-mails) between the initial contact and a sale – this is valuable sales cycle information.

~ If you send out a voucher in the post, you can simply calculate:

  ~ How many vouchers you received back into the shop.

  ~ The amount of extra business that you brought in versus the cost of the exercise.

PUBLIC EXPO

~ If you've invited people to sign up for a free draw with a view to collecting contact details, you can examine:

  ~ The number of leads collected.

  ~ The number of people who responded to your follow-up call to action.

  ~ The number of sales that you generated from this distinct activity, in comparison with the cost of exhibiting, labour costs, transport, etc.

~ If you invited people to buy directly after a demonstration, you could measure:

  ~ The number of people who attended the demonstrations (and how that changed over the course of the day).

~ The number of people who followed through on your call to action (e.g., who bought directly at the stand, who signed up for a follow-up contact, etc.).

~ The revenue made during the entire day and as a result of follow-up, less your costs.

JOINT-VENTURE

Depending on the nature of the joint-venture relationship, you could scrutinize the following:

~ The number of enquiries, leads, sales, etc., that arose from marketing your product to your partner's customers.

~ The amount of revenue that can be attributed directly to the partner's contribution to your business.

It's also important for all parties to consider the impact that they themselves are making on the other. If one person is getting all of the benefit, the agreement needs to be revisited before there are any financial implications or a feeling of bitter one-sidedness creeps into the working relationship.

ADVERTISING AND ORGANIC ONLINE MARKETING

If your call to action is clear, the measurement of the effectiveness of the advert should be quite straightforward, as you can measure how many people actually acted.

~ You can measure:
  ~ The number of people that registered for their free-trial pack on your site.
  ~ The number of people that texted or called the number that you gave out.
  ~ The number of tweets with a certain hashtag.
  ~ The number of hits on a certain webpage.

~ If this is your first point of contact, you will generally follow up with another form of communication (e.g., invitation to an event, direct contact with an e-mail, etc.), so you'll need to measure this form of marketing activity as well.

~ If you want to test different adverts, it's very useful to use two separate 'landing places' to compare results. For example, if I ran two different Google Adwords adverts, I would have two separate landing pages. This would allow me to quantify how many people clicked on one ad versus the other. If there is a vast difference between the two, I could then focus on using the more successful ad, rather than under-utilizing my money on another. (Remember the carton of milk that cost €1 versus €7.50.)

SPONSORSHIP AND PR

Many companies undertake sponsorship and PR activities with the less measurable 'brand building' and 'customer awareness' focus. It is of course possible to measure the number of times that the company is mentioned in traditional media, or the number of people who get a gift pack on their way into an event, but it's very difficult to translate this into directly attributable sales.

For example, I have been on several radio panels to discuss economic affairs, entrepreneurship, financial markets, personal finance, *The Savvy Woman's Guide to Financial Freedom*, etc. However, the interviewer doesn't want me to sit there and blatantly advertise what the company does just so that I can generate sales. They want me to add value through the discussion, point out resources for their listeners, give them actionable information, provide a view on a news story that is currently breaking, etc. While I might have built familiarity with my name or that of the company, I can't link it to a particular portion of our bank balance afterwards, as I could with some of the other portals that I've mentioned.

That absolutely doesn't take away from the efforts that you might make in the area of PR and sponsorship, but it is important to consider this qualitative point when it comes to a decision between 'Do we spend €x on sponsorship' or 'Do I commit to being a columnist in a magazine?'

EVENT-DRIVEN NETWORKING

If you invite people on a mailing list to sign up for a webinar/event, you should note:

- The number of people who open your e-mail.
- The number of people who sign up for the webinar/event.
- The number of people who attend the webinar/event.
- The attention level of people on the webinar.
- The number of people who follow through with the purchase (or other call to action) at the webinar/event.
- The number of people who follow through with the purchase (or other call to action) during your follow-ups after the webinar/event.

WORD-OF-MOUTH

This is the softest, yet one of the most powerful, forms of marketing available. But, although you can prompt people to recommend you if they're happy with your offering, you can't push it too vigorously. I might speak at an event and say afterwards to the organizer: 'If you know of any other event organizers looking for a speaker to examine the current state of the bond market, I would be delighted if you could pass my details on.' She nods and genuinely intends to spread the word to her colleagues. I call her up a week later and ask, 'So have you heard of anybody who might need me?' and I do the same a month later and then again and again. By doing this, I have just made sure that she will never recommend me.

However, it is totally acceptable to say to people who contact you: 'I'm delighted that you called and I look forward to working with you. Do you mind if I ask where you heard about me?' If people respond with 'From a family member/friend/a neighbour/

specific name', you can gauge exactly how much of your business is coming from word-of-mouth marketing.

6. Review

The final step of this process is to take stock of what's working and what's not. In summary, after you

- identify your market
- choose a marketing medium
- articulate your message with the pain or pleasure point to the fore
- give a clear call to action
- follow up effectively and promptly
- measure the impact of the entire process

you need to take stock. What have you learned? Has it been a success, based on what you expected or set out to achieve? What would you do differently? What happened unexpectedly? Have you learned something new about your market? What's important to them, what influences their thinking, how do they like to consume information, what prompts them into action, what holds them back – or is there a whole new dimension to the way you perceive them?

With this in mind, now let's see how we create the bridge from marketing into sales.

Managing difficult conversations

16. *A script for every occasion*

That awkward moment when you meet somebody on a first date; when you walk into a room full of strangers and everybody can see your eyes darting around nervously as you try to find somebody you know; or that first day at a new job, when you don't know if you're using somebody else's mug or sitting in the boss's chair in the canteen – you know the feeling.

There are many occasions in life when everything would be fine, if only we could get past the initial embarrassment. Wouldn't it be great if you could just fast-forward to the point when you can participate in the banter over the photocopier or when you know a couple of people at the school where you drop off your kids, or your shoulders can relax a little as you click with somebody at that party when you're on your own?

Much of what I have talked about so far will require some bravery on your part or pushing out your comfort zone. I certainly have had to do so many times myself. However, it's much easier when you have something to fall back on, and you know exactly how to take those first steps.

First of all, be clear about what you want from the situation, what you're trying to achieve, and why. You won't always be able to predict a specific outcome, but you certainly can enter a situation with a certain goal in mind. As in previous chapters, beginning with the end in mind is the rule here too.

But there's another snag: we often make the mistake of thinking that, once the hard part is over, our job is done. If I walk into a networking event, build rapport with several people, have some great conversations and enjoy the event, that's only the first part of the job. The real value of the time I have invested will have to be mined afterwards, when I follow up promptly and comprehensively. Only then will I enjoy maximum benefit. So many opportunities are lost to the misconception that the achievement lies in overcoming the difficult steps at the beginning.

There will be rejection along the way, and it can hurt. You need to arm yourself against this. It's not you they're rejecting: if you can change your frame of mind, you'll actually get excited about understanding what underpins refusals. I used to get knocked back far too far and far too often when customers didn't choose to avail of the 'once-in-a-lifetime opportunities' that I thought I was giving them. I needed to build a thicker skin – and to start using a spread-sheet (they just have *so* many uses! More on this later).

In this chapter you will learn to decipher the difference between a dead end in a conversation and a simple detour sign. If you know the outcome that you're looking to reach, you need to be prepared to find those 'several ways to skin a cat'; because the route to a better bank balance may not be what you think it is, at all. There will come a time when you're speaking to somebody who is not in your target market, who does not appreciate your offering, and who won't be willing to pay for your product or service. The earlier that you spot this to be the case, the quicker you can move on to make an impact on the life of the person who is waiting for your solution to their problem.

Be aware that not everybody will be a good fit; not everybody is your target market. By cutting short an interaction that wouldn't yield good results anyway, you're being respectful not only of other people's time, but also of your own ambition and of your own clients, whose needs you will be in a position to meet all the more quickly.

I wrote this chapter so that you can dip into it whenever you need to prepare for certain situations. You may find that you don't need to rely on the scripts every time, or that they've served their purpose after a while, or that you have a different approach. That's perfectly fine. I have compiled a toolbox of the most useful lines that I've used, and I've used them countless times to great effect. I hope that they get you past that first awkward stage, so that you can cruise to the place where your new environment becomes part of your comfort zone.

Script 1: Networking

In Step Six, I wrote a lot about networking, the power of it as a marketing strategy and the many ways that you can derive benefit from it. However, I also understand (and know from first-hand experience) how nerve-racking it is to walk into a room full of people you don't know and try to navigate the crowd.

Let's say that you've signed up to go to an event. First, you need to have a plan for what you're looking to get out of the time that you spend there. Refer to Step Six for a list of all the things you might be looking to achieve: for example, you're looking to build your network with a view to meeting new people, contacts, leads and customers. Alternatively, maybe you work in a large company and they've organized a lunchtime seminar. You want to meet with the senior people in the organization, so that you can become a familiar face to them, thereby boosting your chance of getting a promotion.

Networking is certainly not about collecting or distributing as many business cards as possible; nor is it about knowing everybody in the room. What actually matters is . . . what actually matters: the goals that you've thought about in advance.

Consider that I have an ambition to get to know business people in London, and I go to an event hoping to meet new prospects in my target market. I could dart around from person to person every three minutes with a 'Hi, I'm Susan. We work with organizations who want to connect with an audience, to facilitate, design and deliver webinars with a view to boosting sales, retention and engagement. Here is my card. What do you do? [*They start to speak and then I cut them off mid-sentence as I'm hitting two and a half minutes.*] Oh, that's great. It was lovely to meet you. I'll send you a LinkedIn invitation afterwards and maybe we could see if there's a way we could work together. Enjoy your evening.' I then breathlessly move on to deliver the same spiel to somebody else.

It's highly likely that the other party to this conversation would remember me solely for all the wrong reasons, and would be completely turned off by the idea of working with me – clearly, they weren't 'worthy' of my full attention even for a few minutes, so why would they want to work with me? I've seen this happen several times at networking events. People ask you what you do, are turned towards you, but their eyes are scanning the room to see where they're next going to pounce. They go home with a box of business cards, totally exhausted, and having left a less than positive impression. Networking is all about developing rapport: if you talk only to five people at a two-hour event, you can develop a good rapport with all of them; and if you can actually establish how you might be of help to each other, this is a very good result.

If you've decided to take an evening or morning or lunch to spend at an event, you probably have an interest in its theme: maybe you've worked in that sector, want to listen to an interesting speaker or have a desire to upskill yourself in a certain area. You may be feeling shy, but everybody is there because they share your interest; they are most probably like-minded people and have come to speak to others. It can feel like you're barging in on somebody's party, particularly when it appears that everybody knows everybody else. They don't. It can take bravery, but when I'm at an event on my own and don't know anybody at all, I stand in an obvious spot on my own, looking lost. It doesn't usually take more than thirty seconds for somebody to 'come to my rescue'.

But if I were to take out my phone and start looking at my messages, which is such an easy crutch, it would be much harder for somebody to approach me. If I do too good a job of fading into the crowd, I might as well have stayed at home. It's like getting your ears pierced: the pain lasts for a second and then you can enjoy the results pain-free afterwards. If you see somebody on their own, walk over and say hello. Alternatively, hang out where the food or tea and coffee are served. It's a natural attraction point in the room. It's an easy spot to start a conversation and a place that people will generally drift towards. Make eye contact and smile.

If this doesn't work, take a deep breath and gracefully interrupt. Now all that you need to do is to invite the other person to talk about themselves and to establish some common ground to get you started:

ME:	'Hi. Can I join you? I'm Susan.'
OTHER PERSON:	'Hello. I'm [*insert name*].'
ME:	'Hello [*insert name*]. I'm looking forward to hearing the speaker today. The topic sounds very interesting. What do you do?'
OTHER PERSON:	'I . . . [*insert elevator pitch*].'
ME:	'Oh, I see, who would your target market be?'
OTHER PERSON:	'Our customers would be in the [*insert description of*] space . . .'

At this stage, the conversation may develop naturally; if you feel that you like this person/think their offering is worthwhile/would be willing to follow through, after the initial rapport has been established, you could ask:

ME:	'What could I do for you?'
OTHER PERSON:	'Well, if you know anybody that could benefit from our services, I would be very appreciative if you could pass on our details.'

I have often been asked, 'Why would you possibly offer to do anything for anybody, particularly somebody that you've just met, without even telling them about your own business or employment ambitions first?' The reason is that, first, it's absolutely wonderful to see anybody succeed, develop and grow. If I can help them do that in some small way, I get the gift of giving.

Also, there have been many serendipitous events in my life that have happened seemingly without reason. I think that good karma finds its way right back to you.

On a more scientific level, every single person at a networking event is there to promote themselves and to find great opportunities. If I offer to help somebody on their road to success, it's absolutely no secret that I'm on my own journey too. In many cases, people will then turn the question back to me. If they don't, well, then, they don't. I've met people who, at the time, couldn't have done anything for me. Likewise, I've often just benefited from a contact and not been in a position to give anything at that time. However, wouldn't it be awful if somebody held back an introduction to a hugely important lead or didn't tell me about a key event that I should go to, just because I couldn't give them something of equal value at the time? Just go for it: give to the world and it will give back. I have the spread-sheet to back that up.

It's important that you're able to answer both 'What do you do?' and 'What can I do to help you?' clearly and concisely yourself. If you've been following the book so far, you'll know the answer to the former is the 'elevator pitch' and the answer to the latter is the 'call to action'. Please be warned that people are polite. If you see their eyes glazing over or if they nod blankly at the description of what you do, they're effectively saying, 'I'm sorry; I have no clue what you're talking about.' Chalk it down as market research and as a sign that it's time to rework your elevator pitch.

There are some people who don't stop talking about themselves and with whom you won't get a word in edgeways. After you've given them sufficient time to answer the above two questions, don't let thoughts of 'Why aren't they asking me about what I do?' hold you back. It's up to you to take control and to segue from them to you. I have given some examples below depending on the situation that you're in. For example, if you run your own business, follow the [Business] prompts; and if you work as an employee in a large company and are meeting some colleagues that you don't know, arm yourself with the [*Company*] lines. The [*Mixed*] apply, if employees are mixing with owner-managers:

> [*Business*] 'Clearly we're not competitors because we actually target . . .'
>
> [*Business*] 'It sounds like we have a similar target market, but we service them in a different way . . .'
>
> [*Company*] 'In the piece that you wrote for the internal newsletter this week, you mentioned *x*. I'm actually working on a project at the moment where . . .'
>
> [*Company*] 'It's great to get an insight into your department. At this time of the year, we are focusing on *y* on our floor.'
>
> [*Mixed*] 'I'm always interested to hear from business people in the industry, as being part of a company puts you in a slightly different domain.'

If you want to leave the conversation, again, people expect that meetings are transient and everybody wants to make the most of the event, so it's not rude, it's expected. Therefore, you can finish with 'Well, it was very interesting to speak to you. Thank you for your card and enjoy the event.'

Repeat all of the above until you're happy with the 'return on your time'. Please remember that the actual benefit of any networking event is in the follow-up. As I've pointed out, schedule the time in your diary to continue to enter contact details into your database (e.g., into a spread-sheet, CRM system, file the business cards or invite them to connect on LinkedIn), to reflect back on the event and to let your mind process the learning that you took out of it. Then send a brief, personal message to the people with whom you established a connection.

Script 2: Asking for a raise

Asking for a raise requires sensitivity, good timing and preparation, but it can be very rewarding.

First, realize when it's not a good idea to ask for one. One, if you're just 'in the door' and still costing more (in training and time) than your productivity is bringing to the company. Two, if you are doing exactly what you're paid for, your work reflects the agreement that you made with your employer and your salary reflects the industry average. And three, if you're already getting a good deal and/or if your company has made everybody painfully aware that they are really struggling to hold on to staff at the moment and can only do so with rationalized salary agreements.

Conversely, you have solid arguments to present to your employer if:

∼ You've been doing work above and beyond your job description. Gather evidence to support this, so that you can articulate specifically how you add extra value to the organization, e.g.,
  ∼ I generated €x in sales last year.
  ∼ I'm [*fully/partially*] responsible for the retention of y customers.
  ∼ I took ownership of the a, b and c tasks when my colleague left and I've continued to be responsible for them.
∼ You've done your research and can demonstrate that peers in your industry that are doing your job are earning x more than your salary at the moment. (This falls right under market research as discussed in Step Three – talk to recruitment agencies, read industry reports, look at similar job adverts online to see what packages they're offering.)

It's not a good idea to catch your employer off guard at the watercooler and say, 'You know what I was thinking as I watched TV last night; you should be paying me more. What do you think?' Also, I wouldn't just bounce into your boss's office: set up an actual meeting and make it clear that the meeting is about discussing the conditions of your job. There really is a time and place for this. The entire path to the sale that I have been outlining in the book applies almost word for word in this scenario. I would suggest writing an e-mail similar to the following:

Hello [*first name*],

I have now been working with the company for [*x*] years, and I'd be grateful if I could pop into your office at some stage next week to discuss how that period has worked out for both of us, as well as to look at how we might move forward to the future.

   I know that you're busy, so I'm happy to slot into your schedule. What day and time might suit?

   Thanks and regards

[*insert name*]

Before you actually have that meeting, it's important to practise and to think about the ways that the conversation could go. Try it out with the mirror, with your webcam and/or with an honest friend who won't just tell you: 'I would so give you the money. You'll do great.' Ask somebody who will tell you straight that 'Your body language is screaming at me that you don't think you deserve this and are only chancing your arm.'

In addition, go back through your e-mails and look for testimonials or compliments from others. Like a business person developing a sales brochure, you're looking to put your best foot forward to present your skill-set in the most flattering light. For example, let's say that you're responsible for retaining a client and they send you a message that reads, 'Thank you so much for your help. I have to say that your customer service is exemplary and we'll definitely be staying with your company as long as you're managing our account. We really appreciate it.' This type of feedback completely substantiates your argument, and if your employer hasn't seen it before, this particular meeting is a timely opportunity. Don't forget the importance of influencers. Here, the happy client is taking on a key role in your proposal. Invest the time in building as strong a 'business case' as you can for this meeting.

Once I shared the stage with a fabulous woman; she spoke very candidly of her ascension through the ranks of a massive organization in the US. She started off in a junior position and levered herself up to middle management by working hard, thinking smart and upskilling herself. She received an e-mail from a colleague one day to say that a senior position had opened up and she thought, 'Yes. This is my chance. I'm perfect for that job. I'm going to apply and then I'm going to ace that interview.'

She armed herself with all of her achievements, experience and details of her skill-set, and, as she had planned, absolutely blew them all away at the interview. She excitedly opened the e-mail from management that had 'Senior Manager Role' in the subject line – and was devastated to find that she hadn't been chosen. Feeling both indignant and disappointed, she marched down to her manager to ask him, 'What happened here? I thought you were all agreed that I was really suited to the job?'

He told her to sit down and passed on a piece of wisdom to her that she never forgot. 'You've been a hard worker since the day that you walked in the door, but you need something else when you get to senior level. You need to be known. I absolutely sang your praises to the executive team, but they didn't know who you were. They need somebody with charisma and pizzazz. You have plenty of it, but you're crouching behind that computer every day and you're not out there. The rules change as you move up the ladder. It's time to leave night school behind and start networking within the organization.'

She took his advice to heart and joined two of the networks in the company. She started to approach senior people in the corporation to meet for coffee and to discuss how she could do her job in a way that could be of more help to them. She also started to mentor junior people who showed the same ambition, just to give back. It will come as no surprise that she was sporting the title 'Managing

Director' when she spoke that day at the conference. All that she did differently was to identify who her influencers were and to start talking to them, finding out what was important to them and articulating the ways in which she could solve their problems. Her story was a blueprint on how to get a promotion.

There is a distinct possibility that you will be turned down, and it's important to have a Plan B. I was in a situation once when I felt that I was earning less than the entire value of my services. I posed the question in an e-mail to the decision-maker and I have to admit that I was shaking with nerves before I went in to sit down with him. The conversation did start off awkwardly, but I then went on to point out all of the additional benefits that I brought the company, as I outlined above.

He then said, 'Susan, you do know that we've had to cut right back due to the recession, so I'm sorry, but I really don't think that I can do this.' At this stage, I moved to the next option and said, 'I understand. Is there anything we can do about all the extra work that I'm putting into maintaining Client X? They regularly require above and beyond the call of duty, and I'm spending a lot of time working on training materials for them. It really isn't proportional to what I'm being paid, in that specific context.' He thought about that and said, 'In that case, we do need to charge the client for the extra Research & Development.'

We agreed that I could earn this money on a contract basis, and that whenever I was doing extra work on this or any other project, I would flag it up for my employer and it would be taken into account, so that everybody knew from the outset what the expectations were. While I didn't get a blanket increase in my salary, I did negotiate a way to earn extra money in my workplace at the time.

On another occasion, I didn't even attempt to approach my employer for a raise in my salary, as the revenues of the company were falling as fast as the economy itself. Instead, I asked him to sit down with me and I simply put a question to him: 'I want to build up my income in this company. Is there a way that you can help me to do that which would also help you?' We worked out a commission structure in which I would receive 20% of the revenue from the extra products and services that I sold, while the company itself would obviously benefit from the other 80%. Everybody was happy, and I did end up with a bigger pay packet as a result.

If you get a less than enthusiastic reply to your suggestion of receiving more money, have a think about other ways to improve your conditions at your workplace. In the right context, and only if any of the below would actually add value to your working environment and the way in which you do your job, you might ask for:

- Time off in lieu of extra work done.
- Money on a contract basis for extra tasks (as I negotiated above).
- Some education and training.
- Extra benefits – health insurance, gym memberships, mobile devices, etc.
- Opting in to the company pension scheme when the company contributes a certain amount on your behalf (you may not notice an increase in your salary today, but you certainly should when your retirement comes).
- Building your experience in a focused way to increase your earning power in the next role.

I know an astute woman who asked her employer to send her on an 'Accounting Technician' course, as it would enable her to do her bookkeeping job more productively, decrease the amount that the company would need to pay the accountant and allow her to streamline more processes if she learned exactly how all aspects of the accounts fit together. Her manager was only delighted to pay for the course and for her staff member to spend her own out-of-hours time on building her worth to the company. On completion, this particular woman approached a self-employed business person in her local town and started doing some freelance work for them, as she now had the qualifications and experience to offer that service.

I know another woman who loved using the products of a certain company herself and was forever recommending them to others. She signed up as an affiliate and then asked everybody who worked with her to put the order through her if they were going to buy anything from that particular company (of which I was one!). She made 10% commission and increased her monthly income from her workplace without even looking for a raise.

Script 3: Asking for help

There are two forms of help available to you. First, there are government agencies and various companies whose sole *raison d'être* is to help you with money, information, contacts and other resources. I alluded to those in Step Five. I have met with the management, marketing and communications staff of many of these agencies. They spend so much time, effort and money trying to promote their services that they will be delighted to see you coming through the door or calling them for help.

Many of these organizations rely on government departments for funding. If they report back and note that they 'only' helped 3,000 people, for example, their finance may be cut, because the output of the initiative wasn't high enough. You can preserve the jobs of those working in these agencies by asking for help. Also, these bodies have been funded with taxpayers' money. You can choose either to make use of them or to deny yourself the benefit and let others take advantage of your taxes.

Another form of assistance is when you ask others for their time, for information, for contacts, for expertise and for direction. But perhaps the most important thing you can do is to ask them to listen to you. I met with a woman the other day who has been across the entire spectrum in terms of making money: she had a very successful business, was hit hard by the downturn, considered going into employment, raised money by selling equity, developed a product and is now back on the crest of a wave. She has been through it all and was telling me about a mentoring group in which she participates. She said, 'You know, I've been through my fair share of problems and have spent lots of time on a knife-edge in business. But you know what, Susan, there are *no new problems*. All that's different are the people who experience them. So I want to pick up other people's experience and share the lessons in mine so that we can get speedy results all round.'

There will sometimes be people who won't be able or willing to help you. Don't take this personally. They may be under a lot of pressure at that moment. They may worry that you will take their ideas and run with them. They may have given a lot of their time already and you just happened to skate in a little too late. However, there are also lots and LOTS of people who will be only too delighted to help you. I have got so much benefit over the years from so many people and so many organizations. I have rarely been turned down and am just so appreciative of the thousands of people who took me a tiny, small, big or huge step further. Some of them didn't even realize the impact that they had, but without them I wouldn't be as far along as I am now.

So how do you go about this? It's always nice to hear a compliment, but I suggest that you be sincere and meaningful in your approach. For example, 'I would love to buy you a coffee because I think that you're absolutely amazing and I would love to just be in your presence for a while' is simply over the top for someone you don't actually know. Instead, I would send something more businesslike, such as the following: 'I would love to buy you lunch or a coffee, as I admire the way that [*insert specific reason, e.g., "you navigated from a senior position in a corporation to building a very successful company"*]. I find myself in the same position and would love to get some ideas about how I might forge my own way.'

In addition, I would encourage you to find a way to help them also. You may initially think that they are ten steps further on their journey than you are, but you too may have words of wisdom that you can share. Jettison that negative thinking and focus on what you can do.

Once, when I was only starting out in college, I e-mailed Professor Aidan Daly to ask if he would introduce me to the renowned Irish entrepreneur and business author Feargal Quinn. At the time, I was an undergraduate, so I didn't have any contacts or experience in the market place or opportunities that I could offer. However, I did say that if I ever wrote a book of my own, I would mention them and the help and insights that they gave me. These very words are my promise coming to pass.

On another occasion, I was having coffee with an entrepreneur who had multiples of the turnover, staff and profit that I had. She was talking millions while I was doing my best to scramble into the thousands mark, and I was racking my brain to come up with something that I could offer her in return. However, during the conversation, she brought up a problem that she was having: her daughter was worrying and worrying about her exams in school, to the point that she was unable to study at all. I gave her a couple of ideas that I had picked up from going through the experience myself, as well as handling the same issue when I was giving grinds in my college days. She thanked me that day, and I felt that she meant it, from the bottom of her heart. Remember that just because somebody is ahead of you in business, doesn't mean you can't help them. Our lives don't travel a linear path, and our nature as human beings means we may have more to offer than we think. As long as you have the intention of giving back, you will find a way.

Finally, if you ask for thirty minutes of somebody's time, don't ask for anything else unless the conversation allows for it. Read the natural flow of the discussion, so that you don't cross the line into trying to take advantage. For example, compare how these two meetings are wrapping up:

Scenario 1

ME: 'Well, thank you so much for your time today, I got a lot out of it.'

OTHER PERSON: 'Sure, no problem. Best of luck now.'

Scenario 2

ME: 'Well, thank you so much for your time today, I got a lot out of it.'

OTHER PERSON: 'I was delighted to, Susan. Would you like me to introduce you to *x*?'

ME: 'I would be very appreciative if you could.'

OTHER PERSON: 'I will do that. Also, I must send you on details of the event and organization that we spoke about. I think they could be very helpful to you. Will you let me know how you're getting on? I would love to hear about your progress.'

In the first case, the person has given me their time and that really is the end of the conversation. If I was now to start asking them for other things after they have brought an end to the meeting, I'd be overstaying my welcome. I asked them for something, they delivered, I benefited, and that's absolutely fine. In the second case, the other person truly wants to give me more help. I would gladly receive it and send them an e-mail every now and then to show them how I am applying their advice and getting great results. Now that truly is allowing the other person to enjoy the gift of giving.

Script 4: Opening a lead

Opening a lead is the process of taking somebody who doesn't know that you and/or your offering exist, to a point where they may consider working with you or using your solution. There are some cases when this is a straightforward meeting where money is exchanged quickly and without quibble. For example, I want to put milk on porridge for breakfast tomorrow, but I don't have any in my fridge. I go to the closest convenience store that I see and just buy some.

However, on many occasions, it's not quite so easy, and there are a number of steps to building trust before a sale can actually take place. It's important to think this entire process through, be clear on what outcome you're looking for, and encourage your potential leads and customers to just do one thing at a time. Remember that the more painful the problem, the more needed you will be: I can never emphasize enough the importance of market research if you truly want to understand your customer. If your offering truly solves a problem, and solves the exact problem that your target market is experiencing, it will be that much easier to open a lead.

For example, I might work in a hotel where my role is to market our holiday offering to families. We offer a full suite of fun-filled entertainment in a country setting for children, including a 'Kids' Club', crazy-golf course, babysitters on site, bikes to hire, discounts on local activities as well as a fantastic gourmet experience and live evening entertainment for mums and dads, so that the whole family feels renewed and refreshed after their visit to our oasis. The path to a sale might include:

- Take a stand at the 'Family Show' exhibition and invite people to fill out a short form so that they can be entered into a free draw, while simultaneously getting their permission to send them some special offers and useful information.
  Goal: Collect as many names, e-mail addresses and phone numbers as possible.
- Enter all of their contact details into a database and compile a carefully worded, visually exciting e-mail for each of the groups with a clear call to action at the end, which is to book now to secure a 20% discount before the end of the week.
  Goal: Generate as many sales as possible from the direct contact.

~ Send out a reminder text to every person in the database (who hasn't booked already) reminding them that there are just two days left to claim their 20% discount.
Goal: Generate as many sales as possible from the second means of direct contact.

~ Set up a system to send the remaining people regular e-mails and texts about deals, discounts and new packages available in the hotel at different times throughout the year.
Goal: Remind the people on the database of the hotel's offering, to turn the familiarity established at the initial exhibition and subsequent contacts into sales in the future.

There are two ways in which a lead can be opened. Either the customer makes an effort to come and find you when you let them know of your existence, or else you forge your own path to them. In the above example, the hotel would have decided to spend the money on having a stand at the exhibition only if they felt that their target market would be there. As people walk through the doors of the exhibition hall, they are in effect putting a silent, invisible sign over their head which says, 'I'm a captive audience for what you're selling. There is a lot of competition here and I'm looking for an entertaining day out, so you better make it count.'

The people visiting the show come with the expectation of finding companies marketing their products and services. In fact, they will walk right by them, cast an eye over their stands and maybe even approach and ask what's on offer. The chance of this happening increases phenomenally if you put a bowl of sweets in view. Beware that many 'interested' leads may be half talking to you, half choosing which wrapper looks like it could have their favourite flavour. I've often been the person at the other end of that conversation, competing for their attention against a soft caramel.

Hence, if I were to approach them with a smile and ask, 'Would you like to fill out a short form to be in with the chance of winning a family weekend in our award-winning hotel?', it's quite likely that they would be receptive to my invitation. This is all that I would need to do to 'open the lead'. As they're writing down their name, e-mail address and phone number, I have about thirty seconds to ask them if they're interested in having a holiday at home this year. I would then let the conversation develop naturally from there. If I thought there was high potential for a sale, I would call them personally the week afterwards to build on the initial momentum. If there was potential, but not immediately, I would follow through with the process that I described above.

The contents of my e-mail would include:

- My connection with the customer.
- The benefit of my offering.
- A sense of urgency and exclusivity.
- A call to action and contact details so that they can rapidly e-mail me and then I can deal with objections or queries quickly and easily.

For example:

Good morning [*first name*],

It was great to meet you at the recent [*insert name of show*].

We are currently offering an exclusive deal of [*insert offer*] to families who want some rest, relaxation and fun, and to make some unforgettable memories before school starts again in September.

Almost all our rooms have been snapped up, so we're offering this rate only until Sunday [*insert date*] at midnight.

Call us today at [*insert number*] and quote SHOW to claim this super deal.

If you have any questions or comments, please reply to this e-mail and I'll be delighted to help.

Regards

However, it's a completely different kettle of fish when you're marketing to people who have never heard of you and quite possibly don't even think that they need you. Imagine if I were to set up that very same stand in the middle of Union Square in San Francisco. I would stop every single person (whether they have young children, are homeless, are busy professionals rushing to a meeting while talking on their phones, tourists taking a leisurely walk, everybody) and ask them, 'Would you like to fill out a short form to be in with the chance of winning a family weekend in our award-winning hotel in Ireland?' What an inefficient waste of time. You might be thinking that I would be crazy to suggest such a thing, but this typifies a lack of market research and ineffective marketing. And it happens all the time.

It's very important for your offer to be as tailored as you can make it when approaching people who haven't tried, or even thought, to seek you out. For example, in my family hotel marketing role, I would be much better off contacting summer camps around the country with a view to putting a €50 voucher into each of the kids' goody packs for their parents to spend on an overnight package with dinner. I could approach high-traffic parenting blogs and offer to pay them either to put an advert on their site or to send out an e-mail to their database asking the recipients, 'Do you want a holiday where your kids are entertained, in a safe environment, surrounded by nature, while you indulge in some well-deserved luxurious relaxation?' (Can you spot the pleasure and pain points?) The call to action at the bottom of the message would be to click on a specific link to secure a special deal (while also allowing me to track the success of the campaign by measuring the number of clicks).

I could organize an event in the hotel, showcasing all of the activities, complete with nibbles and drinks as well as some novelty entertainment. I could invite local media to come to the launch of our 'School's Out for the Summer' afternoon and to bring along their children, suggest that they interview the managers about how they're offering parents an innovative way of creating action-packed holidays for kids, who are sure to enjoy every minute of our family haven, while their parents rejuvenate content in the knowledge that their kids are learning, exercising and socializing with other children of their own age. I could give flyers to the schools and invite local parents to bring their children; I could ask them to recommend the hotel to their friends with children who might be coming to visit them for an occasion or a holiday. I could open hundreds of leads with this set of activities, because I'm taking the time to think about where to find my customers, what they need, and how to tell them that the hotel recognizes that they need it.

In addition, let's say I go to a networking event at my local Chamber of Commerce and somebody mentions to me that her sister is thinking of starting a dance class for children and was just asking her the other day if she knew of any venues. My mind starts to whirr. If I could encourage the instructor to hold her lessons in one of my rooms during the week, I would benefit from the footfall of the parents coming through the doors. Apart from the opportunity to let these new people gain familiarity with the hotel, there are three potential revenue streams that such a deal might create: the parents might get some coffee or food in the bar or restaurant; the room is generating revenue for me via hiring fees; and the Kids' Club is benefiting if the mums and dads want to have a younger child minded during the class. The dance instructor could be both a buyer in her own right and an influencer within my target market; and it would be worthwhile making just a small profit on her room fees, if this activity could act as a marketing tool. I ask the woman for her sister's number, as I may have a cost-effective solution to her problem.

I would approach the call like this:

Hi, my name is Susan and I'm calling from [*insert name of hotel*]. I got your contact details from your sister [*insert name*]. Am I catching you at a good time?'
  [*If no: ask them when would be convenient and then phone back.*]
  [*If yes: this means you have permission to go ahead.*]

•

[*Now tell them why you are calling.*]

I met her this morning at a Chamber of Commerce meeting and she mentioned that you might be setting up a dance class for children. I was just wondering if you had found a venue yet?

[*Ascertain if there is a need before you try to serve it.*]

We actually specialize in catering for families, so we would have all the facilities that you would need: great location, easy parking and a Kids' Club. We would love to have your business and would be willing to offer a very cost-effective deal. What do you think?

[*Give the potential customers a chance to tell you what they're thinking. If they have any objections, they're likely to come out at this point. If there is any other need that they have that you can service, give them the platform to voice it now.*]

So how would you like to move forward?

[*After giving the customers some time to consider whether your product is a good fit for their need, ask them to give you a clear indication of what they're thinking.*]

Thank you very much for your time today, and I'll get those details right across to you.

Now imagine if I did all of this and then didn't bother to follow up in any way. I take a day off, as I'm due a break after the show, which has been a major success. I come back to find thirty voice-mails and fifty e-mails from people looking to make bookings, seeking more information and a magazine looking for a photo. However, I'm far too busy planning my next set of marketing activities to get back to any of them. Look at all the effort that would be wasted.

This is why I bring it back to the KPIs that matter. My database might be exploding with 'good-quality leads', but I haven't actually made a cent, never mind profit. These marketing activities haven't paid off until the customers actually start paying to stay and using the hotel's facilities. The main thing that you need to do to open a lead is establish a connection, irrespective of how weak it is, but you absolutely need to follow through on it.

I got a call one day that went like this:

ME: 'Hello?'

MAN: 'Hello. Could I speak to Susan Hayes, please?'

ME: 'Yes, Susan speaking. How can I help you?'

MAN: 'Susan, it's great to speak with you. I noticed the piece about your business in the paper this week. Congratulations on that.'

ME: 'Oh, thank you very much. It's great to hear from somebody who read it.'

MAN: 'Well, I thought it was very interesting. I have a graphic design company myself . . .'

This was exactly the way that he opened the lead. He simply found a way to establish a connection with me, despite its being as light as reading a piece about me in the paper. At the end of the conversation, his call to action was an offer to call into my office to show me some of the work that he'd done for other companies. I said that I would be willing to look at it on e-mail and then have a call afterwards instead. He agreed to do that and thanked me for my time. The lead had been opened: I was open to seeing what he could do for me.

What happened next? He never followed up, and I went elsewhere for my graphic design. This has happened to me lots of times over the years.

Outside of our professional life, we are always seeking to connect with others. It's a natural thing to find common ground with another person. After all, when does any conversation get past the weather, the traffic and a big headline that's made the news? It's when we establish a point of interest and common ground with another person. I was at a hen party last weekend and was at a table where I didn't know anybody at all. It wouldn't have been the lively event it was, unless we all found ways to connect. The person opposite me had worked on a cruise ship, and I had been on a holiday on one. The person beside me was planning her wedding, just like I was. The person diagonally across from me had gone to the same university as I had. We had a great chat and are eagerly looking forward to the wedding of said hen.

If you're going to offer to do something or to give something to somebody in exchange for money, you need to remember that lots of other people are trying to do the same thing. You need to be prepared for rejection. Don't let your ego get in the way: people aren't attacking you personally. They're not choosing your product because they don't have the problem that you solve, or they're not having a bad enough time with it to justify handing over the money you're asking, or they have too many other demands on their cash. You personally have very little to do with it. However, to accept that point and act on it is much easier said than done.

I can't tell you the number of times that I've silently wailed 'What's wrong with me?' upon being rejected, when of course my mistake was in thinking that in the first place – especially the last word in that question. I have felt the burning pain of standing in heels for far too long as the clock mercilessly slowed to a crawl, and a string of about twenty people casually walked past our stand at an exhibition and pretended that I hadn't spoken to them, even as I repeated: 'Would you like to sign up for our free draw today?'

I have to admit to often sitting in my car after a meeting that didn't turn out quite as I would have liked, picking up the phone to call my fiancé and being unable to hold back the tears as I tell him what has just happened. Some of you might find this reassuring, because you've done it too. Some of you might think it's weak. Some might even wonder how I can get so emotionally tangled up in my career. However, it doesn't really matter what I thought or how I reacted at the time, but it does matter that I got up and got going again. In fact, that's all that matters anyway. If every single customer bought every single time, we would all be busily running around like headless chickens – and as customers we would all be broke from spending everything we earn. Remember that every time that you get a 'no', it brings you closer to the 'yes'.

Then again, when opening a lead it's important to be mindful and respectful of time. Let's go back to my example of representing my hotel at the exhibition. A person stops to fill in the form for the free draw and we get chatting. Thirty minutes later, we find out that we have a friend in common, have both been to Malta and – the icing on the cake, this – we both love spread-sheets! Now, while this would be a great conversation to have, my job was to create a sales funnel for the hotel that day; not to increase the number of friends that I have on Facebook. Fifty potential clients might have walked past the stand during that time period, and they certainly weren't going to interrupt an animated conversation so that I could sell to them.

I had a meeting in New York one time when I made that very mistake. I met with a fantastic woman who was making significant waves, not just in her business but in her industry. I eagerly listened to her synopsis about how she got to that place and where she was headed next. She proceeded to ask me about my background and, being a chatty Irish woman, I started at the very beginning. We had lots in common, and it sounded like her path had started off in a similar way to mine.

I had just reached my first year after college when she suddenly said, 'I have to go in ten minutes, so what can I do for you?' Now I was in a pickle. I had to shortcut the rest of the way through what we did, ask for her help and find a way to offer my own in about five minutes. I had had the opportunity to put forward my (and the company's) best foot, but I frittered it away in conversation. I left that meeting having made only a shadow of the impact that would have been possible had I kept my story to the highlights and found a way to segue into how we could help each other much earlier.

'Getting down to business' might happen in two ways. Ideally, the problem that you can solve will come up naturally in conversation and you can magically swoop in with 'I can actually help you with that.' Notice that the language I use is 'help you with that' – as opposed to 'I could flog my product and you could pay me.' Let's say I'm at the exhibition representing the hotel. An exhausted young mother is pushing a buggy and dragging her feet while her little boy is buzzing around the stands, laughing hyperactively from a sugar rush because he's eaten half a box of chocolates. She's been up all night with the baby, who now looks like butter wouldn't melt in his mouth and is happily catching up on the sleep lost to teething in the early hours. I walk over to her and she says, 'I could really do with a holiday. I wish that somebody would run the legs off my little fella and I had nothing to do but read him a story before bed.' I warmly reply with 'Well, you'll never guess, but that's exactly what I can make happen for you.'

It might sound too good to be true but it does happen (hear the magical words: 'Do your market research'). If, however, the conversation swerves into a totally different domain you'll have to find a way to steer it back into sales mode, which is of course the reason why you're there. Remember that when you're clearly in a marketing space, it's completely expected. For example, let's say a man is filling out his details for the free draw and he asks me if we have a golf course. As I'm giving details of the discounts that we've negotiated with the local golf club, we get talking about where my fiancé is a member, how I couldn't watch anything over the weekend because the Masters was on, how he once went to St Andrews and how he was giving his wife lessons for her birthday. Now, this conversation could continue in this vein, but it's up to me to bring it back to sales with something like:

- ◠ 'Maybe she would like a weekend of quality time with you at a fabulous hotel instead?'
- ◠ 'We have lots of parents that relish going out on the first tee while their children are busy having fun at our Kids' Club.'
- ◠ 'If you wanted something different, but yet with a physical exercise element to it, you might like to go for a family cycle through the woods. It's a great day out and you can still pick up the sunshine.'

As you can see, I'm offering him the opportunity to think about enjoying the benefits of the hotel without bringing price into the discussion. I've listened to his situation while we were chatting and tailored my suggestions to that. I've put it to him that he should now move forward with the idea or give me an objection. It will become clear within the next couple of sentences whether he's seriously interested in buying from me or not. Of course, if I hadn't brought the conversation around to sales, I would have learned a lot more about his golfing interest, without having made any impact at all on my marketing KPIs that day. You can still be a kind, caring, interested person while moving towards your sales goals.

Finally, if you find that somebody wants to buy from you without going through the process that I've outlined above, just go with it. When a lead converts earlier than planned, don't try to address objections they don't have. If somebody came up to me at the stand and said, 'I heard about your hotel from a friend of mine. She told me that it's absolutely fabulous. Actually, now that I'm here, do you have availability for the bank holiday weekend in October?' I would pick up the phone right away to my sales team and confirm the reservation. I wouldn't say, 'Why don't you fill in your details for the draw and then we'll e-mail you?' There would be absolutely no need to put them through the sales funnel when they want to be a customer straight away. If somebody wants to leapfrog your sales process, that's fantastic. You can address a need right now and it's probably a result of word-of-mouth marketing or brand awareness that has built up over time. Well done.

Script 5: How to avoid being strung along

I don't know anybody who wakes up in the morning and says, 'I want to be rejected today. I'm going to bounce out of bed and I'm going to chase rejection. I'm going to make fifty calls and I just can't wait to hear "no", "it's not for me", "please go away". I love it. Let's get stuck in.' The thing is that we've all experienced this and we know that it hurts. So we don't really want to inflict it on anybody if it can be avoided.

In a previous job, I used to make follow-up calls after a free event with a view to securing the sale on the phone. The customer had already met us, sampled our offering and had the opportunity to voice their objections, buy at the event or simply leave. There were several occasions when people didn't want to buy, but nor did they want to turn me down. They often took the easy route of saying, 'Could you send me an e-mail on that?' or 'I will take a look again and get back to you.' However, in many cases, they just wanted to get off the phone and out of an awkward situation where they didn't want to offend me by saying no.

Let's roll forward now: I write the e-mail or I put a note in my diary to call them back. This is a pure waste of time, but since the potential customer hasn't actually turned me down, I don't know if I'm leaving a sale on the table or if they're actually not interested (and they simply won't tell me). So how do I spot the difference?

A participant at a business course I was attending spoke of his massively increased productivity when he gave a clear, unequivocal 'out' to people who sounded like they were stringing him along. He told us that all he said was: 'I can certainly do that [*e.g., send the e-mail or call back again*]. I would imagine that you're probably a very kind person who doesn't want to say no to somebody who's in a sales position like I am, and I appreciate that. However, to be quite honest, if you tell me to call you back in a week, I actually will. So just to make sure that we don't waste each other's time, do you really want me to follow up or is it that you don't want to hurt my feelings? I can take it.'

In this scenario, you're asking the potential customer to come clean. You're giving them a clear opportunity to end the conversation there and then. You've also made it patently obvious with carefully chosen words that they're wasting your time if you have to put more work into this sale when they have no intention of buying. This simple question also speeds up the sales process, as people will reveal if they're actually interested or not at this point and you can then focus on serving those who give you the green light.

If you're being given the 'put it on an e-mail for me' line, you can loop the conversation back round again by using either of the following approaches:

- Have the e-mail ready to go in advance of the call and send it immediately after they ask you to. Ask them if they're at their computer or mobile device? If they say yes, take them through the contents.
- Alternatively, you could say, 'I will certainly do that. While I have you on the phone, could I just ask if [*insert next question that identifies if they're interested or not*]?'

Remember that a sales process acts like a funnel. There may be ten people who express an initial interest for every two people who actually buy. The objective of the above conversations is not to be pushy, but instead to shorten the time it takes to ascertain if the person at the other end of the exchange is one of the 'eights' or is one of the 'twos'. The faster you can find out if somebody is one of the eights, the faster you can get on to finding the twos.

It is very true that you don't always get the sale the first time round, and that you have to be persistent. But in the interests of efficiency, try progressively to change the focus to less personal, less time-intensive contact points. After, say, two calls, move to an e-mail, then to a blanket e-mail (i.e., a more generic e-mail that goes out to a larger list), then to relegating that person to your general mailing list. You still have a number of touch-points to remind people of your existence, but you're not spending your days chasing uninterested cold leads.

Script 6: Dealing with objections

Somebody has agreed to listen to your pitch. How do you get them to state their objections, and how do you deal with those? Objections are easily observed, if you'll only listen out for them. People will tell you what they don't want, what they're worried about. If you're being rejected, write down a list of why, and make sure to address those objections – what will solve those problems for your customer?

'Susan, get yourself a coffee there and let's have a chat about your sales technique.' This was the beginning of a conversation I had several years ago that I thought would end with 'And you're fired.' I was working in a job where sales were a key part of the role, and my employer had brought in a coach to talk to me about how to boost my results. Initially, I had the reaction: 'Uh, oh, I'm not good enough, and this is a pretty clear sign from my boss that I'm not performing.' Now that I'm an employer myself, I understand that it really meant: 'You're showing promise in this area, and now I'm willing to invest in you for our collective benefit.' We focused on retention that day: that is, people who had bought the product in the past and whom I was now calling to ask if they wanted to renew the service. However, the exercise could be used in any sales scenario.

The coach started off by asking me, 'So, tell me, why don't people renew?' I rolled my eyes and said, 'There are lots of reasons that people give me.' He replied, 'So give me as good as you get. Tell me every single reason that people have given you.' I expected to be going through objections for about two hours, but I found it very hard to list more than four, because every time I came up with another answer, he said, 'That's not another objection; it's simply a different way of putting one that you've already mentioned, for example, "I don't think it's worth the money", "It's too expensive", "I don't get that much use out of it."' He was correct. In each of these cases, the issue was with perceived value relative to price.

He went on to say, 'Do you really think the issue is price or is there something else that they're not saying or that they don't even know themselves?' I thought about that for a minute and said, 'In most cases, the problem is that they don't actually know what they're missing out on. They use only 10% of the product and forget that the other 90% is there, even if only 50% would really appeal to them. I wish I could just tell them that.' He then asked me the obvious question: 'So why don't you?'

I was giving up too early. As soon as I heard the initial objection, I interpreted it as a total rejection. He went on: 'Do you really believe that what you're selling to them is worthwhile?' I emphatically replied, 'Yes, of course I do. I wouldn't work with this company if I didn't. I've seen the results, and I've witnessed lots of disastrous consequences when customers are left with the problem unsolved.' In a brilliant example of reverse psychology he said, 'So there are people who could really do with this product. Why, then, are you leaving them to fend for themselves, when an extra five minutes with you could enlighten them about the benefits that they're missing?' Now I was feeling guilty. He was correct again: I was safeguarding my feelings at the expense of the customer, and that was the wrong way around – the customer should come first.

The next thing that we did was to list every category of objection:

- There isn't enough perceived value (relative to the price).
- I don't have enough time to use it.
- I use a competitor's product.
- I don't have a use for it at all.

Also, while this isn't a separate category, there is another type of customer who gives objection after objection after objection. In this case, they just don't want the product. They may need it and possibly could be convinced to buy, but they show all the signs of being a difficult client who would demand a lot of customer service and simply be looking for a way to criticize. The profit would evaporate with the time that it would take to cater to their every whim, and it simply wouldn't be worth it.

Next the coach and I discussed which of the above issues we couldn't solve, and which we should choose not to solve. If somebody didn't have a use for the product, there wasn't any point in pursuing the conversation. However, it was important to let them know that we would always be willing to serve them again if the need arose in the future, or if they knew of anybody else who might benefit from our service. Similarly, if I got the feeling that somebody was being repeatedly negative about the potentially positive impact of our product, I should politely thank them for their time and move on.

We spent the remainder of the morning writing a short script for me to fall back on in those instances when there was a possibility of winning back the customer, much to their benefit. The objective of this persistence on my part was to help me distinguish between clients who were still trying to figure out if they really didn't have a use for it and those who just didn't want to buy at all. I finished the session by articulating the following goal: by the end of each renewal sales conversation, someone with one of the first three objections should have been answered in full, so that I could have a much better chance of progressing towards a sale; and no further time should be wasted on those identified as belonging to the final, 'non-buyer' category.

The script we ended up with went like this:

CUSTOMER:	'To be honest, I don't think that it's worth the money.'
ME:	'I appreciate that feedback. Could you tell me what you would expect from an offering like this? Maybe you have an idea of what would be worth the price?'
CUSTOMER:	'Well, it would be great if it had x, y and z.'
ME:	'While we don't provide z, we actually do have x, it's in the [*specify which*] section. It actually leads you into y.'
CUSTOMER:	'Oh, I didn't realize that.'
ME:	[*After a short silence so that the customer has time to give me their feedback*] 'Does this have an impact on your decision to renew today?'

Notice that I've answered two of the three issues here, and I'm inviting the client to buy again without using overly pushy sales language. At this point, the customer may change their mind. You will notice that I didn't promise to deliver z. Don't promise a result you can't deliver. If you overpromise, that sale is going to cause you problems. If what you sell doesn't do something, don't fabricate functions just to get the sale. You will regret it later.

CUSTOMER: 'I'm not sure. It's still a lot money.'

ME: 'How about I extend your usage period of the product for another two weeks so that you can see for yourself the benefits of x and y? I'll call you at the end of that period and you can decide if it's for you?'

Here I'm giving the client some time to reconsider the product. In addition, during this time period, they will clearly decide if they're interested or not. If they do use the features that they thought weren't part of the offering, they may very well renew. If they ignore the extended access period, the objection was simply a veiled attempt to get me off the phone; and it's very likely that they would have found yet another objection to the sale. They don't want to buy, and it's not in my interest or theirs to push them into it.

Remember to take yourself out of the picture. It's not about you. The path to a long-lasting relationship with any client – your employer in a job, your clients in a casual income stream or customers representing a large account with a multinational corporation – is to look after them to the best of your ability. If you just want to 'flog stuff off', it's not going to endure. Sales is all about helping the other person identify whether you have something that can help them, making it as easy as possible to buy from you and then going the journey with them.

Script 7: Asking for the sale

Have a plan, have a plan, have a plan. If you're not tired of hearing it by now, I'm not tired of saying it again. Your plan projects you into the future – once you've achieved the current step, what's next?

What's on the other side? Ostensibly, a sale is the exchange of a product and/or a service for money. However, there can be several steps before that: in the example of the hotel, I outlined the different steps that led from a leisurely stroll at an exhibition to actually making the booking.

A 'sale' happens when you convince someone to do something that would benefit both them and you. But it is not necessarily the exchange of something for money. It could be asking somebody to:

- Give you their contact details.
- Take a phone call.
- Have a meeting with you.
- Put you on a supplier list.
- Consider a proposal.

All these activities lead up to the monetary sale, which is the end goal after all. It's important that you ask only for one 'sale' at a time, as you need to build trust and avoid overwhelming the other party. Let me set the scene for the three ways that a phone call with a target customer could go. Let's say I'm selling software with a €100 per month price tag:

ME: 'Good morning, Mark. Susan here, we met last week at the business breakfast.'

MARK: 'Oh, hello, Susan. Thank you for following up.'

ME: 'You're very welcome. I enjoyed the event last week. Did you find it beneficial?'

MARK: 'I met a couple of people that I had been meaning to catch up with for a while, so from that perspective, it was worthwhile.'

ME: 'That's good. Mark, I just wanted to pick up on our conversation, as you mentioned that you might be interested in what we offer.'

MARK: 'Sure, go ahead.'

The conversation goes on for about ten minutes: I answer all of Mark's questions confidently and capably.

MARK: 'That sounds interesting, and we've been thinking about a way to solve our problem.'

Scenario 1

ME: 'So may I have your credit card details and I'll create a twelve-month order for you?'

Scenario 2

ME: 'Well, if you have any questions in the future, you have my number.'

Scenario 3

ME: 'I'll be in your area next week – why don't I call in, while I'm there and I can give you a demonstration.'

MARK: 'Sure, that sounds good. I'll be here for most of the week. Give me a call when you know your schedule.'

ME: 'Why don't we confirm a time since we're on the phone? Let me just check my calendar here . . . would Thursday at 3 p.m. suit?'

Let's consider what happened in each of the three cases. In Scenario 1, I jumped right into asking for a sale from somebody who had just met me the week before, who didn't have any experience of our product to date, and who was asked to commit to a twelve-month contract costing €1,200 in the first ten minutes of conversation. It's not very likely that I will be successful with this scenario. In fact, it's far more likely that he'll quickly make his excuses to get off the phone and avoid me at any future networking events. This is too pushy: I've completely jumped ahead without giving him a chance to see how he might benefit.

In Scenario 2, I left the opportunity on the table and walked away. He gave me some positive cues that he was interested, but since he didn't expressly use the words 'I would like to buy from you', I didn't progress the sale to the next stage. I have to admit that I fell into this trap lots of times in the early days, because I just didn't have the confidence to steer the conversation into the next phase. However, practice helps a lot, and, again, if you really believe in what you're selling, leaving a sale on the table denies the other person the opportunity to benefit.

In Scenario 3, I've asked for a little more commitment on the part of the potential customer. I'm asking him to tell me straight if he's interested: 'Yes, Thursday at 3 p.m. is fine' or 'I'm actually out at that time – could we meet earlier in the day?' If he's not interested, he now has an opportunity to tell me: 'Why don't you let me look at your website instead and I can call you back, if we want to take it further.' If somebody makes a move to end a conversation before any concrete plans have been made, the simple question of *Do you have your diary with you and we could put a provisional time down now?* will uncover whether they're seriously interested or not. If he agrees to the meeting, I have a chance to show him exactly how the system operates, what it can do and how it could work for him; and I can draw out his objections. At the end of that second conversation, the right time to ask him for the monetary sale will have arrived.

I was home last month, and my mother asked me to take her to a homewares store to buy a fold-up bed. We went to the first shop and asked an assistant to point us in the right direction. He brought us down to the relevant section in the store and pointed to the bed. I folded it out and my mother asked, 'Would that base take the weight of a six-foot man? The bands across it seem quite fragile.' He replied, 'Ah, they would, ya. That's what they're for like, so it would be grand.' My mother gave me a silent look that said, 'I don't believe him at all', so I thanked him for his time and we quickly left the shop.

We drove to the next shop and the salesman there wheeled out a similar bed. My mother posed the very same question. He said, 'It would be absolutely fine. Lie down there on it and see for yourself.' I found myself looking at the ceiling, and we all waited to see if I would burst through the base and land on the floor with a loud thud. As soon as the bed passed the test, I stood up and Mam gave me another silent look, which the salesman correctly interpreted as 'It seems OK, what do you think?' He simply asked, 'Would you like to take this one, so?' We walked over to the till, she paid for it, and it's now comfortably behind the couch at home. Had he not put that question directly to her, we could easily have gone to another shop to check out another, and he would have left the sale on the table (or on the bed in this case).

It's important to ask explicitly for the sale. In a sales situation, people are expecting to be asked to buy. We didn't recoil in horror or feel insulted when the salesman asked my mother if she wanted to buy what she had clearly come in looking for. Nobody will be surprised if you ask 'So would you like to buy?' when you feel the time has come. There are many gentle ways to nudge a 'lead' into becoming a customer. For example:

- 'How would you like to move forward?'
- 'So you can get started by *x* time/date if you want to approve the order now.' (Meaning, you can enjoy the benefit as soon as this technicality, that is, payment, is taken care of.)
- 'If I send you in a proposal with some details of logistics, will you take a look at it and let me know your thoughts?'
- 'Would you like to put some dates in the diary?' (For example, for training, coaching, house repairs, etc.)
- 'Would you like to take a trial?'
- 'Will I put you down for *x* units?' (For example, a box of five.)
- 'So is this the one you would like to take?' (If the customer is faced with a choice.)

It's also a good idea to build in a special offer for a finite period, to focus people's attention on whether they want to buy or not, and to nudge them to make that decision there and then. There are lots of times during our lives when we genuinely intend to buy, sign up or register for something, but then we get a call or move to another webpage and it goes right out of our head. For example, if you tell your leads something like 'Special show offer of €29 – ends at 5 p.m. today', they have a sense that they're taking advantage of a bargain. Rather than putting your offer on the long finger, if they want to buy it, they're better off doing so now, as opposed to waiting until tomorrow, when the price goes back to normal. This gives you the opportunity to shut off all the distractions that are waiting for them as soon as real life tugs at their sleeve and thoughts of buying your product or service go out of their head.

Again, be aware that your offering may be rejected at this stage too. People will decline; they will fill out the form and then tell you that they didn't realize they had to pay for it; they will say, 'I'll think about it', which really translates to 'no'. However, the earlier this happens, the better. If the customer doesn't want to buy, asking explicitly for the sale brings it out into the open. You can then make sure your time isn't wasted and move on to bringing the benefits of your product or service to those who do need and want them.

That doesn't take away from the fact that this can be very demotivating. After a couple (or maybe more than a couple) of polite refusals, you can begin to question yourself. I learned how to turn this on its head by taking note of the number of 'yeses' that I get in comparison with the 'nos'. Let's say I'm manning a stand at an exhibition and two out of five people fill out the form for the free draw. If three people in a row say no to me, I know the person ready to say 'yes' is close by, and my motivation to find them actually grows after each refusal. I did this with my calls when I was marketing my mentoring services. On average, I found that two out of every ten people who had attended the training course would at least be interested in, or even book, a mentoring session.

My mother was sitting beside me one day when I was doing the calls. I had got eight 'nos' in a row, and she couldn't understand my growing excitement. She said, 'Don't take this the wrong way, but none of them want you. What are you so happy about?' Her sage daughter (who was all of twenty-one) corrected her: 'First,

Mam, it's not that they don't want me; they just don't have a burning need for my offering today. Second, it's clear that I've saved the best for last, because my two orders are currently waiting on the other side of my next two calls.' Cynically, she watched me dial in the number. Thirty seconds later I winked knowingly at her as I said to the person I had phoned, 'Of course, have you got your diary to hand and we can slot in a date and time while I have you on the phone?'

I have to say that this technique of removing me from the equation and relying on the mathematical probabilities of the situation was what kept me going when the recession dug its heels in. The numbers changed from two 'yeses' out of ten to one out of twenty. However, I knew that there was money to be made, assuming that I just kept at it every single day. It's pretty rough by the time you get to the seventeenth 'Ah, no, I don't think so, but thanks for calling anyway', and if I hadn't had my spread-sheet of data, I may well have given up and resorted to blaming the bond market, the government and every other macroeconomic trend, instead of just picking up the phone one more time.

At this point, it's important to encourage you to think about how you can improve those numbers. For example, you could:

- Focus on people who are more likely to need what you have (e.g., refine and improve your market research).
- Articulate your offering in a more pointed way (e.g., improve the manner in which you tell your market how you can solve their problem or give them much needed pleasure).
- Incentivize others to refer you to their family and friends, so that you leverage the good impression that you have made on previous customers and give them a reason to act as your sales team.

Sometimes there can be some ambiguity as to whether the offering is free or not, particularly if you use language like 'trial' and 'approve the order'. Then people might think they're getting something for free. You can remove this uncertainty with:

- 'How would you like to pay?'
- 'If you just give me your credit card details, we'll have everything sorted.'
- 'That will be €x, please.'

I once organized a course that I was delivering myself. I couldn't take money at the door as well as speak at the top of the room, so I asked somebody else to manage the registration desk for me. I told him that the entry fee was €20, gave him the list of registrants and answered any questions that he had. About half an hour before the event was due to start, a few people started to trickle in. I went over to ask if everything was OK with him. 'Everything is great. It's just that nobody is giving me €20.' I said, 'Have you been asking them for it?' He said, 'No, I thought they knew that already, so I just assumed they would give it to me on their way in.' I pointed this out to him: 'If you saw two people in front of you walk into a room for free, you could easily assume that the number after the euro sign was a misprint and that you could just slink in behind them.' Needless to say, we collected the full amount after I shared this tip with him.

Script 8: Asking for payment if it's not forthcoming

Clarity is the most important thing when it comes to matters of payment. If you agree to do something for a certain price and you deliver on it, you have every right to chase the money for executing the task. It's essential to state your price in writing (e.g., an e-mail) in advance of the customer committing to their purchase. Otherwise, ambiguity can be grounds for backing out of an agreement that you thought was clear – and this will happen after you've already done the work, which puts you at a serious disadvantage. You can prevent so many issues from arising if you use simple, clear language that leaves no room for misunderstanding. If you have any doubts about whether the client will pay, you can either ask for payment references, ask them to sign a detailed contract or request an initial deposit, if appropriate. If they put up a strong resistance, it's a red flag that you ignore at your peril.

I was asked to speak at an event one time, based on a recommendation from a colleague of the organizer. I subsequently had a meeting with them, and we got so caught up in the discussion of the content of the presentation, the location of the venue and the needs of the audience that they asked me to put the date in my diary and didn't even discuss price. I followed up afterwards with an e-mail confirming all of the details and a paragraph to outline the content, but also stating my rate for the research as well as for the delivery. As the date drew nearer, they e-mailed to confirm my availability. I delivered the seminar and followed up with the invoice. While they never actually replied to my e-mail stating the price, they did confirm the booking after I had sent it and I knew they had seen it, because they used the paragraph that I had written in their promotional material. As a result, when it came to sending the invoice, I had a paper trail to document my original quote. I didn't need it in the end, because they were forthcoming for that amount, but I had covered myself in advance.

It's important that you state on the invoice or the request for payment the timeframe in which you expect payment. For example, an employment contract should say that you'll be paid on the same day of the month. If you offer credit to the party buying your product or service, you need to state 'payment due within x days of the invoice date'. After this period has elapsed, you have every reason to go back and in effect tell the client, 'I've delivered the service / product, stated my credit terms and hence there isn't any reason why the payment should be delayed any longer.'

In several cases, people and businesses will hold on to their money until the end of that credit period for the purposes of managing cash-flow. However, if they haven't paid when the x days are up, simply forward the e-mail you sent previously with:

Dear [*insert first name*],

I just wanted to follow up on my e-mail dated [*insert date*] regarding Invoice Number *xxx*.

   [*This reminds them that the credit term has actually elapsed without the need to click on the attachment to read the date on the invoice.*]

   You might take care of payment, as we haven't received the funds into our bank account as of yet.

   Regards

This is a simple yet firm reminder that will prompt people into action who genuinely forgot to pay. I have had to send this e-mail on many occasions, and, thankfully, it sorts out the majority of outstanding payments.

If the matter persists, you need to call the office, speak to 'Accounts Payable' and say the following:

My name is [*insert name*] and I'm calling with reference to Invoice Number *xxx*. I sent it on [*insert date*] and followed up a week ago via e-mail. I haven't heard a response and was just wondering what the status of payment is, please?

If, after all of this, you still don't get what you're owed, there is a possibility that you won't be paid. Cut out the chatty tone and send a terse letter, simply listing the sequence of events:

Dear Mr/Ms [*insert last name*],

I am writing to you, as the terms of credit, as stated on Invoice Number *xxx*, have expired and payment is well overdue.

I initially sent said invoice on [*insert date*]. I have followed up on two occasions: an e-mail [*insert date*] and a telephone call with [*insert name of person with whom you dealt*] in your Accounts

Payable Department on [*insert date*]. However, we have not received payment, nor any communication from your company regarding the reason for the delay.

I would appreciate if this matter could be brought to a prompt conclusion, as this has gone well beyond the stated terms of contract.

If the money has been transferred to us before the arrival of this letter to your attention, please disregard same.

Yours sincerely

I attended a course on cash-flow management a number of years ago, and the consultant/trainer suggested that if a client is a 'repeat offender', you could apply the bank rate of overdraft interest to the outstanding balance. When they query it, you could reply with 'If I don't receive your money in the time that we both agreed on, I have to find short-term finance elsewhere. This is a cost that I have to bear solely due to the delay of your payment, and hence it is an additional cost of doing business with you. Our existing price structure isn't designed to absorb this.'

Unfortunately, if none of the above works, you'll have to write it off as a bad debt and learn how to perform more thorough credit checks on your future clients, or else seek legal advice on your rights in the situation.

Troubleshooting: 'It didn't work – what now?'

17. 'I've tried the sales and marketing, but where's the money and the profit?'

By now, I hope that you've been following the process and that your efforts are producing tangible dividends. However, I'm sure that you've hit some bumps along the way. This is going to happen whether you're hoping to make €500 or €500,000. The ways in which the challenges are dressed and addressed are different, but I would be very surprised if the journey has been completely smooth.

The important thing now is to find a way through, over, under or around the issue that you're facing. Hopefully, you'll look back sometime in the future and say that this was an opportunity in disguise, a learning experience that might have acted as a stabilizer when you were trying to go too far too fast. It's not the runner who runs the fastest that wins, but the one that just keeps running.

So you've hit a wall, within yourself ('I'm too scared') or in your environment ('This piece of marketing hasn't delivered for me in any way whatsoever'). You just can't see a way forward. But, trust me, there is one. There were moments in my business when I cried, moments when I rang my fiancé in despair. I knew things wouldn't get better if I didn't take drastic action, but what was that drastic action?

There was always a way out and a way up. Let me share with you some hard-earned wisdom.

'I haven't made any sales'

First things first: let's look at your spread-sheet. How many people have you approached for a sale? Then – how many 'nos' did you get?

If the first one or two people say no, that's not really a problem, so you shouldn't be worried, that's an expected part of the process.

It's also important to differentiate between 'no, thank you' – after you've asked for the sale – and 'thank you for your time' – after you didn't put the question to them directly and they walk away. How many sales conversations have you had recently? Not networking conversations, not establishing rapport, not meeting somebody for coffee, but asking somebody whether they would like to buy from you. Very often we shy away from asking directly: and we think that, now people know we have an offering, they'll express an interest and ask to buy if they want the product or service.

You have to ask for the sale. People expect you to initiate this exchange, since you're the person selling something. I'll repeat it: *you have to ask for the sale.* Directly. As in 'Would you like to buy?' Not 'This is a wonderful product, isn't it? [*hint, hint*]' Go back through the various different ways that you can progress the sales conversation in Step Seven.

If real 'nos' keep piling up, something in your offering or your marketing needs to be adjusted. Perhaps you're not solving a real problem, or not solving it in a way that makes sense to those who have that problem. You need to consider the information that you gathered from the people who didn't choose to buy from you. Did they say it was too expensive? That they didn't really have a need for it right now? That they preferred to buy from a competitor? This is valuable information that you can add to what you learned during the market research stage in Step Three. Perhaps you're not targeting the right people; your pricing needs to be revised; or you need to add some extra value to your offering.

Maybe your customer would be ready to buy, but they have an influencer who is convincing them to decline. The missing link could just be that influencer, who can also tip them favourably from being a prospect to an actual customer. Revisit Step Four to find ways to identify and communicate with them.

Alternatively, perhaps you need to change the way that you articulate the benefits of your product or the method that you're using to reach people. Go through the Marketing Framework in Step Six and figure out ways that you could tweak the medium, the message, the call to action and the follow-up. What could you do differently?

Remember my story about my eLearning venture: there was a gap in the market, but there wasn't a market in the gap. My offering got turned down, again and again and again. And I was approaching companies that had already worked with me, that knew me and had been very satisfied with other work I'd done for them. And they still said no. However, there was a lot to learn from this, and I had to go back to the lessons in Step Two, change direction and figure out a new way forward.

'How do I make the first sale?'

This is a variation of the first issue. I get it. There's a bit of a chicken-and-egg problem when you're just starting out: to buy from you, people will want to know whether you can deliver, whether others have been happy to buy from you; but if nobody has ever bought from you because you've just started out, what do you do?

Sometimes the way to the first sale is to provide the service without charge or to give a free trial to potential customers. It's free in so far as you're not asking for money, but be very strategic about how you'll benefit afterwards. This is effectively a sales contract, so give it the importance it deserves. Have a record of something in writing:

Dear [*insert first name*],

Thank you for agreeing to work with me over the coming [*insert timeframe*].

I very much appreciate that you will give me [*insert benefit, e.g., a testimonial if you're happy with my work, a written review to post on my website, a phone call to discuss feedback*].

If you're happy to continue after this time, my rate will be [*insert pricing structure*].

I look forward to working with you.

Regards

This is how one of my providers approached me: she had heard me speak at a networking event and noticed that my blog (www. thepositiveeconomist.com) wasn't very lively. She offered to work with me on a content plan, a calendar, some research for posts, etc. As she was just starting out herself, she offered to work for free for a few weeks. She set a specific end date to the experiment. By the time that date arrived, the amount of value she had provided was extremely clear to me. In fact, I approached her with an offer before the time period expired, because I wanted to continue to use her services.

At the beginning of our expansion into the eLearning world, we developed a webinar offering for companies. We would manage the technology, develop the content and provide analytics of webinars to train staff, boost sales, increase engagement and grow productivity in a very efficient way. However, nobody knew us in this area, and we didn't have a track record with a client at that point. Our office was in an incubation centre on a university campus, so I started to work with the business school, delivering a three-week programme to a group of Master's Degree students that included webinars, exercises, resources, corrections and insightful analytics at the end of the session. The business school was very happy with this, as it gave their students some tuition for free; in return we got the kudos of calling a large, well-known, reputable institution a client. That's all we needed to do for free in order to get up and running with this offering.

I used to be a member of a business forum that had about 20,000 members, and it had built up a lot of traffic. One woman had set up a new business that offered copywriting services to website owners. She had been participating in online conversations on the forum for a couple of months, so the community became quite familiar with her and her ability to give tips and advice on a range of topics. I remember the day that she announced to the forum that she was developing this new service. She offered to review five different sites for the members on two conditions: first, they had to allow the feedback (good or bad) to be posted on the forum so that potential customers could see the depth of her analysis; second, if they were happy, they had to give her a testimonial for her own website. I quickly replied to the post, and she actually did a review of the site of the company that I was working for at the time. When I spoke to her afterwards, she told me that the offer had been snapped up within fifteen minutes and that she'd had her first sale by the end of the week.

'Free' should always be a springboard to 'paid', so, once again, think it through before you start. Also, be wary of people asking you to work for free 'because you will gain exposure'. Is this exposure actually going to benefit you? Will you be put in front of your target market? Can they quantify the number of people or website hits that they're expecting? In many cases, these opportunities are exactly that, and this platform can be fantastic. However, sometimes they aren't a great fit, and remember that your time is finite – spend it wisely.

If your product is complex and therefore difficult to explain or to visualize or your audience just can't grasp what you do, create a demo if at all possible. I designed an innovative budgeting tool that I use all the time for myself in Excel. It has got some built-in formulas and macros to make it easy to navigate and mine the most important information out of one's income and spending. I made it available for download on www.savvywomenonline.com for the readers of *The Savvy Woman's Guide to Financial Freedom* (you're very welcome to use it too). A number of people e-mailed me, as they weren't sure where to put an entry, how to incorporate an exceptional item or what a particular indicator was for. As a result, we developed a step-by-step eLearning suite on the site to highlight all the functionalities of the spread-sheet as well as to show other businesses how we can develop content to bring the same kind of value to their customers.

'The marketing isn't working'

OK, let's break this down. Tell me exactly how it isn't working. Have a think about the following questions:

- Does your medium have the audience that you're looking for?
  If not, you need to revisit Step Six to change the platform that you're using.
- Is your market connecting with your message?
  If not, you need to revisit Step Six to change the way that you articulate the benefits.
- Is your market responding to your call to action?
  If not, have you tested the link/number/e-mail address to make sure that it's working?
  Is the link/number/e-mail easily confused with another?
  Is the call to action clear and unambiguous? People are busy: they need to understand what you want from them in a split second. Make it easy for them.
- Are you following up promptly and effectively?
  If not, how could you increase your resources to be able to do so?
  If not, maybe you should slow down and deal only with what you can?
- Do you have the data to be able to answer any of these questions?
  If not, revisit Step Six to go through how to measure marketing results.

We once worked with a group of students at Dublin City University who orchestrated a Google Adwords campaign for us. To use Google Adwords, you choose a number of keywords: these are recorded by Google on the basis of real searches that people have done. The keywords chosen by the students are a good straightforward example for illustrating the concept. We wanted to target people interested in the stock and options markets. A lot of people search for 'how to choose stocks': you choose that string of keywords and pay Google to display your ad when somebody types this particular phrase into their search engine (i.e., pay per impression) or you pay Google when somebody clicks on your ad (pay per click). The students were getting the hits, but their money for the experiment was running out fast, because they had chosen expensive keywords: 'how to choose stocks' would yield a high volume of searches and encounter lots of competition. It was the method that they needed to refine, by choosing more niche keywords (e.g., 'how to choose stock options', 'how to choose fundamental value stocks', 'how to choose income-generating stocks'). They changed their keywords to terms with less competition, fewer hits and hence a lower cost. However, since these keywords were more targeted, the potential 'clicker' was far more likely to be a motivated customer for the site, or, to use the language that we have grown accustomed to, a 'targeted lead', meaning they were much more likely to buy the end training product. This is why it's so important to engineer your marketing so that you gather a lot of data and respond to the feedback that the market is giving you.

You also need to make sure that it's really your marketing that's not working, and not something else. A company that I was working for asked me to manage a stand in a trade show in the Netherlands. I don't speak Dutch, so I had an interpreter with me. I delivered a presentation about the product in front of an eager audience – but very few people actually signed up. What happened? The only form of payment I could receive, due to the company's systems, was credit card. However, the culture at the time was that the Dutch generally didn't use credit cards, and, when they did, it was for emergencies. All our KPIs were telling us that everything was great – we had the right numbers for footfall, interest, hits, etc. – so marketing wasn't the problem here. It was something else entirely.

If you feel that your marketing is indeed at fault – have you tried different versions? Have you tested different ads? To refine your marketing, change one variable and see if the ad performs better. For example, put two slightly different ads (different wording, or different call to action, or different design if relevant) in the same place (same magazine, same website, same radio show). Alternatively, put the same ad in different places. Make sure to change only one variable at a time, so that the differences in outcome are clearly attributable to one factor – and record every piece of data that you can. Compare results, see what you can learn, keep the better ad, and then test another variable. I've told you about the entire process that I went through when managing a LinkedIn advertising campaign for our client. At the time, we had five different ads, and two were clearly performing much better on every level. We dropped the other three within two days and spent our marketing dollars in the most efficient way.

Remember that nothing is ever wasted. If one marketing strategy doesn't work at all, learning that it doesn't work is in fact very valuable. At least you know that you can eliminate it from your plan. You're bound to come across some absolutely useless marketing plans on your journey, so put it down to experience, extract all the learning that you can from it and get ready to make the next attempt a success.

'There isn't any profit in this'

You metaphorically punch the air. You got an extra €500 in. That's great. However, on examining your bank balance, you realize that you're €100 down. What's going on? It might be that you forgot to factor in certain costs – like transport, taxes, etc. As we discussed in Step Two, there is a cost to making money. Depending on where you work and whom you work with, you might have to invest in your appearance (e.g., suits, shoes, cufflinks, make-up, briefcase); you might have to factor in the time and money of a commute; or you might have to incur expenses that would usually be borne by an employer (stationery, a printer, dedicated software . . .).

This is a very common discovery after some initial success, particularly if you start off without thinking everything through. This has happened to me more times than it should have over the years, and that's why I'm really trying to drive the point home. Experience is a great teacher.

Let's figure a way out of this. First, is this a temporary thing? Do you need to just hang on a bit longer before you see results?

For example, if you're putting a lot of time into getting new clients, as soon as they start handing over money (and on a regular basis), you'll see a lot more profit later on than you do today. Maybe you didn't factor in the time that you would have to spend writing copy for a website, going forwards and backwards with a web designer on tiny details, and getting through all the paperwork needed to enable a website to take credit card details. These tasks are one-offs, and when they're done, they're done. I don't want to compound your workload, but I would strongly encourage you to take the advice I give in Step One and keep a time record of everything that you're doing. Identify where your time is going, note the tasks and ask yourself if this is work that you'll need to do on a regular basis or just once because you're beginning a new initiative.

Then there is the permanent sort of 'no profit in this'. You need to address this as early as you can. Perhaps you didn't anticipate how much time ongoing customer service actually takes: opening a lead, sending through a proposal, following up, replying to e-mails, sending invoices and following up to ask for money. Maybe you priced a product by taking the cost of materials and applying a margin to it without factoring in the 'cost' of your own time. Maybe you just wanted to get started and didn't want to charge a prohibitive price (remember the scenario of the person who was going to give facials for €20). Perhaps you need to spend some more time working out the cost of your inputs and filling out the calculator to 'find your profit within your revenue' on www.savvymoneyguide.com.

When I started mentoring people in the stock market, the price

I was charging was far too low, considering the value my customers were getting. I had lots of clients, but I made all of the above mistakes and ended up with very little profit. I turned it completely around by making two changes.

One route to increasing your profit is increasing your price. Some of you will recoil in horror at this suggestion. You'll tell me that it was hard enough to get your customers in the first place; the last thing you want to do is to increase your price, particularly in a recession. However, if you're not making any profit, what's the point in doing it at all? As I mentioned to you much earlier in the book, when I increased the price for my mentoring sessions, a frequent reaction from clients was 'Now you're getting some sense. I was wondering when you would actually value your time.' My own resistance was the only issue: they didn't have any problem with the rise in price. I have brought this topic up at a number of presentations that I give to businesses, and I have often had another objection levelled at me: 'You can't just increase your price, especially for clients who have been with you a long time.' In that case, remember my tip for making your customers feel cared for in the midst of a potential price rise. You can test the water by saying, 'I'm planning to increase the price of my service next month due to [*insert valid reason, e.g., rise in the cost of inputs, increase in qualifications, extra value-adding element, etc.*]. However, you have been with me for a long time, so I'm going to hold our current agreed price with you for the next six months. How does that sound?'

Another avenue is to do something differently. I used to drive all over Ireland to give mentoring sessions, travelling an awful lot, eating out and sometimes paying for overnight accommodation. I was also paying a high-opportunity cost, as I couldn't pursue other money-making activities during that travel time. I turned to my business adviser (aka my fiancé, Ardle, my trusted fountain of knowledge) and we went through exactly what the offering was. We pared it right down into its individual elements. Customers weren't actually paying for my physical presence, but rather for my personal, tailored tuition and step-by-step guidance on the technical side of investing. All that they really needed was to hear my voice and to see the screen on which I was demonstrating what they needed to do. If I could find a way to make my voice and my laptop screen travel to their computer, I wouldn't need to move an inch. I started to use Skype to let them see my desktop; or I used screen-sharing software to take control of their computer remotely to demonstrate the steps. This absolutely revolutionized my profit margin. Now sessions started at the time of the appointment, not three hours earlier when I climbed into the car. In addition, I could record the session, so that a tailored, step-by-step video guide was created for them, which added value to the service itself. I was able to sell more billable hours, and my mentees didn't have to tidy their sitting rooms for the visitor and buy biscuits to make tea for me. That was the only downside for me, as I did miss the Mikados and Jaffa Cakes.

If you have agreed to take on extra work in your workplace, you need to apply the same logic. You might end up doing five hours, when you're paid three. Now, if it happens that you're going through a very busy time for two weeks and you stay late every evening, I'm sure your employer appreciates that very much. As an employer myself, I would indeed be appreciative, and I'm sure you'll be rewarded in some way, e.g., leniency if you're looking for some time off, a voucher, doing their very best to make sure that you hold your job if tough decisions are needed down the line.

However, if this is happening day after day and week after week, you need to bring it to their attention. Revisit the script in Step Seven and ensure that you have your market research from Step Three done. Present your case: your job description expressly states that you earn x per hour, you are actually doing the job of [*e.g., a personal assistant, when you're paid the salary of an office administrator*], you have delivered y results and if they were to replace you, by current industry standards, it would cost them an extra €z per week.

I was having lunch with business associates in Canary Wharf last week, and we were discussing this very topic. One of them was telling us that her job description and her previous experience are in the area of fund accounting. She has progressed to team manager now, and her salary is commensurate with her title. However, her manager had given her a 'new challenge' the week before, which was to recruit two new staff on top of her existing heavy workload. This woman works in a huge organization, and they had a whole floor of HR professionals, but he gave her the task. She didn't have any experience in recruitment whatsoever and had no idea where even to start. She put this to her boss and he dismissed her with 'You always make a success of whatever you do. Have a look around on LinkedIn, and if you need a budget for advertising the positions, we can talk about that. We wouldn't want you to get bored now, would we? Ha, ha.' She went back to her desk and spent her lunch break panicking. She looked at her diary, which was already bursting at the seams, and her inbox, which was blowing steam; and then she gazed blankly at her homepage on LinkedIn. Next, she did a little googling and came up with the daily rate that a recruitment professional would be paid to find the calibre of person that she was supposed to hire. She gathered her 'business case' together and asked her manager if she could pop in. In a ten-minute conversation, she pointed out all that she had on her plate at the moment, her actual job description and the distance between her daily rate and that of the recruitment consultant. She then said, 'Therefore, as I see it, the way in which we can assure the best outcome for the company is for me either to delegate one of my core projects, perhaps [*she specified the one that was going to be most time-consuming*] or I could come in on evenings and weekends, which I'm prepared to do in exchange for €x. This is about half of the incremental cost a recruitment company would charge, but, given that I don't have the experience that they would bring to the table, I'm happy to go along with this. Which would you prefer?' This was the way that she negotiated a 10% temporary pay rise for the duration of this task. She was already planning how she could ask for a higher salary when the time came to search for a new job or when going for that promotion, given that she would have specialist recruitment experience on her CV.

'I've tried the sales and marketing, but where's the money and the profit?'

I called in to visit a friend of mine the other day who decided to mind children in her own home, as her children were of pre-school age. She took on children only when she liked the parents, and initially everything went fine. They dropped them off at 8.30 a.m. and picked them up at 4.30 p.m. This worked very well for a couple of months, until one set of parents pushed 4.30 to 4.45 when they stopped at the shop on the way home for bread and milk. A week later, they didn't come until 5 p.m., apologizing profusely for having got caught up at a meeting in work. However, in this one particular week, they arrived at 5 p.m. on two evenings, at 5.30 p.m. the next two evenings and at 6 p.m. on the Friday with a casual 'Well, I don't know where the time went today.' At this stage, my friend was getting totally fed up with this intrusion on her own family time. The mother handed over the money and my friend said, 'You're €50 short.' The mother looked puzzled, counted the money out in front of her and said, 'No, it's all there.' My friend looked her straight in the eye and said, 'If you stay late in work, you get paid overtime. All of this week and in fact for several weeks before this one, you've had me work extra hours. I charge €*x* per day, and if you add up all of the extra time that I've put in for this week alone, it comes to €50.' The mother found a way to be punctual in the future, and when she was going to be late, she checked in with my friend to ask how much it would cost.

'I'm doings lots of work all right, but I don't see any money'

If this is the case, you need to ask yourself: what was the original path? Revisit the 'sales cycle KPI' that we discussed in Step Two. How were you supposed to get your money? What has happened to that? For example:

~ Are you actually finding people who might be willing to buy? *If not, look back at 'The marketing isn't working' point that I addressed above.*

～ Are you putting lots of people into your database, but the money from sales isn't coming through?

If so, look back at the 'I haven't made any sales' issue that I discussed at the start of this chapter.

You'd be surprised how many people have a wobbly business model or none at all. Facebook started off as an experiment to see if one computer genius could hack a database, upload details of his college peers and get people to approve ('like') and comment on their friends' statuses. The money-making idea of companies using Facebook to advertise to highly targeted groups, utilizing the sheer volume of detailed information that they gave away about themselves, came afterwards.

You may also have heard of bloggers who hoped to make money out of their blog in the long run, only to find their readers weren't interested in buying from them, and advertisers didn't think the blog had enough readership or influence to warrant advertising on it. This was because the business model wasn't clear from the outset, and the blogger didn't think clearly about what they were offering, who their target market was, what problem they were solving or what pleasure they were providing. That's why the issues that I invited you to think about in Step Two are so, so important.

If you're working with a company on a commission basis, perhaps it's time to talk to them about your journey so far. I told you earlier how I started off with the stock market training company on a commission basis. I was full of enthusiasm, but didn't quite know how to expend my energies after I had looked in the obvious places. This wasn't a failing on my part (as they pointed out to me), but rather the start of a learning curve. I called the person who was responsible for dealing with me specifically and told him openly and honestly that I really wanted this to work, both for me and for the company, but that I needed some direction. It was simply a matter of communication. We set up a meeting, and over the course of three hours we identified some key ways that I could move forward in the coming months. For example, the company was taking a stand at an exhibition and I asked to go along to learn how to position the offering to new people. I went to their free workshops to learn how they answered questions and overcame objections from potential customers. I went to local enterprise groups to be around other people who did this all the time, to build up my confidence and learn some new skills at their training events. I didn't know it at the time – then I was simply doing what I could to move in the direction that I wanted to go – but I now recognize these activities as marketing and networking with a view to building a sales funnel.

If you've engaged in affiliate selling or multilevel marketing, you might need to ramp up your own marketing, rather than just relying on that of the company whose products you sell. Depending on the terms on which you have become a reseller, you could ask for support. If the organization for which you work is not paying you on time, or if you're asked to work overtime and not really getting paid for it, you need to ask them whether anything is amiss. Perhaps it's a logistical issue. For example, if you are selling with multilevel marketing and the organization pays out every thirty days, and you submit your own invoice to them on Day 30, you may have to wait another thirty days before you finally get paid.

If your model for making money is sound – that is, if you know who is going to give you money and the problem you'll be solving for them is a real problem – but the money still isn't there, retrace your steps. Where were you headed? How far are you from there? Did you get sidetracked? If it seems that you're one or two steps back from where you thought you were, this is not in and of itself a problem: things are taking longer than you expected, so factor that in, learn from it and see whether there is any way you can speed things up in the future. Re-evaluate where you are and be realistic about any cash-flow issues: if you were planning to have the money in your account by August, and you now realize it won't be there until December, can you hold out that long? If not, revisit Step Five and find people to talk to who can help and give advice about what to do next.

'I don't have the time – I'm exhausted'

You might realize that your new money-making ventures are taking up a lot of your time and that you're really tired from all the activity. Of course being exhausted isn't all fun, but this is actually a good measure of initial success. Congratulations. Try to shift your thinking from 'I'm exhausted – this is all bad' to 'I'm tired, but this is part of the result that I'm trying to achieve.' However, let's examine the source of your tiredness: is it because this is all new and you need to adjust before your schedule becomes second nature? Whenever we try something new, we have to utilize more cognitive resources to deal with all the learning and adjustment that's taking place. After a while, the new thing becomes a habit and we're partly on autopilot: we've adjusted to the new environment, and we're not so tired any more. But it might be that you're tired because you truly are doing too much, you don't have time to recuperate, and you're over-stretched. This is not sustainable in the long term, so you need to find a way to do less.

I decided to take on a personal assistant, as things had come to a head. For a full month before she started with me, I was berating myself about how I couldn't handle my workload. I saw this as an inability to keep up, I needed to be stronger, I should have been able to get up earlier and keep going for longer. However, it wasn't until the board meeting where Ardle and I discussed taking her on that I realized the huge positive in my perceived negative. It was a fantastic thing for our business that I wasn't able to do everything any more. This level of activity was reflected in our financial statements and the full pipeline for the months ahead. It was a clear signal that we were progressing. Yet I was wondering why I couldn't handle it all on my own. If I continued to process the entire workload myself, we would never be able to see significant growth. It was a wonderful thing that I had work to delegate, on a consistent basis, so that I could focus on those activities to which I could really add value.

I was giving out to myself because we were actually achieving what we had set out to do.

I was at a networking lunch recently and I got chatting to a woman, both a wife and a mother, who had recently set up a side business in her home. She found herself with a much busier day and needed some time to concentrate on the task at hand. She spent a couple of hours on the laptop during the week when the kids had gone to bed. However, she asked her husband to take care of the children on a Saturday afternoon, so that she could dive deep and not think of anything other than her work. They all sit down together on a Saturday night to have a takeaway, and she listens to their stories of the park or the cinema or playing with their friends.

She had a glint in her eye as she told me that her household had benefited immensely from her new venture. First, they're financially better off, but also her husband and her kids now look forward to this new-found quality time with Daddy. She finds that she has oiled a lot of previously rusty skills, has a lot more confidence and is getting a great deal of personal satisfaction from this new interest. The only things that have fallen by the wayside are house chores. She now finds that she hoovers the house once a week instead of twice, the dishwasher might have to wait until the morning until it's emptied and she doesn't watch that movie on a Wednesday night like she used to. If you've done the time-logging exercise in Step One, you'll have a written list of activities that take up your time. Which ones can be totally eliminated or can become less frequent with few to zero consequences? Which ones can be delegated to your partner or your children? Which ones can be delegated to a hired helper, if the money you can earn in the time that is freed up is more than what you pay to that person?

If you don't have anyone to delegate to or you can't pick and choose your time, what do you do? When I was in college I had a packed week (I made sure of it). I did all of my studying and social-izing during the week. I had a recuperating lie-in on a Saturday morning, worked in a convenience shop from 12 till 9, and then went babysitting in the evening (which took care of any spill-over study from during the week). I worked another shift on Sunday from 10 till 6; then on Sunday evening I would give grinds to second-level students. There was no break at all, and I couldn't have been more efficient with my time than I already was. I had one Sunday off out of three, when I would thoroughly enjoy visiting family. I certainly wasn't ready to give anything up. I was happy with this as it was, but my schedule was as full as it possibly could be. See if there are any movable parts in your week: can you become more efficient with your time, can you give up a low-priority, low-profit task?

'I'm lonely'

Due to your circumstances, you might have decided to leave your job and set up a business at home; or to start making money online; or you might have taken the plunge to change your working environment so that you travel a lot for work or do more work from home. In any one of these cases, you may find yourself spending your days around a lot fewer familiar people than before, a change that you might not have anticipated when you made a decision based on numbers.

I have been in both of these situations. In Step Five I told you about the claustrophobic feeling of being confined within the four walls of the tiny office I had set up at home. There is only one solution to this: you need to get out of the house. Go for a walk in the morning so that you have a journey 'on the way to work'. Go out for a coffee and bring a notebook to write down your list of things to do. Go to a networking event, go to Toastmasters, join a class, anything, even if it's not directly related to what you're doing, as long as it gets you out and about. Feeling lonely might be a source of boredom and even burnout in the long term; socializing is the direct antidote, and you owe it to yourself to make your money-making efforts sustainable.

I have been travelling a lot on behalf of my own business, and, although you might be surrounded by hundreds of people, there can be a different type of loneliness in this lifestyle. Often the issue here is that your life becomes one-dimensional. You get up in the morning in your accommodation and have breakfast, read the paper, go to a meeting and then it's go-go-go all day. You get back to your hotel at night, open your e-mails and work until your eyes can't see any more. You get up the next day and repeat a pretty similar process. You miss cooking for yourself or seeing a loved one before you go to bed at night. Is it any wonder that negativity begins to permeate your days? Taking care of yourself while on the road or in the air is not optional – it's vital. If I spend five days travelling around Ireland for meetings, I always pop into the home of a friend or family member (as they're dotted all over the place) for a cup of tea if I'm passing. If I'm in London, I meander around Borough Market or go to a show in the West End or go for a cycle through Hyde Park or do one of the billion things that there are to do in such a vibrant place. I'm going to Malta next week for two days, and I'm already planning to visit my favourite coffee shop, walk from St Julian's to Sliema and go to one of their national feasts.

If you're working away from home, the natural distractions aren't there to unglue you from work and your computer. In my experience, that's where it goes wrong. I always try very hard to be a tourist for an afternoon or an evening when I'm away. Find ways to nourish yourself when you travel on business and then you can enjoy being at home all the more on your return.

'I've bitten off more than I can chew'

So you went ahead and boldly sold a product or a service to an enthusiastic client, or you've convinced your boss that you can add value to the company by doing something new in your workplace (and getting paid for it). But now you find yourself with a tall order. First, your ambition is a good sign. Stay hungry. Any new activity is going to have a learning curve, which might be rather steep in the beginning. It's normal and expected. It's happened to me many times, and I've grown to love feeling my heart beating out of my chest as I know that I'm pushing out of my comfort zone. Although it's scary, it's also very exciting. I love it, and I love rising to the challenge. The rush of excitement and positive stress is part of your growth.

But, still, it doesn't alter the fact that you might not be able to pull it off. So let's think about that. What is the exact problem?

Is it a skill you don't have?

Do you know anybody at all who could help you with this? Go back through Step Five and think about who you could turn to. Can you look it up online? Could you do an eLearning course at home at night? Do you know somebody who has done it successfully – could you ask them for some advice?

Do you have a deadline that's too close?

Communicate clearly and early with your customer or employer, and talk it out with them. I was doing a professional exam last year, and a client asked me to do a project for them during the month leading up to the exam. The actual task took much longer than either of us had envisaged, due to complications that we came across. I got through the first half and told him three weeks before the exam that I really needed to put the second half on hold until after the exam was done. The project wasn't time-dependent, so he was very happy to agree. I completed the entire job the week afterwards and thanked him for his flexibility.

Let's say that you've signed up to organize the Christmas party at your office. This is the first time you'll be doing this and you have no precise idea of all the work that's involved: how do you select a venue? What kind of food do you go for? What is a successful office Christmas party, anyway? First, do some market research. What type of party would staff enjoy? When? Where? Would they like a theme? Are they looking for something different or just a couple of drinks on a Friday? What type of budget is going to be provided? Does your boss have any restrictions on what you can do? At least if you find out all that you can, you can plan your next steps, go through your network to see who can help you and get some novel ideas on board.

Sometimes what seems like an impossibility is only a lack of self-confidence. It's not that you've bitten off more than you can chew: it's that you don't know how much you can actually chew. A friend of mine was once asked by a magazine editor to write an article about a foreign-aid programme. She wrote back to the editor in a bit of a panic, saying, 'But I know nothing about that.' The editor, whom she had worked for before, simply replied, 'We aren't looking for specialist expertise, but a well-written article making complex information clear to our general readership. That's what you excel at, so simply do what you always do, but just apply it to a new subject.' My friend wasn't an expert on foreign aid, but that wasn't what was expected of her. Once she realized that, she was able to deliver the kind of article that the editor wanted.

Break down the task into SMART goals, and then strategize. The R in that acronym will help you distinguish between a physical impossibility (no, you won't be able to deliver 10,000 widgets one week from now, because your machines simply can't crank them out this fast) and a lack of confidence. Sometimes we think we're not capable, when in fact we very well are. Again, ask for help and advice, and reassurance if necessary. Write down every single possible idea, person that you could contact, and resource that you could use to move one step closer to delivery of this task. Put your entire focus on what you can do. Use the GROW MORE! system from Step One. Draw out any issues that you believe you have and come up with a way in which to go over, under, through or around them.

'I'm trying so hard but I'm getting nowhere'

Yes, there are times when no matter how hard you work, it seems you're going around in circles. It might be of little comfort right now, but I can tell you with the benefit of hindsight that, no matter how bad it is, you will learn, you will benefit, something good will come of this. For me it was the lesson I learned when our first foray into eLearning didn't work. I was so sure we had a winner: it was solving a real problem, one people were actively trying to solve themselves. There was an absolute gap in the market. We had poured many hours of work and a great deal of money into it. And still it was getting nowhere. I remember it was, ironically, on 1 June, a day of new beginnings, that I came out of yet another unsuccessful presentation. Around me everyone was enjoying the sunshine; it seemed I was the only one walking around with that little grey cloud over my head. I thought, 'You know what, Susan Hayes, you just have to take the rest of the day off, because this isn't working.' Sitting down and looking out over the city, I was sipping yet another coffee, when the realization sank in. 'You just have to listen to the market, and the market is telling you no . . .'

It might have been hard while I was living it, but beyond the disappointment there was little damage. Thanks to asking 'What's the worst that could happen?', we had made sure that the money and time invested in the project couldn't put our company and our livelihood in jeopardy. We had made sure to diversify our sources of income and to retain all of our previous clients. And, though I had to let go of the idea, I did realize that I had gained a great deal nonetheless. I had learned an awful lot about market research, how to open new doors with existing clients and how to hone a sales pitch; and the process had prompted lots of ideas about how we would go about delivering the service itself. I felt my sales skills had sharpened from having to handle so many objections. And I knew that I understood my customers much better as a result.

But sometimes trying too hard is part of the problem – maybe you need to work smarter, not harder?

Success in business is hardly ever a matter of putting things on autopilot: it comes as a result of testing and tweaking, trying again, iterating. Just because it's hard now, doesn't mean it will be hard forevermore. For example, let's say that you're working in a sales and marketing role in a hotel. You've exhibited at shows, spent money on advertising, used some Google Adwords and gone down all of the traditional routes to bringing in more wedding business. How about bringing people to your hotel now, instead of putting yourself out to them?

Perhaps you could drastically increase the number of wedding parties who might choose your property, if you held a wedding fair? Rather than approaching potential customers on a couple-by-couple basis, you could talk to a hundred leads in one day. Design some visually exciting e-mails and invite everybody with whom you've spoken in the past six months who still hasn't decided where to hold their reception. Dress your function rooms to look their absolute best. Invite local bands, jewellers, artisan cake-makers, travel agents, etc. Open the bubbly and order in some nibbles. Now that you've seduced a pool of buyers into visiting your wedding fantasy land, you have a platform for demonstrating how you can provide a couple with their perfect day, and you can do so very efficiently. This can be achieved, however, only after you've gone out there and collected details of people to invite. I'm sure you won't be surprised when I tell you that this is exactly how my fiancé and I decided on our own wedding venue.

Some periods are harder than others. That is actually a measure of success: just as you're about to grumble about how tired you are, stop and take a moment to congratulate yourself. It's a nice problem to have. I remember that there was one week last year when I had criss-crossed the country on business engagements, then flown to London, landing around 8 p.m.; by the time I had made it out of the airport, into the City, got a bite to eat and finally settled down at my hotel, it was 11 p.m. I immediately sat down to make the final touches to a set of slides for a client, because they absolutely needed the materials that week. By 1 a.m., alone in my room and the rest of the world asleep outside my window, I took a minute for a bit of self-pity. 'This is so hard. My eyes are burning the whole way through to the back of my head with tiredness.' I was finally in bed at 2.30 a.m., up again at 7.30 a.m. and off to Trafalgar Square. That's when I walked right into the meeting that would turn out to be one of my biggest business opportunities to date. Even though these times are not exactly relaxing, they are part and parcel of my business journey, and I love the rush of adrenalin that comes from dealing with everything that's thrown at me. Of course, it's important to mention that these are relatively rare occasions, as otherwise I would be suffering from regular bouts of burnout. The point I'm trying to make is that we all go through spots of really having to dig deep, so keep going and reap the rewards.

Sometimes you start to think, 'There has to be an easier way.' And very often there is one, all right. But be careful what you wish for. We all know that a large part of success is just the sheer volume of effort. If it were all simple, straightforward and easy, everybody would do it. An easier way might be to make your processes more efficient, which is the whole premise of this book. But when a source of income is guaranteed and risk-free, very often the return will be puny. You could always fill out surveys for a couple of euros during your lunch break. Sometimes that is all you can do, and even just a couple of euros might be exactly what you need at that time. But the easier way is very likely to be the less profitable. And when you're thinking, 'Why is everything so hard? I can't go on like this. Should I give up?', remember to check your KPIs and hang on in there some more. You have to believe that karma will look after you, and that, in time, the accumulation of a slew of small, incremental actions will eventually have a positive effect.

'Somebody said no. This is awful.'

You'll meet with rejection, quite possibly on a regular basis. In some cases, it will be up to you to draw out customers' objections, as I detailed in Step Seven. Often this 'no' will bring you closer to a 'yes', and on other occasions the 'no' will be only temporary.

A few months back I met with a prospect to showcase what my financial training could do for them. Hearing nothing from them, I followed up by e-mail a couple of times. I persisted and called them, only to hear: 'We're currently reviewing all our training processes.' I have learned over the years that this is code for 'Please go away.' However, that's not to say that they won't come back at some stage. I've heard hundreds of these rejections dressed up as platitudes during my career, but many of them have turned into something: doing business with them in the future, an introduction to a potential client who is actually looking for our services, a phone call from somebody out of the blue who worked in that company but has now moved and wants me to come in and meet the senior team for a much bigger deal entirely.

It's worthwhile looking into the reasons why your potential customer said 'no' with such questions as:

- 'We were just wondering if you had any feedback about the event that you attended with us?'
- 'We thank you for letting us know of your decision. We'd be keen to serve you again in the future and would love to hear how our offering could be made more suitable for your needs?'
- 'Would you mind just letting me know if there were any particular factors that led to your decision?'

Make sure to ask these questions, as this is valuable market research that has moved from the theoretical to the practical. You've actually gone to market, and the market hasn't wanted or needed the benefits that you put forward. The answers to these types of questions will teach you something that you can use to improve your whole sales process, if you feel that changes need to be made.

If you know your offering is solid, your market research is spot on and your marketing is good, then you need to keep up the calls until you find the customer who's been waiting for you all along. That's why you have KPIs: you need to know how many sales you're closing, in comparison with how many leads you're opening, etc. As you continue to compile data from your activities, you can go back to Step Six and refine your sales and marketing processes, until you're happy.

'I'm so scared I can't do anything'

This is completely normal when you're venturing far outside of your comfort zone. I have learned to love the feeling, but there were times when I was scared into immobility. When the alarm rings at 7 a.m. and you know you'll be cold-calling by 8 a.m., you're not exactly bounding out of bed full of enthusiasm. It's very tempting to hit snooze and snuggle back under the duvet . . .

You need to go back to the marathon story in Step One: just put one foot in front of the other. As when I first went to Malta, take each step automatically, as if you were simply hired by somebody else to write e-mails and call people. Pretend it's not your venture, it's not your baby, you're just taking care of this for somebody else. For a little while, completely put your emotions to the side and go through the motions.

I met a woman a couple of years ago who was going on maternity leave and was afraid she would be bored (I realize mothers reading this will be amused by that!) and so decided to start a local magazine. She told me that every single month, when she set about getting the next issue off the ground, she was terrified, even though the previous month had been fine. She was afraid that this month there wouldn't be any advertisers, readers or money, and all she could see in the future was a dark pit of anxiety. However, after a couple of months, she realized that she needed no more than a tiny jolt to spur her into action. The first enquiry she received from somebody wanting to place an ad and she was up and running again. As long as there was some sort of positive response from her market, some sign of engagement, she didn't have any difficulty in finding the motivation to dive right in. Keep going, focus on the next step only. Then, once you've taken it, consider the step after that.

'There aren't any events in my area'

The first solution is to get online: there are few things that you can't do online, especially when it comes to making contact with people. However, if you do want to interact with 'real' people, you might consider organizing an event or starting a network in your area. Is there a suitable forum online where you could post: 'Who would like to meet for an informal coffee for people working from home next week at [*insert name of location*] at [*insert time*]?' I used to see this happen all the time on online forums, and it can be a great way to translate online networking into in-person meetings. What if you're the only one who turns up? What's the worst that could happen? You can have a coffee on your own with your notebook to record some thoughts (that's always my default option). But imagine if ten people are there: you have a great morning and it's the start of a social outlet that everyone can look forward to each month . . . and it's all thanks to you. That might just be worth the risk.

A couple of years ago, one of my business acquaintances decided to take matters into his own hands just like that. It was a particularly festive time of year, and he rang me to say: 'Do you know what I don't like at all about being self-employed? You can never have a Christmas party when you're working for yourself. Sure, where would you go? Who would you go with? So I think it would be a good idea to take a table at one of the Christmas party nights in the city. We can pay as individuals and enjoy the night as if we were a corporate! I'm asking everybody that I know who works on their own. Will you go?'

'I don't know anything about x'

We aren't born fluent in computer-programming languages, knowing what to put in a suspense account, able to pick holes in a legal contract or with an innate understanding of how to interpret a tax code. That's why the training, learning and education sector is the second biggest in the world (healthcare is the largest). However, there is an abundance of people who can teach you any topic or subject in the world.

I have gone on all types of courses throughout my career. Some were expensive; some were government subsidized (because I went looking for them, as I described in Step Five); some were part of networking-group offerings; some were online. I've learned an infinite amount from doing, practising and just having a go. I've also made mistakes too numerous to count – some of which I've shared with you in this book. But then how else can I expect to learn?

Ardle took me to a three-day programme on websites, hosting, blogging, SEO and online marketing. I didn't know what any one of them meant at the time, never mind how they worked together. Afterwards, I put some of the lessons into practice, and supplemented them with videos on YouTube and articles that I had googled. I was only starting off in the world of self-employment at the time, and the two of us sat down one Sunday and created our very own website. It didn't have any bells or whistles, but we had learned enough to get started. Fast forward a couple of years, and we now have a wonderful web designer and general IT whizz in our team. He of course knows infinitely more than I do about that whole world, but at least I'm able to talk to him in his techie language. I know enough to be able to ask for specific things, to measure the immense value he is bringing, and to know what I don't know.

If there's something you don't know, find somebody to teach you; or take an eLearning course so that you can learn enough to get by until you can afford to pay someone to do it for you. If you don't have the money to pay for the course or for the help, see if you can barter. You might be able to trade IT services for bookkeeping, graphic design for executive coaching, marketing training for dog walking, anything. And remember to ask for help – your local Chamber of Commerce or another organization might have funding available, grants, free events, you name it.

Now that we've solved the problems that you're most likely to encounter and you've been through the entire process, how would you like to proceed?

Redirecting your efforts towards your desired goal

18. *So what now?*

At this stage, I hope that you've thought about how to get started, performed some market research, found effective ways to articulate your message, got some help from the abundance of assistance that's out there, followed up, asked for the sale and taken steps to address any difficulties along the way.

Now would be a good time to stop for a moment to reflect. Think back to the goals that you set in Step One. What did you – specifically, measurably, attainably, realistically – want to achieve, and in what time-frame? Did you want to earn an extra €300 a month? Did you want to set up a small business and generate €10,000 at the end of the year in profit? Did you want to explore new markets and find five new clients? Did you want to earn more money in your workplace and raise your income by 10%? Did you want to strengthen your money-making ability in the company where you work and increase your sales by 20%?

How has your experience been? Did you achieve this number? Was the goal unrealistic? Did you do better than you had thought? What surprising sources of assistance did you find along the way? What elements soaked up more time, effort and resources than you expected? Do you feel more confident now? What skills have you learned? What do you know about yourself that you didn't previously?

I strongly suggest that you take an hour to really think about these questions and to gather all this information about yourself, as if you were being your own executive coach.

Where next?

There are four different directions that you can take from here. Finish the sentence for yourself: 'Now I would like to . . .'

301

Cruise

Right, I've got my €300 extra a month and I just want to be able to maintain this until I want it to change. It's been an interesting journey that has forced me to push out my comfort zone quite a lot and I'm happy with this new income every month. At least I know how to do it again, when I want to do it again, and I now see that money-making isn't luck but a skill, and I've found a framework that works.

Get bigger

I love it. I'm delighted with my new money and the excitement of making it. I find the process of aspiring to and achieving higher and higher goals hugely exciting, and I want to move on to the next level. I want to expand my market, grow my team, increase my sales and my scale, and accelerate my profit. I want to reach for the stars. If I could achieve this much in this period of time, and have learned all of these new lessons, what could I do in the same amount of time again?

Get niche

While I love having my new money, I don't want to have to put quite so much time and effort into it. There were some aspects that I really enjoyed, but some that I didn't. There are certain customers or jobs or projects that I preferred over others. In fact, if I were to change course a little, I would love to earn x in y number of hours working on z. Now that would be ideal.

Get out

I gave it a good go. I tried it out, but it just wasn't for me. I loved the money, but not the work. I would either like to change the type of work that I'm doing or the way in which I'm doing it. Perhaps, I'm at that stage where I want to try something new entirely. I know that this is a robust framework, though, so now I just need to apply it in a different way to produce a different outcome.

You will probably choose each one of the four at a different point in your life. As your value system grows and develops, claims on your time change and your priorities move around, you'll want to change what you do and why you do it. Let's think about how to progress forward as you'd like to.

Retaining any business you have generated

No matter which route you take, please make sure that you get the maximum benefit out of the efforts that you have already poured in. If you have brought somebody to the point where they're willing to hand over money in exchange for your product or service, do all that you can to retain them. You've done all the work of getting a raise, or starting to give piano lessons, or grinds; or you implemented a new marketing activity in your job or took on new tasks; or you have set up a business. You should really make the effort to let that generate a benefit for you over and over again.

Go back through all of the leads that you opened in Step Six. Did you follow up with everybody who left their contact details with you when you exhibited at a show? Did you send a LinkedIn invitation to everybody that you met at every networking event that you attended? Did you actually send that e-mail to the editors of five high-traffic websites that you identified and for which you would like to write an article?

As I noted much earlier in the book, accepted business wisdom says that it is four times easier to sell to an existing customer than it is to sell to a new prospect. If your employer has agreed to pay for some extra tasks in the workplace this month, are there other ways that you could help out next month? You've already figured out what would be of assistance (you gathered the market research), had the conversation with them about doing this work in exchange for more money (marketing), and they agreed (closed the sale). Now how could you retain them 'as a client'? If somebody signed up for your gym classes, how could you encourage them to come back again for the next season? If somebody bought your book-keeping services, organized their Christmas party in your hotel, booked three coaching sessions, made a catering order or got all of their stationery from you this quarter, how could you encourage them to come back to you again next time?

There are two steps to this process. First, at a minimum, you need to deliver on your promise and outperform their expectations if you can. If you said that your one-day training course can benefit staff, take a measurement beforehand using a questionnaire, deliver a great course and then ask the participants to take the question-naire again. The difference in the scores is your measurable impact, which you can show to your client to demonstrate the quantifiable difference that you made on the day. If you told your boss that you could take care of setting up a new filing system, add in some-thing extra, like a branded step-by-step document, so that it can be e-mailed to everybody in the office and used to minimize the time involved in adjusting to the new process. If somebody hires you to be a photographer at their special occasion, print off one shot that doesn't need any work, put it in a spare frame and give it to them as an extra. Just do something that leaves them with that feeling of 'Ah, thanks a million. I'm really delighted with what you've done.'

Also, it's a small thing to do, but just say thank you. So many times I've been sent an invoice, I've paid it and that was it. I never heard from them again. It's not that I'm expecting more: they did the job I asked them to do and they delivered what they had prom-ised. However, it's the very fact that I'm not expecting more that gives them the chance to exceed expectations: when they do some-thing on top of that, it makes them stand out. My company has been paying invoices for years, and I can count on the fingers of one hand the providers who have said thank you in a memorable way. It's just not done, and it's a simple, yet highly effective way to differentiate your offering.

If they have been with you for a while, send them a small gift: a box of chocolates, a bottle of wine, a small hamper or a card. If they become a regular customer at your market stall, give them a small token every now and then, just to say that you appreciate their business. I often encourage people to adopt this practice when I speak to entrepreneurship groups, and I've been met with the following cynical comment: 'Isn't that just a blatant way of giving them a guilt trip into giving you more business?' No. The objective of this exercise is to show, in a meaningful way, just how much we appreciate their business. Without our clients, there wouldn't be a company. I wouldn't be able to live my life the way that I enjoy, and there wouldn't have been the adventures, learning, fun and excitement of my career. They're extremely important people, and I just want to tell them that. If they choose to buy from us again, that's great, but I trust that the quality of what we deliver will make that decision, not the gift of appreciation.

The second thing that you need to do is to remind your customer of your existence. I often get a laugh out of this at presentations when I ask the attendees, 'How many of you are sitting here today thinking, "I wonder how I could get Susan Hayes more money, improve her balance sheet? The amount of money she earns? Do I know anybody who would want to hire her? Is there any way I could buy five books even though I don't have anybody to give them to?"' No. Of course they don't. They came along to that presentation to see what nuggets of learning they could pick up from me to benefit their lives. It's not their responsibility to figure out a way to help me.

If you're giving out in your own head to your boss because he hasn't suggested that you go to the training course you came across last week, ask yourself how he's supposed to know that you even saw it, unless you say it to him? I was on a course once where the group met once a month. We had all got to know each other quite well by this particular Wednesday afternoon. One person was telling us that he had been interviewed on a big show by a famous host. 'We got a substantial number of enquiries and quite a number of sales after we followed up.' The group congratulated him on this big coup. I then asked, 'And now are you going to go back and see if you can do another interview? Since it's coming up to Christmas, you would have some very suitable topics to talk about, given the nature of your business?' He said, 'Oh, I will if he asks me.' I wouldn't have been so straight if I hadn't known him, and direct speech was encouraged on that particular course, but I said, 'Do you think he's sitting in a meeting right now thinking, "We'd love to get that person we interviewed for three minutes last month. I bet you that he has lots of interesting things to tell our listeners, and it would just be fantastic if we could get him in the studio." No offence, but they have about thirty slots a day on that show, they've probably forgotten you. You've now built up some rapport with the team, so you're ahead of the competition that's vying for their attention. Build on it. It's your job to remind them of your existence; don't expect them to remember.'

I'm going to give you three conversation-starters to use when you want to go back to people that you might have worked with in the past. They won't all work for every type of client, but take them in context and apply your own judgements.

'I just thought I'd give you a call, as I haven't heard from you for a while'

If you've built up a significant rapport with a client, it can be as simple as this to initiate the conversation. I had been doing a lot of business with one particular client, and I hadn't heard from them for a couple of months, which was unexpected. I called up my contact and used these very words. The conversation finished with 'Susan, thanks a million for calling me. You reminded me that I need to send that e-mail, follow up on that lead and return a call from earlier. If we have any developments after that, I'll be right back to you.' He called me three days later with a booking and two weeks later with a further four orders. All I did was to bring my company and our offering right in front of them again, as they had lots of things going on themselves at the time. I just prompted a little more activity on their part, which delivered extra business. If it hadn't, what's the worst that could have happened? It was good to touch base with them and 'the most appalling result ever' would have been that we had a polite conversation.

'We have a new [insert attention-deserving item] at the moment'

Apart from people that you know well, there are many that you wouldn't necessarily call to say 'I haven't heard from you for a while', so you need another reason to ask for their attention. For example, 'I just wanted to let you know that we have a special offer at the moment – 10% off all orders over €100. In case you're running low, you'd get a good deal if you put in an order around this time of year.' Alternatively, could you give something of value to your clients and leads? For example, if you're involved, either as an employee or as a business owner, in an accounting business, you could develop a branded 'Budget Briefing' five-page summary to inform your clients and potential clients of how changes in government spending and tax will affect their businesses. I wrote a piece on my blog last month that could be of use to many of the people who attended my entrepreneurship presentations over the past year. I contacted all of the event organizers who had originally booked me at the time, as well as others who would be in my target market. I invited them to share the piece with their members or anybody else who might benefit from the content. Within an hour, I had some speaking events booked; and I was able to connect with and give value to the attendees long after I had met them. This method of contact is a way in which you remind your clientele that they're important to you, and also that you're alive, kicking and ready to serve them.

'I was thinking of the work we did for you recently, and I think you might benefit from x. Could I send you something to look at?'

I chose those words thoughtfully, as it's important to convey what you actually mean. 'I was thinking about the work that we did for you recently' highlights that I put a lot of thought and effort into what I did for you. I take pride in my work, and you, as a client, are important to me. 'I think that you might benefit from *x*' illustrates that I think that you could leverage what I did for you by taking an extra step. In my opinion, you would benefit from this additional product or service. 'Could I send you something to look at?' is a very soft approach to a non-monetary sale. You don't want to be pushy: all you're asking for is a sliver of their attention while they consider if your idea is worthwhile. Again, I have got several proposals to clients in this way. Many have been turned down, but others have been accepted. The point here is that I built fresh income streams from existing sources by finding new ways of working with them. So what if some got rejected? They all would have been if I hadn't put them forward in the first place. Remember that if you don't ask, the answer is always no.

This could also be used to segue from one agreement with your employer into another. For example, 'I was thinking about the Christmas party that I organized last week, and it occurred to me that we could hold a fantastic event here in our offices for our top fifty customers. We could create a branded e-mail; invite a guest speaker and offer wine and canapés. I think it would certainly boost retention. Could I send you some thoughts in an e-mail?'

Here I must address an objection that has often been levelled at me when I bring this up. Many, many people have said to me, 'I don't want to be annoying people. If they want me, they know where to find me.' I reiterate the point that I made earlier. We are extremely busy people in a world that is spinning ever faster. We move fast, think fast, consume fast. A thought may flicker in your client's head that they must call you with an order and then their phone rings, or an e-mail pops into the bottom corner of their screen, or they think of something else. I met one of my suppliers by chance at a social occasion a couple of months ago. I said, 'Hello, it's great to see you. I've been meaning to call you, as I've a big order to send you.' He replied with 'I thought I hadn't heard from you for a while, but I didn't want to be annoying you.' I said, 'It's a pity that you didn't, because it would have taken one more thing off of my to-do list.' Of course, I'm not suggesting that you call your clients or pop into your boss every week with new suggestions of how they could pay you more. However, using your judgement, it's very worthwhile, both from a financial and a customer-care point of view, to check in with them regularly. They hand over money because they value what you do for them more than the money in their pocket. If your offer was annoying, they wouldn't buy it.

In summary, let's consider our KPIs in this scenario. If you work with a paying customer over and over again, it shortens the sales cycle considerably, because the trust is already built and they may be very open to buying from you again. This reduced marketing time and cost feeds into a greater margin, and your market replenishes itself as you serve the client again and again. From personal experience, I know that you really can keep retention levels high if you do these three things well:

- Deliver a good product or service as agreed.
- Say 'thank you'.
- Keep in contact.

Networking within your network

There are a lot of people who aren't in a position to help you at the moment, but they may buy from you or might act as an influencer in the future. Instead of just going to new networking events, cultivate the contacts you already have. Last week I got a call from a previous contact. She asked me if I would speak about personal finance to a group of their staff, but they didn't have a budget for the event. However, she offered me the opportunity to promote the book to the audience (which is my exact target market for the book); and she said she'd introduce me both to a major radio station broadcaster (which would be a great addition to our PR marketing strategy) and to their London branch (where I could have another speaking opportunity to a new audience). In addition, she invited me to write a piece about the book in the corporate newsletter that's distributed to everyone in the company. So I didn't have to find three distinct, new contacts to access these opportunities; a person in my own network had the perfect connection to all three. Also, this is an example of doing something for zero money but reaping lots of other benefits instead – it's not just for beginners.

While she wasn't a buyer, as I described in Step Four, she was a key influencer. It takes time to build up your network and contacts. You've expended energy going to certain events, following up, sending e-mails, having a meeting over coffee to figure out what you can do for each other, etc. However, it's not always about increasing the number of new people that you meet; it's also important to remind the people you already know of your existence, even if they're not going to buy directly from you – they could be an influencer instead. You need to network within your network. There are lots of things people can do for you along the way that don't necessarily involve an invoice number.

Now let me give you some ideas on how you can either instigate or reciprocate:

∿ If you're going to an open event, why not invite a couple of people who might enjoy it or meet some people in their target market to come along? This not only enables you to catch up with them but also to give them something of value; and you help the event organizer by boosting the number of people who turn up. This radically improves the 'return on your time' of taking a morning out to go to a breakfast briefing.

⟋ If you've written an article that would be useful to other people in your network, come across a business looking for their service or an online discussion where they could add value, send them a quick e-mail to let them know. It takes two minutes, and it can be highly appreciated.

⟋ If you have two people in your network that could benefit from connecting with each other, take thirty seconds to send an e-mail introducing them to each other. For example, let's say that they have the same target market, but their offerings don't compete. If they meet and are happy to refer each other's services, they could act as key influencers for one another. Your introduction, which takes very little time, could have a significant impact and open doors for both individuals.

How to cruise

In order to progress your money-making achievement from this month to every month, you need to do two specific things that fall under the category of retention. First, you need to deliver upon your promises; and, second, you need to translate a temporary agreement into a permanent contract.

I alluded to the first element earlier in this chapter, but the second element requires you to think further about how you can help the person willing to pay. If you can negotiate a pay rise, you've obtained an agreement that will repeat the effect of that initial conversation month after month. However, if you've found a one-off way of helping an employer or a client, one that has monetary value during a single pay period, how could you do it again during the next period?

I was in a meeting with a company a couple of years ago in which a proposal to deliver a couple of days' training here and there throughout the year was being discussed. While this was good, I knew it would be a lot better if we could get the client to agree to a fixed number of days every month, with an option to increase that number at any time if they wanted to. I also knew that we could absolutely deliver on it. I then suggested that we would decrease our price by 10%, if they were willing to work with us on that basis. You might wonder why I suggested such a thing, particularly since this reduced our margin. With a repeat contract, I could plan our cash-flow more solidly; and, on top of that, the 10% that I was offering was actually lower than the cost of the marketing resources and time that I would have had to pour into finding several new one-off clients. I had factored this into the price back in Step Three. They agreed and signed off on the deal.

If the type of offer that you have isn't conducive to a retentive contract like this, you need to set up some sort of a practice that keeps your pipeline flowing. I remember the summer that I started mentoring, I was working at my new initiative with gusto, and I was really getting places too. To keep the figures round, let's say that I was taking twenty appointments every month at €60 per session, so I was making €1,200. I was putting in plenty of effort, and reached my targets for May, June and July. In fact, at that stage, I was actually getting repeat calls, as people wanted to learn more and were inviting me to come back. I was a couple of months into my new money-making activity when I found that my conversion ratio (the number of sales as a percentage of leads) was growing and that people were giving me great feedback, as they really were benefiting. However, when things start to happen regularly, we can get lulled into a false sense of safety – 'This is just what happens now.' I went to visit one of my college mates in New York and, when I returned in August, thought that I would just slot right back into things. I woke up on a Monday morning to face a big, blank, white, appointment-free page staring back at me. The work had dried up because I hadn't put any effort into filling the sales funnel while I was away. This is where your spread-sheet, your knowledge of your market and your KPIs will come in handy. From the information that I had been gathering as I went along, I knew that I needed to make ten calls to get two appointments. Therefore, I reserved the hour between 10 a.m. and 11 a.m. every day for making fifteen calls to new leads and five to existing customers to build my pipeline right back up again. If you want to maintain a level of income every month, you need to deconstruct how you got the money in the first place, month by month. Now break it down into a step-by-step guide for yourself, as we did in Step Six. Put the process in place so that you can mechanically and enthusiastically reach your goal every single month.

19. *Dreaming bigger dreams*

Now that you've started on this journey and seen that you can get past the initial barriers, delivering results that come from a combination of your own skill-set, tenacity and drive, the question is what's next? If you've achieved something that you thought would be difficult, or even impossible, what else is hiding in your future?

It's almost like being a child who learns to cycle for the first time without stabilizers: you're able to steer a series of working parts independently on a defined path. Over time, you'll get faster, more confident and be absolutely able to hold your own. In fact, you may just need a bigger bicycle with more than one gear . . .

In Step One, I asked you to think about your understanding of success. Now I'm going to ask you to do the same thing about growth – when you think of expanding, growing what you're doing and becoming bigger, what exactly do you mean? Do you want to:

1. Increase the amount that you're getting paid in your job again?
2. Increase your sales to your existing market?
3. Expand your market?
4. Expand your offering?

If you want to increase the amount that you're earning in your workplace and you've already negotiated a raise, it's very unlikely that you can do that again in quick succession. Instead, after you've adjusted to your new expectations, perhaps you might consider going for a promotion – more money for greater value-adding responsibility? Alternatively, you could start to look for a new job: a new challenge would help you to build your CV, qualifications and experience. Remember in the last chapter how I emphasized the importance of delivering on your promise. If you've achieved better working conditions, don't leave your employer in the lurch a week later by announcing that you're now off to greener pastures. Plan the process by starting in Step One with your new higher goal, doing your market research, gathering your business case and articulating your new skill-set.

If you want to increase your sales within your existing market, you need to undertake more marketing or else increase the effectiveness of your current activities. Revisit Step Six to refresh your thinking on this. Perhaps you've been investing in advertising and now you need to engage in some sponsorship to build brand awareness. If you've been doing a lot of networking, perhaps you need to think about how to build on that with a direct e-mail marketing campaign. If you have been working hard on organic SEO online traction, perhaps you need to pair it with a paid platform. Maybe you need to take a stand at an exhibition to meet new people in your target market? Could you send out a press release to mainstream media to boost the effectiveness of your social media efforts?

Also, have you thought about encouraging your customers to refer your services to their family, friends and colleagues? After you've finished doing a job for them and they've expressed their approval of your work, have you asked them, 'Do you know of anybody who could benefit from my service?' I spoke earlier of ways to remind your customers of your existence and networking within your network. If somebody recommends you to a friend or colleague, this is far more credible than you recommending yourself. Ensure that they have all that they need to tell others what you do (in other words, don't ask them to come up with ways to market you – arm them with a simple description) and your contact details to hand – make it as easy as possible for them and they may become a powerful influencer in your market place.

If you want to expand your market, you need to identify some new geographic, demographic and psychographic characteristics of customers in an expanded part of your market. Start the process from Step Two and pay particular attention to the market research stage as demonstrated in Step Three. If you're moving into previously unknown geographical territory, particularly if you want to expand internationally, you need to learn all about the conditions of doing business with your new customer. It may not be the case that the benefits that you offer here are going to be accepted as such when you go to a new place; and, conversely, you may have extra attractions that might be overlooked at home. For example, as an international trainer in Malta, I had certain advantages: a more dynamic understanding of the European debt crisis and related economic issues, given that I was coming from outside their own country. However, I also had certain disadvantages: because of the importance that they place on doing business face to face, our webinar offering didn't solve a problem for them, particularly as eLearning hadn't taken off when I first started going there. There were also other things to be considered, including a different tax system, the much larger time and financial cost of flying across Europe to have follow-up meetings and attend networking events, and the requirement to develop a new set of training materials with their own local colour, infused with their news stories, current affairs and financial nuances. In addition, my previous influencers in the form of testimonials from well-known Irish companies didn't hold any weight when I went to a new country, as neither the referee companies nor the people who worked in them were known to my leads. I had to start from scratch.

This advice regarding geography doesn't just apply to business, but also to any job abroad with the reward of a higher salary. You too will need to consider many of the same things. As soon as I embarked upon my summer in Edinburgh, I had to deal with the upfront cost of renting an apartment and buying one-off household goods and groceries to make a house a home. I had to familiarize myself with a new tax system and go through the horrendous process of setting up a bank account (when I didn't have any utility bills in my own name). Similarly, I didn't have any influencers in the labour market: my recruitment consultant wasn't familiar with any of the companies that I had worked with in the past and I had to defend my own merit in order to influence them into placing me with their client, who would be the buyer of my labour. The cost of visiting home was now much higher, as it involved flights, time off work and transport to and from the airport. This sort of thing needs to be factored into your decision and then managed as well as possible.

If you want to expand your offering, you need to go back to Step Two and figure out ways to complement your existing product or service. Let's say I'm a life coach. I could write my own book, design a course to deliver to groups, create an online course, generate commission from an author whose books I recommend and go on to sell, etc. I could start a blog, build my audience and sell advertising and sponsorship. Revisit the brainstorming framework to come up with other ideas and then proceed to the market research stage.

I want to insist on one point. There have been millions of people who have expanded their horizons, just like you're doing. You don't need to go it alone. It's so important to talk to the relevant state agencies that can help you to do these things. Go back to Step Five with your renewed vision. Maybe there's funding that you can apply for? Perhaps there are trade missions, delegations, specialist offices or networks that could be invaluable when getting started. Personally, I found the Irish International Business Network to be of phenomenal help when I started to expand into the UK. I made lots of contacts through them, went to their events, joined their online forum and then worked my way from there. As I mentioned earlier, we got feasibility funding from a state agency to discover how we could develop an eLearning offering. The Enterprise Europe Network was instrumental in helping me to get started in Malta. I've been on countless subsidized training courses and couldn't even hazard a guess at the mass of information, direction and advice that I've picked up from all these sources. Remember that for all of this help that you get, you can give back in so many ways. I've paid thousands and thousands in tax, created employment, shared this knowledge with other people, built awareness about these programmes, among other things. Life is all about give and take.

If you're going to go down the route of taking on staff, the entire framework of this book will apply in a similar way. Start with your goals in Step One. What do you want this member of staff to do? How will they help your business or your team? Do you want to take on somebody with initiative, or to carry out tasks diligently so that you have more time to focus on value-adding tasks? Describe your ideal candidate. Next, work out what you can afford to pay them, how they will bring more value than their salary, and how you would like them to fit into your team. Ensure that you have enough work for them to do on a consistent basis as opposed to just clearing a backlog. Do your market research and, again, learn as much as you can about HR from the different resources that are available to you. There are libraries full of books about how to recruit, manage and get the best from your staff. I'm not going to attempt to cover it all here, but I'd say, from personal experience, be prepared for a learning curve. You'll hit the jackpot, and you'll make mistakes. Learn and move on.

Perhaps you want to do everything. You want to increase your market, your offering, your staff numbers, your sales, etc. That's fine if you're a multinational and you have a separate team that can focus on every single one of these respective aims. If not, take them one by one, give each ambition the time and resources that it needs and then progress to the next. If you allow your enthusiasm to lead you into a chaotic life, the whole thing could fall apart. Remember the person I told you about in Step Three who wanted to open a kitchen and a personal training studio as well as lots of other things? Don't weaken the whole edifice by putting too heavy a roof atop thin walls.

How to 'get niche'

Right: let's figure out exactly what you want. Do you want to charge a higher price? Do you want to put in less time? Do you want to focus on a certain group or within a certain area of an industry? Do you want all three? It's important that you clarify precisely what you're in search of so that you can point yourself in the right direction. If you try lots of different ideas, you'll find yourself getting very busy. This happens as you become more proficient at opening leads, closing the sale and spotting opportunities. You then see that making money isn't something that happens to lucky people, but rather to those who have chosen to learn how. You get to the point where you can select the best route forward, depending on what's important, e.g., the money, the time or the task. Next, let's see if we can figure out a way to increase the amount of value that you can offer to this niche. You need to revisit the KPIs that we developed in Step Two to find the data you need to help you to make a decision.

I recently spoke to a woman who was running three Weight-Watchers classes in her local community centre as well as holding a part-time job. It was her aspiration to grow the amount of money that she was making at WeightWatchers, so that she could leave her part-time job and enjoy more time at home as well as do other things. She wanted only to maintain her level of income, not to grow it. In this case, she needed to 'go niche'. Given that the room could hold up to forty people each time, she knew that she had the capacity to serve a larger group. In fact, if she'd wanted to, she could have doubled the number of classes that she was holding, but this didn't interest her. She had a set amount of money that she wanted to earn and was looking for a way to get that from her classes. Her first plan was to keep in regular contact with her current clients to encourage them to come back week after week to achieve their target weight (i.e., retention of her existing client base). Next, she focused on communicating with people who had come once or twice and then fallen off the wagon. These people had effectively opened themselves up as a lead and were a captive audience (i.e., sales funnel). Finally, she poured her efforts into marketing – organic web advertising, putting up posters around the area and direct e-mail contact. As soon as she hit the necessary number, she left her job and switched gear from 'niche' to 'cruise'.

I sat down recently with an enthusiastic man who really wanted to bring his coaching service to the market for the betterment of his future clients. However, he valued his family time and wanted to compress this new business into two days a week, during which he would make enough money to sustain the other five. He was so focused on his plan that he was animatedly talking with his hands, pointing to an imaginary whiteboard on to which I'm sure he was beaming figures from his head. 'I'm gonna be charging €80 a session, do ten sessions a day and take home €1,600 a week.'

I had to point out the holes in his argument:

∼ He was thinking only about revenue and not about after-tax profit. I could see him going straight to the 'There is no profit in this' passage of Step Eight a couple of weeks after starting, with a bewildered look on his face as he thinks about how all that money could disappear.

∼ It would have been immensely difficult to get all ten sessions into one day due to time constraints, but, on top of that, where was the time for marketing, administration, cancellations, follow-ups and the other less obvious tasks that qualify as 'urgent'? He was also dangerously on his way to the 'I don't have any time' passage in Step Eight. Alternatively, he could hire some help to take care of these administrative tasks and that would eat further into the profit margin.

∼ He was actually aspiring to make a certain amount of money during a particular (finite) period of time, but was trying to stretch the day out too far instead of increasing the value, which was a variable over which he had complete control.

Since time is finite and fixed, the only other thing he could change was his price. I suggested that he should find ways to bring the value of his sessions up to €135 and to go in search of only six appointments per day.

He looked at me and said, 'Susan, I thought you studied economics. Don't you know that the higher my price, the fewer the number of people who will come to me? I don't want that to happen!' I went straight back at him with 'Exactly. That's what you do want to happen. Now you can make the same amount of money without burning yourself out, and you can factor in the time that it will actually take to bring in the business.' We brainstormed with a couple of ideas: travelling to people's homes within a certain radius; becoming a specialist in a particular area and building his brand around that; creating a tailored package for each client with resources, exercises, a CD and a branded piece of stationery to document their journey. I left him looking forward to comparing each of these ideas using KPIs and then testing them out with his market.

How do I get out?

Tell me, out of what exactly do you want to get?

Is it that you want to wind down your business or a particular brand and get a job instead? If so, you could look into selling the entity that you've created. If you speak to your local enterprise centre and some business brokers, they'll be able to give you some information about your options. Revisit Step Five to get some ideas about other organizations that might help you.

If you want to go the other way around and potentially leave your job to pursue a business idea, you need to look at how exactly you might achieve that. Revisit Step One and use the GROW MORE! model. What do you want to do and why? What are the realities of the situation that you can't change, but need to work around? If you don't have the safety net of a salary every month, do a set of projections for your income and expenditure and then figure out a way to potentially lock in some sort of regularity. You want to get out of one income stream while growing another, much bigger one, so I would refer you to the specific section on growth earlier in this chapter.

Maybe you don't like what you do, period, and you want a change. You've given it your all. 'I love to bake so I decided to sell croissants and muffins at the local farmers' market. On a Sunday I get up at 3 a.m. to bake my produce. The smell is fabulous. Then I go to sit in my tiny stand in the cold all day and sell only half of what I've baked. I do it all over again the next week, taking care to bake fewer croissants and more muffins, because I've noticed that's where the demand is. I do this for six weeks in a row. I'm totally miserable. I hate getting up so horribly early, as it completely throws me for the rest of the week. I realize I don't like selling my own products. Instead, I enjoy seeing the look of pure indulgence on people's faces when they bite into my pastries. Yes, I'm making money, but I hate sitting hours on end in the biting cold. I've had enough.'

Fair enough: you've given it a good go. And what you've achieved is truly impressive. Now take a step back. What have you learned?

- What do you now know about yourself that you didn't in the past?
- What way would you prefer to spend your time and how could you make money that way instead?
- What market research did you glean?
- Did you solve the problem or bring the pleasure to your market that you thought they wanted?
- If not, why did they pay you? How could you make money by solving that problem or providing that means of pleasure instead?
- Which marketing techniques worked?
- Did you find ways to measure your marketing?
- Did you learn how to sell, deal with objections, open leads and ask for the sale?

Look at all that you have learned!

The question you should ask now is: what might you do differently? Where can you change the focus? Baking in and of itself, and being paid for your baking, is apparently not the problem: the smell in your kitchen might have been the only thing keeping you going during all those early-morning baking sessions. Let's think back to Step Two and list every other way that you could make money from your love of baking. Could you be involved in catering perhaps? You could approach a caterer about providing the bakery element to their offering in a joint-venture partnership, or the caterer could be your reseller. You could choose whether simply to bake and send off your pastries, or to accompany the caterer on site to serve the pastries – and enjoy that appreciative look of enjoyment on people's faces, while looking to your KPIs for guidance on the best way forward.

If something hasn't worked out, it's because you brought it to its natural conclusion, and this piece of market research led you to a new finding. It's not a negative. It's not a failure. It shouldn't be a disappointment. You learned what you like and don't like, so instead of giving up, why not adapt? I guarantee that you're now in a position to choose a more suitable route the next time round. You'll be able to get up and running more quickly, more easily and more efficiently because you can apply all the lessons that you've already learned.

What's next for you?

Conclusion

We have been through quite a journey together. My hope is that you'll dip into this book at various stages throughout your career. In Step Nine, I wanted you to see that we often come across the same issues, but on a larger, deeper and more complex level. If you read this book again after a month or after two years or after ten years, you'll read it with a more substantial bank of experiences and in a different way. However, the framework will work for you over and over again.

I have two parting requests to make of you, to ensure that you'll be feeling the benefits of this book for years and years to come.

Please let extra money be extra money . . .

In *The Savvy Woman's Guide to Financial Freedom*, I coined the phrase 'financial thermostat' in an attempt to discuss an incredibly widespread phenomenon. I think that we all have an amount of money in our head that we're comfortable having. When you have more than that in your bank account, you find a way of getting rid of it: you go on a shopping spree, change some furniture or treat your friends to lunch. You may not realize it, but money burns a hole in your pocket when it's above the level of your financial thermostat. You're uncomfortable with that much money and you spend your way right back to your subconsciously chosen 'number'. Conversely, if your bank balance falls below this level, you become uncomfortable, as you feel exposed. You find that you redouble your efforts to earn more and to save whenever your bank balance goes below this 'number'. I couldn't possibly begin to count the number of people who have told me how much this resonates with them.

If you've been thinking, 'I'm working so hard. I soooo deserve nice things/this new tablet computer/this manicure/this set of golf clubs / this dress. Besides, now I have the money to afford them', it might be your financial thermostat making you uncomfortable with all that 'extra' money. Of course getting those nice things might be the reason you started to work on making more money to begin with. If you've decided that that's the way you want to spend that money, that's perfectly fine. It becomes a problem when you are spending the money as fast as, or faster than, you're making it.

There are a number of ways around this. First, if you think this could happen to you, simply being aware of it might be enough to help you check yourself when, say, you find yourself choosing to go out for breakfast instead of making it at home, just because you have the money to do so.

In my own case, I log the money that I make outside of my fixed salary in a separate part of my budget spread-sheet under 'variable income'. As I work out how much I have against how much I spend, I leave the variable income totally outside of the equation and consider only my fixed income. As a result, *extra money is actually extra money*. If I need to supplement day-to-day spending because of a lump sum that needs to paid, such as car insurance, I consciously dip into my variable income. It's right there waiting for me when I have an unexpected or infrequent expense.

Otherwise, I decide exactly what purpose I'm going to use it for. I might save it; at the moment, I'm putting it towards a 'wedding fund'. I don't just let it slip through my fingers unnoticed. I'm in control of my financial thermostat. If you need further protection from yourself, the solution might be to set up a separate account that is more difficult to access, like a credit union account or a deposit account, in order to protect your new money. Then you can let it grow into something substantial and use it for a larger, more significant purpose. But, please, if you're going to go to the effort of following the steps in this book, please let yourself actually enjoy the benefits of this extra money by achieving your true goals – getting a few expensive things that you don't need just because you can certainly won't have the same impact.

. . . *and please learn a little about savings, investments and pensions.*

You make money by working hard, working smart and working effectively. Why not put your money to work for you in exactly the same way?

I've devoted a large part of my own career to studying investment, teaching people about the financial markets and personal finance, and working with organizations and corporations to train their staff to understand the intricate world of finance.

Yet it never ceases to amaze me just how little people know about where to put their extra money or how to plan their way to a solid financial future. I often hear that people are intimidated or bored by the complexity of the jargon. I have heard far too many stories of unscrupulous 'advisers' taking advantage of this lack of knowledge and pushing people towards investments with disappointing returns and totally unsuitable risk levels as well as underfunded pensions, with the person selling the financial product putting their own desires before the needs of their clients.

I think the industry has a lot to answer for in this regard; meanwhile, I would urge you to take matters into your own hands. A little information can go a long, long way. For example, it will take you very little time to understand:

- The various differences between savings accounts in terms of interest, safety and accessibility.
- The difference between investing and speculating in the stock market.
- The main categories of pension structure, and the range of products that exists in each category and how to maximize tax efficiency.

If you can learn these fundamentals, you'll be able to have a much more informed discussion with your financial adviser, which will in turn give you greater control over the management of your savings and investments in the long term. Again, there are government-funded cost-comparison websites that spend millions of your taxes on marketing this personal finance education every year to anyone willing to soak it up for their own benefit. Since this is such a huge passion of mine, I've created some free resources and a directory of services on this very topic at www.savvymoneyguide.com.

It has been an absolute pleasure to share this journey with you, and I'd be delighted if you were to drop me an e-mail at susan@savvymoneyguide.com to let me know how you're getting on.

My warmest wishes for your success.

Susan

Acknowledgements

First and foremost, I would like to express my deepest gratitude to each and every one of those people who sent me e-mails after reading *The Savvy Woman's Guide to Financial Freedom*. I'm so proud of how much action they took and of the extraordinary progress that they've made. Some have made psychological discoveries; some have developed new financial habits; and they're all closer to financial freedom. I have been truly humbled by the words that have graced my screen from all over the world. You are my inspiration.

This is the second time that I have been fortunate enough to work with such a fantastic publisher; Michael, Patricia D, Cliona, Patricia M, Brian, Keith, Holly Kate, Lisa and their teams at Penguin, and also copy-editor Donna Poppy, have made the process an absolute pleasure. I am very grateful to them for all the time and effort that they put into *The Savvy Guide to Making More Money*.

It would have been utterly impossible to write this book and to pack it full of anecdotes and stories without all the people who acted as clients, prospects, colleagues, influencers, mentors and business friends over my fifteen years of generating an income. Life is full of learning and milestones, and it is because of all of you that I can pass on my knowledge and experience to others.

Mam and Dad led the way as hard-working, kind people who were always ready to help others. They instilled values of belief and respect as well as the skill of conversation in Conor and me. It's as impossible to quantify the worth of these intangibles as it is to quantify the love, appreciation and admiration that I have for them. They brought us into a wide-ranging, but tightly knit family of individuals who went on to succeed in so many facets of their own lives.

I would also like to mention Marion, Thomas, Barbara and Pearse Culleton for their support and encouragement through all the ups and downs of the past year. It's wonderful to be marrying into a family that has given me such a warm welcome.

My thanks to Julie Duran for her help, wisdom, feedback and encouragement, which she provided at every word, every paragraph and every chapter. Destiny held a wonderful surprise when Julie was introduced to me a number of years ago. She has an awe-inspiring command of the English language, and I hold her in enormous esteem as a professional, a colleague and a friend.

Finally, as I am about to begin married life with Ardle Culleton, I can't find words to express the heart-bursting anticipation I feel at the thought of spending my life with him. He is my business adviser, my Salmon of Knowledge, my best friend, my soulmate and such fantastic company! I thank God that I get to spend every day with him, and if I were asked to design the husband of my dreams, I wouldn't change a thing. He truly is 'my hero'.